A TERM OF OVID

STORIES FROM THE METAMORPHOSES
FOR STUDY AND SIGHT READING

BY

CLARENCE W. GLEASON, A.M. (HARV.)
OF THE ROXBURY LATIN SCHOOL

REVISED

AMERICAN BOOK COMPANY
NEW YORK   CINCINNATI   CHICAGO   BOSTON   ATLANTA

PREFACE

Ovid is an author far less difficult than Vergil, and more interesting than either Vergil or most of the prose writers generally read in schools; hence he deserves a place in our courses of study. In many courses, if not most of them, the aim is to crowd as much of the bare essentials of Latin as possible into the smallest amount of time; thus a literature at best impoverished is bereft of one of the most charming and interesting of the few authors available for school use. The agile pupil is made to vault from his condensed beginner's book into Caesar, from Caesar either into Cicero by way of Vergil, or into Vergil by way of Cicero. But a few weeks spent on the Metamorphoses of Ovid need not be considered an unnecessary digression from the straight path to the desired goal, or in any sense a waste of time, for besides the great literary gain of reading the tales of Greek and Roman mythology told in a most delightful way, there is a distinct value in using Ovid as a stepping-stone from the level (though — in Caesar, at least — rough) roadbed of prose to the more difficult and to many pupils dangerous heights of Vergil. A glance at the vocabulary of the present volume will perhaps make this plain. The extracts from the Metamorphoses were selected without reference to choice of words, or to their ease or difficulty in translation, but solely from a literary point of view, for the beauty and interest of the

3

stories themselves. Yet when compared with the first book of the Aeneid, which logically follows in a well-rounded school course, the similarity is seen to be striking. The vocabulary to the first book of the Aeneid contains about 1460 words; of these all but 300 (exclusive of proper names) are contained in the present volume. So that the pupil is not only reading the legends of gods and heroes written in a most entertaining style, but is lessening the greatest gap in a continuous Latin course by becoming familiar with the vocabulary of Vergil in easier verse.

The present volume is designed to fit the needs of several classes of schools. For those which have not hitherto included Ovid in their curricula it offers a short and convenient book of representative selections. For courses which take up Ovid before Vergil it forms an intermediate step between prose and verse by the adoption, to a limited extent, of features which the editor has found useful in previous books.

The volume contains about 2075 lines, with full notes and vocabulary. The first hundred lines are divided into feet for scansion, with accents and caesuras. The division of the second and third hundred lines is marked in a different way. The ordinary Latin prose order is given for the first three selections, or until the student may be supposed to be familiar with the general differences of structure in prose and poetry. In the prose version the quantities are marked, and also the common synonyms of the more unusual words or words with special poetic uses are given. The notes contain a short introductory sketch and summary of each chapter, tables of genealogy of the principal persons, and references to the more available books of reference and to other literary helps. Words also found in the first book of the Aeneid are marked in the vocabulary with an asterisk.

The text used is in most cases that of Merkel (1875). With a few exceptions the hidden quantities of vowels in the vocabulary and synonyms are marked according to Lewis's Elementary Latin Dictionary.

CLARENCE W. GLEASON

Roxbury Latin School

The stories of *Ceres and Proserpina* and *Jason and Medea* have been added in response to a number of requests for additional material for sight reading, and the *Cadmus* and *Daedalus* selections to fulfill the requirements of the College Entrance Examination Board.

CLARENCE W. GLEASON

CONTENTS

* Required by the College Entrance Examination Board.

IN nova fert animus mutatas dicere formas
corpora.   Di, coeptis (nam vos mutastis et illas)
adspirate meis, primaque ab origine mundi
ad mea perpetuum deducite tempora carmen.

Metamorphoses, Book I, lines 1-4.

OF bodies changed to various forms I sing: —
Ye gods, from whom these miracles did spring,
Inspire my numbers with celestial heat,
Till I my long laborious work complete;
And add perpetual tenor to my rhymes,
Deduced from Nature's birth to Caesar's times.

Dryden's Translation.

ATALANTA'S RACE: POYNTER.

I. ATALANTA'S LAST RACE

A MAIDEN OF MATCHLESS BEAUTY AND FLEETNESS

Fórsitan ₁ aúdie₁rís ‖ ali₁quám cer₁támine ₁ cúrsus
vélo₁cés supe₁rásse vi₁rós. ‖ Non ₁ fábula ₁ rúmor
ílle fu₁ít; ‖ supe₁rábat e₁ním. ‖ Non ₁ dícere ₁ pósses
laúde pe₁dúm ‖ for₁maéne bo₁nó ‖ prae₁stántior ₁ ésset.
Scítan₁tí Deus ₁ huíc ‖ de ₁ cóniuge, ₁ 'Cóniuge,' ₁ díxit,   5
'níl opus ₁ ést, ‖ Ata₁lánta, ti₁bí..‖ Fuge ₁ cóniugis ₁ úsum.
Néc tamen ₁ éffugi₁és; ‖ te₁queⁱ ípsa ₁ víva ca₁rébis.'
Térrita ₁ sórte de₁í ‖ per o₁pácas ₁ ínnuba ₁ sílvas
vívit, et ₁ ínstan₁tém tur₁bám vio₁lénta pro₁córum

Forsitan audieris aliquam virginem certāmine cursūs vēlōcēs
virōs superāsse. Ille rūmor nōn fuit fābula; superābat enim.
Nec dīcere possēs pedumne laude an fōrmae bonō esset praestantior. Huic dē coniuge scītantī Deus dīxit: 'Tibi, Atalanta,
nīl coniuge opus est. Fuge ūsum coniugis. Nec tamen effu-
giēs, vīvaque tē ipsā carēbis.' Territa sorte deī per silvās opācās
innuba vīvit, et condiciōne īnstantem procōrum turbam fugat

3. nōn: neque. — 4. laude: virtūte. fōrmae: pulchritūdinis. — 6. fuge:
vītā. — 7. carēbis: prīvāberis. — 8. sorte: respōnsō. — 9. īnstantem: im-
portūnam.

cóndici¡óne fu¡gát : ‖ ‘Nec ¡ súm poti¡únda, ni¡s',’ ínquit,   10
‘vícta pri¡ús cur¡sú. ‖ Pedi¡bús con¡téndite ¡ mécum.
Praémia ¡ vélo¡cí ‖ con¡iúnx thala¡míque da¡búntur ;
mórs preti¡úm tar¡dís. ‖ Ea ¡ léx cer¡táminis ¡ ésto.’
Ílla qui¡d^{em} ímmi¡tís : ‖ sed ¡ tánta po¡téntia ¡ fórm^{ae} est,
vénit ad ¡ hánc le¡gém ‖ teme¡rária ¡ túrba pro¡córum.   15

HIPPOMENES FALLS A VICTIM TO HER CHARMS

Séderat ¡ Híppome¡nés ‖ cur¡sús spec¡tátor in¡íqui,
ét ‘ Peti¡túr cui¡quám ‖ per ¡ tánta pe¡rícula ¡ cóniunx ? ’
díxerat ; ‖ ác nimi¡ós ‖ iuve¡núm dam¡nárat a¡móres.
Út faci¡^{em} ét posi¡tó cor¡pús ‖ ve¡lámine ¡ vídit,
quále me¡úm, ‖ vel ¡ quále tu¡úm, ‖ si ¡ fémina ¡ fías,   20
óbstipu¡ít : ‖ tol¡lénsque ma¡nús, ‖ ‘ Ig¡nóscite,’ ¡ díxit,
‘ quós modo ¡ cúlpa¡ví ; ‖ non¡dúm̄ mihi ¡ praémia ¡ nóta,
quaé pete¡rétis, ‖ e¡ránt.’ ‖ Lau¡dándo ¡ cóncipit ¡ ígnes

violenta. ‘Nec sum potiunda,’ inquit, ‘nisi prius cursū victa.
Pedibus contendite mēcum. Vēlōcī coniūnx thalamīque praemia
dabuntur ; mors erit (dabitur) pretium tardīs. Ea estō lēx certāminis.’

Illa quidem erat immītis : sed tanta est fōrmae potentia, temerāria turba procōrum ad hanc lēgem vēnit.

Hippomenēs sēderat cursūs inīquī spectātor, et ‘Cuiquam coniūnx,’ dīxerat, ‘per tanta perīcula petitur?’ ac nimiōs amōrēs
iuvenum damnārat. Ut faciem tamen virginis et corpus positō
vēlāmine vīdit, quāle est meum, vel quāle tuum, Adōnis, sī fēmina
fīās, obstipuit, manūsque tollēns, ‘Ignōscite,’ dīxit, ‘vōs quōs
modo culpāvī. Nōndum nōta mihi erant praemia quae peterē-

---

12. coniūnx: uxor. — 14. immītis: crūdēlis. — 15. temerāria: imprū-
dēns. — 19. positō: dēpositō, dēiectō. — 21. ignōscite: parcite. — 22. nōta:
perspecta.

ét ne ˌ quís iuveˌnúm ‖ curˌrát veˌlócius ˌ óptat
ínvidiˌáque tiˌmét. ‖ 'Sed ˌ cúr cerˌtáminis ˌ húius   25
íntempˌtáta miˌhí ‖ forˌtúna reˌlínquitur?' ‖ ínquit.
'Aúdenˌtés ‖ deus ˌ ípse iuˌvát.' ‖ Dum ˌ tália ˌ sécum
éxigit ˌ Híppomeˌnés, ‖ pasˌsú volat ˌ álite ˌ vírgo.
Quaé quamˌquám Scythiˌcá ‖ non ˌ sétius ˌ íre saˌgítta
Áoniˌó viˌsᵃ ést iuveˌní, ‖ tamen ˌ ílle deˌcórem   30
míraˌtúr magis. ‖ Ét curˌsús facit ˌ ílle ‖ deˌçórem :
aúra reˌfért ‖ abˌláta ciˌtís ‖ taˌlária ˌ plántis ;
térgaque ˌ iáctanˌtúr criˌnés ‖ per eˌbúrnea, ˌ quaéque
póplitiˌbús subeˌránt ‖ picˌtó genuˌália ˌ límbo :
ínque puˌéllaˌrí corˌpús canˌdóre ‖ ruˌbórem   35
tráxerat, ˌ haúd aliˌtér quam ˌ cúm super ˌ átria ˌ vélum
cándida ˌ púrpureˌúm ‖ simuˌlátas ˌ ínficit ˌ úmbras.
Dúm notat ˌ haéc hoˌspés, ‖ deˌcúrsa noˌvíssima ˌ métᵃ est,

tis.' Laudandō illam īgnēs concipit, et optat nē quis iuvenum
vēlōcius illā currat, invidiāque timet. 'Sed cūr fortūna hūius
certāminis intemptāta mihi relinquitur?' inquit. 'Audentēs deus
ipse iuvat.' Dum Hippomenēs sēcum tālia exigit, passū ālite
volat virgō. Quae quamquam Āoniō iuvenī nōn sētius īre vīsa
est Scythicā sagittā, ille tamen decōrem ēius magis mīrātur. Et
ille cursus decōrem facit : aura tālāria citīs plantīs ablāta refert ;
crīnēsque per terga eburnea iactantur, genuāliaque pictō limbō
quae poplitibus ēius suberant ; rubōremque in corpus ēius puellārī candōre cursus trāxerat, haud aliter quam cum vēlum pur-
pureum super candida ātria simulātās umbrās īnficit. Dum hospes
haec notat, dēcursa est mēta novissima, et victrīx festā corōnā

26. intemptāta : inexperta. — 27. audentēs : audācēs. — 28. exigit : vol-
vit. passū : gressū. — 29. sētius : aliter. — 31. decōrem : fōrmam, 4. —
32. plantīs : pedibus, 11. — 35. puellārī : virgineō. — 38. dēcursa : praeterita.

ét tegi₁túr fe₁stá vic₁tríx ‖ Ata₁lánta co₁róna.
Dánt gemi₁túm vic₁tí, ‖ pen₁dúntquᵉ ex ₁ foédere ₁ poénas.   40

THE CHALLENGE

Nón tamen ₁ éven₁tú ‖ iuve₁nís de₁térritus ₁ hórum
cónstitit ₁ ín medi₁ó, ‖ vul₁túquᵉ in ₁ vírgine ₁ fīxo,
'Quíd facil₁ém ‖ titu₁lúm supe₁rándo ₁ quaéris ₁ inértes?'
Mécum ₁ cónfer!' ‖ a₁ít, ‖ 'seu ₁ mé for₁túna po₁téntem
fécerit, ₁ á tan₁tó ‖ non ₁ índi₁gnábere ₁ vínci.   45
Námque mi₁hí geni₁tór ‖ Mega₁reús ₁ On₁chéstius : ₁ ílli
ést Nep₁túnus ‖ a₁vús : ‖ prone₁pós ego ₁ régis a₁quárum.
Néc vir₁tús ‖ ci₁trá genus ₁ ést. ‖ Seu ₁ víncar, ‖ ha₁bébis
Híppome₁né vic₁tó ‖ ma₁gnᵘᵐ ét memo₁rábile ₁ nómen.'

ATALANTA WAVERS BETWEEN PITY AND DUTY

Tália ₁ dícen₁tém ‖ mol₁lí Schoe₁néia ₁ vúltu   50
ádspicit, ₁ ét dubi₁tát ‖ supe₁rárⁱ an ₁ víncere ₁ málit.

Atalanta tegitur. Victī gemitum dant, penduntque ex foedere poenās.

Iuvenis tamen hōrum ēventū nōn dēterritus in mediō cōnstitit, vultūque in virgine fīxō, 'Quid facilem titulum inertēs superandō quaeris?' ait. 'Mēcum cōnfer. Seu mē potentem fortūna fēcerit, ā tantō vincī nōn indīgnābere. Namque Megareus Onchestius mihi est genitor : illī Neptūnus est avus : itaque ego pronepōs sum rēgis aquārum. Nec citrā genus est virtūs mea. Seu vincar, māgnum et memorābile nōmen Hippomenē victō habēbis.'

Mollī vultū tālia dīcentem eum adspicit Schoenēia, et dubitat

---

41. ēventū : exitiō. — 42. vultū : oculīs. — 43. titulum : glōriam. inertēs : ignāvōs. — 44. cōnfer : congredere.

Atquᵉ ita, ｜ 'Quís deus ｜ húnc ‖ for｜mósis, ｜ ínquit, ‖ in｜íquus
pérdere ｜ vúlt, ‖ ca｜raéque iu｜bét dis｜crímine ｜ vítae
cóniugi｜úm pete｜rᵉ hóc? ‖ non ｜ súm, me ｜ iúdice, ｜ tánti.   54
Néc for｜má tan｜gór, — ‖ pote｜rám tamen ｜ hác quoque ｜ tángi —
séd quod ad｜húc puer ｜ ést. ‖ Non ｜ mé movet ｜ ípse, ‖ sed ｜ aétas.
Quid, quod in｜ést vir｜tús ｜ et ｜ méns in｜térrita ｜ léti?
Quíd, quod ab ｜ aéquore｜á ‖ nume｜rátur o｜rígine ｜ quártus?
Quíd, quod a｜mát ‖ tan｜tíque pu｜tát co｜núbia ｜ nóstra
út pere｜át, ‖ si ｜ mé ‖ fors ｜ ílli ｜ dúra ne｜gárit?   60
Dúm licet, ｜ hóspes, ‖ ab｜í ‖ thala｜mósque re｜línque cru｜éntos.
Cóniugi｜úm cru｜déle me｜ᵘᵐ ést. ‖ Tibi ｜ núbere ｜ núlla
nólet; et ｜ ópta｜rí ‖ potes ｜ á sapi｜énte pu｜élla.
Cúr tamen ｜ ést mihi ｜ cúra tu｜í, ‖ tot ｜ iᵃᵐ ánte per｜émptis?
Víderit! ｜ ínteré｜át, ‖ quoni｜ám tot ｜ caéde pro｜córum   65
ádmoni｜tús non ｜ ést, ‖ agi｜túrquᵉ in ｜ taédia ｜ vítae. —

utrum superārī an vincere mālit. Atque ita 'Quis deus,' inquit,
'fōrmōsīs inīquus, hunc iuvenem perdere vult, cāraeque vītae
discrīmine hōc coniugium petere iubet? Tantī nōn sum, mē
iūdice. Nec fōrmā illīus tangor, — hāc tamen quoque tangī
poteram — sed quod adhūc est puer. Nōn iuvenis ipse sed aetās
ēius mē movet. Quid est quod virtūs eī inest, et mēns lētī interrita? Quid, quod quartus ab aequoreā orīgine numerātur? Quid,
quod amat et tantī nostra cōnūbia putat ut pereat, sī mē fors dūra
illī negārit? — Abī, hospes, dum licet, thalamōsque cruentōs relinque. Crūdēle enim est meum coniugium. Tibi autem nūbere
nūlla virgō nōlet; et ā sapiente puellā optārī potes. Cūr tamen
mihi est cūra tuī, tot aliīs iam ante perēmptīs? Vīderit ipse!
Intereat, quoniam tot procōrum caede nōn est admonitus agiturque

52. fōrmōsīs: pulchrīs. — 53. discrīmine: perīculō, 17. — 55. tangor:
moveor. — 56. aetās: adulēscentia. — 58. orīgine: stirpe. — 64. perēmptīs:
occīsīs. — 65. vīderit: cōgitet. — 66. taedia: odium.

Óccidet ǀ híc igiǀtúr, ǁ voluǀít quia ǀ vívere ǀ mécum,
indiǀgnámque neǀcém ǁ pretiǀúm patiǀétur aǀmóris?
Nón erit ǀ ínvidiǀaé ǁ vicǀtória ǀ nóstra feǀréndae.
Séd non ǀ cúlpa meǀ^a ést. ǁ Utiǀnám deǀsístere ǀ vélles!   70
Aút, quoniǀ^{am} és deǀméns, ǁ utiǀnám veǀlócior ǀ ésses!
Át quam ǀ vírgineǀús ǁ puerǀíli ǀ vúltus in ǀ órᵉ est!
Á! miser ǀ Híppomeǀnés, ǁ nolǀlém tibi ǀ vísa fuǀíssem!
Vívere ǀ dígnus eǀrás. ǁ Quod ǀ sí feǀlícior ǀ éssem,
néc mihi ǀ cóniugiǀúm ǁ faǀtᵃ ímporǀtúna neǀgárent,   75
únus eǀrás ǁ cum ǀ quó sociǀáre cuǀbília ǀ véllem.'
Díxerat; ǁ útque ruǀdís ǁ priǀmóque Cuǀpídine ǀ tácta,
quíd facit ǀ ígnoǀráns ǁ amat ǀ ét non ǀ séntit aǀmórem.

VENUS SUMMONED TO THE LOVER'S AID

Iám soliǀtós posǀcúnt curǀsús ǁ popuǀlúsque paǀtérque:
cúm me ǀ sóllicoǀtá ǁ proǀlés Nepǀtúnia ǀ vóce   80

in taedia vītae. — Occidet hīc igitur, quia mēcum vīvere voluit,
necemque indīgnam amōris pretium patiētur? Victōria nostra
invidiae erit nōn ferendae. Sed nōn est culpa mea. Utinam
dēsistere vellēs! Aut, quoniam es dēmēns, utinam essēs vēlōcior!
At quam virgineus est vultus in ōre ēius puerīlī! Ā! miser Hippomenēs, nōllem tibi vīsa fuissem! Namque vīvere erās dīgnus.
Quod sī essem fēlīcior, nec mihi fāta importūna coniugium negā-
rent, tu ūnus erās quōcum cubīlia sociāre vellem!' Tālia dīxerat,
utque puella rudis, prīmōque Cupīdine tācta, ignōrāns quid faci(a)t
amat, et amōrem suum nōn sentit.

Iam populusque paterque Atalantae solitōs cursūs poscunt, cum
prōlēs Neptūnia Hippomenēs sollicitā vōce mē invocat, 'Cytherēa'-

---

68. **indīgnam**: immeritam. — 77. **rudis**: imperīta. — 79. **solitōs**: cōn-
suētōs. — 80. **sollicitā**: anxiā.

ínvocat ǀ Híppomeǀnés, ǁ ' Cytheǀréaque ǀ cómprecor, ǀ aúsis
ádsit,' aǀít, ǁ 'nosǀtrís ǁ et ǀ quós dedit ǀ ádiuvet ǀ ígnes.'
Détulit ǀ aúra preǀcés ad ǀ mé non ǀ ínvida ǀ blándas ;
mótaque ǀ súm, ǁ fateǀór. ǁ Nec oǀpís mora ǀ lónga daǀbátur.
Ést ager, ǁ índigeǀnaé Tamaǀsénum ǀ nómine ǀ dícunt,   85
télluǀrís Cypriǀaé ǁ pars ǀ óptima, ǁ quám mihi ǀ prísci
sácraǀvére seǀnés ǁ temǀplísquᵉ acǀcédere ǀ dótem
hánc iusǀsére meǀís. ǁ Mediǀó nitet ǀ árbor in ǀ árvo,
fúlva coǀmám, ǁ fulǀvó raǀmís crepiǀtántibus ǀ aúro.
Hínc tria ǀ fórte meǀá veniǀéns ǁ deǀcérpta feǀrébam   90
aúrea ǀ póma maǀnú : ǁ nulǀlíque viǀdénda niǀsⁱ ípsi
Híppomeǀnén adiǀí ǁ docuǀíque quis ǀ úɔus in ǀ íllis.

THE RACE

Sígna tuǀbaé dedeǀránt ǁ cum ǀ cárcere ǀ prónus uǀtérque
émicat ǀ ét sumǀmám ǁ celeǀrí pede ǀ líbat haǀrénam.

que ait, ' comprecor, ut ausīs nostrīs adsit, et īgnēs quōs dedit
adiuvet.' Aura nōn invida precēs ēius blandās ad mē dētulit ;
mōtaque sum, fateor. Nec opis longa mora dabātur. Est ager,
pars optima tellūris Cypriae (indigenae Tamasēnum nōmine eam
dīcunt) quam prīscī senēs mihi sacrāvēre, templīsque meīs hanc
dōtem accēdere iussēre. Mediō in arvō nitet arbor, fulva comam,
rāmīs ēius fulvō aurō crepitantibus. Hinc veniēns tria aurea pōma
forte ferēbam manū meā dēcerpta : nūllīque videnda nisi ipsi Hip-
pomenēn adiī, eumque docuī quis ūsus esset in illīs.

Tubae sīgna dederant, cum uterque ē carcere prōnus ēmicat, et
celerī pede summam harēnam lībat. Illōs siccō passū freta rādere

---

81. comprecor: quaesō. ausīs: inceptīs. — 85. indigenae: accolae.
— 86. prīscī: antīquī. — 87. accēdere: iungī. — 88. nitet: splendet. —
89. fulvō: flāvō. — 90. dēcerpta: dērepta. — 94. ēmicat: āvolat. lībat:
tangat.

Pósse pu｜tés il｜lós ‖ sic｜có freta ｜ rádere ｜ pássu   95
ét sege｜tís ca｜naé ‖ stan｜tés per｜cúrrer⁣ᵉ a｜rístas.
Ádici｜únt ani｜mós iuve｜ní ‖ cla｜mórque fa｜vórque
vérbaque ｜ dícen｜túm, ‖ 'Nunc, ｜ núnc in｜cúmbere ｜ témpus,
Híppome｜né, ‖ prope｜rá ! ‖ Nunc ｜ víribus ｜ útere ｜ tótis.
Pélle mo｜rám, ‖ vin｜cés !' ‖ Dubi｜úm Mega｜réius ｜ héros   100
gaúdeat án virgó ‖ magis hís Schoenéia díctis.
Ó quotiéns ‖ cum iám possét transíre morát⁣ᵃ est
spéctatósque diú vultús ‖ invíta relíquit !
Áridus é lassó ‖ veniébat anhélitus óre,
métaqu⁣ᵉ erát longé.

THE GOLDEN APPLES

Tum dénique dé tribus únum   105
fétibus árboreís ‖ prolés Neptúnia mísit.
Óbstipuít virgó ‖ nitidíque cupídine pómi
déclinát cursús ‖ aurúmque volúbile tóllit :

et segetis cānae stantēs aristās percurrere posse putēs ! Clāmorque
favorque animōs iuvenī ādiciunt, verbaque eōrum dīcentum, 'Nunc,
nunc est tempus incumbere ; properā, Hippomenē ! Nunc ūtere
tōtīs vīribus. Pelle moram, nam vincēs !' Dubium est utrum
magis Megarēius hērōs an virgō Schoenēia hīs dictīs gaudeat. Ō
quotiēns, cum iam trānsīre posset, morāta est, invītaque vultūs diū
spectātōs relīquit ! Āridus veniēbat anhēlitus ex ōre lassō, longē-
que erat mēta.

Tum dēnique mīsit prōlēs Neptūnia ūnum ē tribus fētibus arbo-
reīs. Obstipuit virgō, cupīdineque nitidī pōmī cursum dēclīnat,
aurumque volūbile tollit : praeterit eam Hippomenēs : resonant

95. freta : aequora. — 96. stantēs : ērēctās. — 97. ādiciunt : addunt. —
104. āridus : siccus, 95. lassō : dēfessō. anhēlitus : spīritus. — 106. mīsit : abiēcit.

praéterit Híppomenés : ‖ resonánt spectácula plaúsu.

Ílla morám ‖ celerí cessátaque témpora cúrsu   110

córrigit, átquᵉ iterúm ‖ iuveném post térga relínquit.

Ét rursús ‖ pomí iactú remoráta secúndi

cónsequitúr ‖ transítque virúm. ‖ Pars última cúrsus

réstabát. ‖ ' Nunc,' ínquit, ‖ ' adés, ‖ dea múneris aúctor ! '

ínque latús campí ‖ quo tárdius ílla redíret   115

iécit ab óbliquó ‖ nitidúm iuvenáliter aúrum.

Án peterét ‖ virgó visᵃ ést dubitáre : ‖ coégi

tóllerᵉ et ádiecí subláto póndera málo,

ímpediíquᵉ onerís ‖ paritér gravitáte moráque.

Néve meús sermó ‖ cursú sit tárdior ípso,   120

praéteritᵃ ést virgó : ‖ duxít sua praémia víctor.

spectācula plausū. Illa celerī cursū moram temporaque cessāta corrigit, atque iterum iuvenem post terga relinquit. Et rursus secundī pōmī iactū remorāta virum cōnsequitur trānsitque. Ultima pars cursūs restabat. ' Nunc ades,' inquit ille, ' dea, mūneris meī auctor ! ' aurumque nitidum ab oblīquō in latus campī, quō tardius illa redīret, iuvenāliter iēcit. Dubitāre vīsa est virgō an peteret pōmum : tollere eam coēgī, et mālō sublātō pondera adiēcī, pariterque oneris gravitāte morāque eam impediī. — Nēve sermō meus tardior sit ipsō cursū, dīcam, praeterita est virgō : dūxit sua praemia victor.

109. **praeterit**: trānsit, 102. — 114. **restābat**: supererat. **ades**: prōpitia estō. — 118. **pondera**: gravitātem.

II. PYRAMUS AND THISBE

THE EASTERN LOVERS

Pýramus ét Thisbé, ‖ iuvenúm pulchérrimus álter,
áltera quás Oriéns habuít ‖ praeláta puéllis,
contiguás tenuére domós ‖ ubi dícitur áltam
cóctilibús murís ‖ cinxísse Semíramis úrbem.   125
Nótitiám ‖ primósque gradús ‖ vicínia fécit:
témpore crévit amór; ‖ taedaé quoque iúre coíssent,
séd vetuére patrés. ‖ Quod nón potuére vetáre,
éx aequó captís ‖ ardébant méntibus ámbo:
cónscius ómnis abést; ‖ nutú signísque loquúntur.   130

LOVE WILL FIND A WAY

Quóque magís tegitúr, ‖ tectús magis aéstuat ígnis.
Físsus erát tenuí rimá, ‖ quam dúxerat ólim

Pȳramus et Thisbē, alter iuvenum pulcherrimus, altera puellīs
quās Oriēns habuit praelāta, domōs contiguās tenuēre, ubi Semīramis urbem suam altam mūrīs coctilibus cīnxisse dīcitur. Vīcīnia
nōtitiam gradūsque prīmōs fēcit; amor tempore crēvit; taedae
quoque iūre coīssent, sed patrēs vetuēre. Ambō ex aequō mentibus captīs ārdēbant, id quod patrēs vetāre nōn potuēre: omnis
cōnscius abest; nūtūque sīgnīsque loquuntur.
Quōque magis tegitur, eō magis aestuat īgnis tēctus.   Pariēs

---

126. **nōtitiam**: cōnsuētūdinem. — 127. **crēvit**: auctus est. — 128. **vetu-**
ēre: prohibuēre. — 129. **ex aequō**: pariter, 119. — 130. **cōnscius**: testis. —
132. **dūxerat**: trāxerat (cf. 567, 1246).

cúm fierét, ‖ pariés domuí commúnis utríque.
Íd vitiúm ‖ nullí per saécula lónga notátum —
quíd non séntit amór? — ‖ primí vidístis, ‖ amántes,   135
ét vocís fecístis itér ; ‖ tutaéque per íllud
múrmure blánditiaé minimó ‖ transíre solébant.
Saépe ubi cónstiteránt, ‖ hinc Thísbe, ‖ Pýramus íllinc,
ínque vicés ‖ fuerát captátus anhélitus óris,
' Ínvide,' dícebánt, ‖ ' pariés, ‖ quid amántibus óbstas?   140
Quántum erat út sinerés ‖ totó nos córpore iúngi,
aút hoc sí nimiúm ‖ vel ad óscula dánda patéres !
Néc sumus íngratí ; ‖ tibi nós debére fatémur
quód datus ést verbís ‖ ad amícas tránsitus aúres.'
Tália díversá ‖ nequíquam séde locúti   145
súb noctém dixére valé ‖ partíque dedére
óscula quísque suaé ‖ non pérveniéntia cóntra.

commūnis utrīque domuī fissus erat tenuī rīmā quam ōlim cum
fieret dūxerat. Id vitium nūllī per saecula longa notātum, vōs,
amantēs, prīmī vīdistis — quid nōn sentit amor? — et vōcis iter
fēcistis ; tūtaeque per illud minimō murmure blanditiae vestrae
trānsīre solēbant. Saepe, ubi cōnstiterant, hinc Thisbē, Pȳramus
illinc, anhēlitusque ōris in vicēs fuerat captātus, ' Invide pariēs,'
dīcēbant, ' quid amantibus obstās? Quantum erat ut tōtō corpore nōs iungī sinerēs, aut si hōc est nimium vel ad ōscula
danda patērēs ! Nec tamen sumus ingrātī ; tibi enim nōs dē-
bēre fatēmur quod trānsitus ad amīcās aurēs verbīs nostrīs est
datus.'

Tālia dīversā in sēde nēquīquam locūtī, sub noctem valē
dīxēre, ōsculaque nōn contrā pervenientia partī suae quisque
dedēre.

THEY PLAN AN ELOPEMENT

Póstera nócturnós ‖ auróra remóverat ígnes
sólque pruínosás radiís ‖ siccáverat hérbas :
ád solitúm coïére locúm. ‖ Tum múrmure párvo   150
múlta priús questí, ‖ statuúnt ut nócte silénti
fállere cústodés ‖ foribúsque° excédere témptent,
cúmque dom° éxierínt ‖ urbís quoque técta relínquant ;
néve sit érrandúm ‖ lató spatiántibus árvo,
cónveniánt ‖ ad bústa Niní ‖ lateántque sub úmbra   155
árboris : ‖ árbor ibí ‖ niveís ubérrima pómis
árdua mórus erát ‖ gelidó contérmina fónti.

THISBE IS FIRST AT THE TRYSTING PLACE AND MEETS WITH AN ADVENTURE

Pácta placént ; ‖ et lúx tardé discédere vísa
praécipitátur aquís ‖ et aquís nox súrgit ab ísdem.
Cállida pér tenebrás ‖ versáto cárdine Thísbe   160

Postera aurōra īgnēs nocturnōs remōverat, sōlque radiīs suīs
pruīnōsās herbās siccāverat : amantēs ad solitum locum coïēre.
Tum multa prius murmure parvō questī, statuunt ut nocte silentī
custōdēs fallere ēque foribus excēdere temptent, cumque domō
exierint, ut urbis quoque tēcta relinquant ; nēve eīs sit errandum
in lātō arvō spatiantibus, statuunt ut ad būsta Ninī conveniant,
lateantque sub umbrā arboris : namque arbor ibi erat, gelidō contermina fontī, ardua mōrus niveīs ūberrima pōmīs.

Pacta placent ; et lūx, quae amantibus tardē discēdere est vīsa,
praecipitātur aquīs, et nox ab īsdem aquīs surgit.   Thisbē callida
per tenebrās cardine versātō ēgreditur fallitque custōdēs suōs,

---

152. temptent : cōnentur. — 155. būsta : tumulum. — 157. contermina :
contigua, 124. — 157. gelidō : frīgidō. — 158. pacta : condiciōnēs, 10.

égreditúr ‖ fallítque suós ‖ adopértaque vúltum
pérvenit ád tumulúm ‖ dictáque sub árbore sédit.
Aúdacém faciébat amór. ‖ Venit écce recénti
caéde leaéna ‖ boúm spumántes óblita ríctus
dépositúra sitím ‖ vicíni fóntis in únda.   165
Quám procul ád lunaé radiós ‖ Babylónia Thísbe
vídit et óbscurúm ‖ trepidó pede fúgit in ántrum,
dúmque fugít ‖ tergó velámina lápsa relíquit.
Út lea saéva sitím ‖ multá compéscuit únda,
dúm redit ín silvás, ‖ invéntos fórte sinᵉ ípsa   170
óre cruéntató ‖ tenués laniávit amíctus.

PYRAMUS MISSES HIS APPOINTMENT AND JUMPS AT
CONCLUSIONS

Sérius égressús ‖ vestígia vídit in álto
púlvere cérta feraé ‖ totóquᵉ expálluit óre
Pýramus. Út veró ‖ vestém quoque sánguine tínctam

adopertaque vultum ad tumulum pervenit, dictāque sub arbore
sēdit. Audācem amor eam faciēbat. Ecce leaena tamen recentī
boum caede oblita rictūs spūmantēs, venit sitim in undā fontis
vīcīnī dēpositūra. Quam Babylōnia Thisbē procul ad lūnae radiōs
vīdit, et trepidō pede in antrum obscūrum fūgit, dumque fugit
vēlāmina sua ā tergō lāpsa relīquit. Lea autem saeva ut sitim
multā undā compescuit, dum in silvās redit, amictūs tenuēs forte
sine ipsā inventōs ōre cruentātō laniāvit.

Pýramus, sērius ēgressus, in altō pulvere certa ferae vestīgia
vīdit, expalluitque tōtō in ōre. Ut vērō vestem quoque sanguine
tīnctam repperit, 'Ūna nox,' inquit, 'duōs amantēs perdet; ē

161. adoperta: vēlāta. — 164. rictūs: ōs, 139. — 166. radiōs: lūcem,
158. — 169. compescuit: dēposuit, 165. — 172. sērius: tardius, 158.

répperit, 'Úna duós,' ‖ inquít, ‖ 'nox pérdet amántes: 175
é quibus ílla ‖ fuít longá ‖ digníssima víta,
nóstra nocéns ‖ animᵃ ést: ‖ ego té, ‖ miseránda, ‖ perémi,
ín loca pléna metús ‖ qui iússi nócte veníres
néc prior húc vení. ‖ Nostrúm divéllite córpus
ét sceleráta feró consúmite víscera mórsu,   180
Ó quicúmque ‖ sub hác habitátis rúpe, ‖ leónes.
Séd timidⁱ ést optáre necém.'

HIS LIFEBLOOD DYES THE MULBERRIES RED

Velámina Thísbes
tóllit et ád pactaé ‖ secúm fert árboris úmbram.
Útque dedít notaé lacrimás, ‖ dedit óscula vésti,
'Áccipe núnc,' ‖ inquít, ‖ 'nostrí quoque sánguinis haústus!' 185
Quóquᵉ erat áccinctús ‖ demísit in ília férrum;
néc mora, ‖ férventí moriéns ‖ e vúlnere tráxit.

quibus illa dīgnissima fuit longā vītā, nostra anima est nocēns;
ego, Ō miseranda, tē perēmī, quī iussī ut in loca metūs plēna
nocte venīrēs, nec prior hūc vēnī. Dīvellite nostrum corpus,
Ō leōnēs, quīcumque sub hāc rūpe habitātis, et scelerāta
vīscera morsū ferō cōnsūmite. Sed optāre necem est hominis
timidī.'

Velāmina Thisbēs tollit, et sēcum ad umbram arboris pactae
fert; utque nōtae vestī lacrimās dedit, ut ōscula dedit, 'Accipe
nunc,' inquit, 'nostrī quoque sanguinis haustūs!' ferrumque quō
erat accīnctus in īlia sua dēmīsit; nec erat mora, sed ferventī ē
vulnere moriēns tēlum trāxit.

---

175. **repperit:** invēnit, 170. — 177. **perēmī:** perdidī, 175. — 180. **scele-**
rāta: impia. — 182. **necem:** mortem, 13. — 183. **pactae:** dictae, 162. —
186. **dēmīsit:** īnfīxit. **īlia:** latus, 115.

Út iacuít ‖ resupínus humó ‖ cruor émicat álte :
nón alitér ‖ quam cúm vitiáto ‖ fístula plúmbo
scínditur, ét tenuí ‖ stridénte forámine lóngas   190
éiaculátur aquás, ‖ atque᷄ íctibus áera rúmpit.
Árborei fetús ‖ aspérgine caédis in átram
vértuntúr faciém, ‖ madefáctaque sánguine rádix
púniceó ‖ tinguít pendéntia móra colóre.

THISBE FINDS HER LOVER'S BODY

Écce metú nondúm positó, ‖ ne fállat amántem   195
ílla redít, ‖ iuvenémqu᷄e oculís animóque requírit
quántaque vítarít ‖ narráre perícula géstit.
Útque loc᷄ᵘᵐ ét visá cognóscit in árbore fórmam,
síc facit íncertám ‖ pomí color : ‖ haéret an haéc sit.
Dúm dubitát ‖ tremebúnda vidét pulsáre cruéntum   200
membra so‖lum ‖ re₁troque pe₁dem tulit, ‖ oraque ₁ buxo

Ut iacuit humō resupīnus cruor altē ēmicat : nōn aliter quam
cum fistula plumbō vitiātō scinditur, et tenuī forāmine strīdente
longās aquās ēiaculātur, atque ictibus āëra rumpit. Arboreī fētūs
aspergine caedis in ātram faciem vertuntur, rādīxque sanguine
madefacta mōra pendentia pūniceō colōre tinguit.

Ecce illa, metū nōndum positō, nē amantem fallat, redit, iuve-
nemque oculīs animōque requīrit, quantaque perīcula vītārit nār-
rāre gestit. Utque locum fōrmamque in arbore vīsā cognōscit,
sīc color pōmī eam incertam facit : haeret an haec sit arbor
dicta. Dum dubitat, tremebunda membra cruentum solum pul-
sāre videt, retrōque pedem tulit, ōraque buxō pallidiōra gerēns

---

189. vitiātō: ruptō. — 191. ictibus: impetū. — 192. fētūs: frūctūs. —
193. faciem: colōrem. — 194. pūniceō: rubrō. — 195. positō: dēpositō,
remōtō, 148. — 197. vītārit: effūgerit, 7. gestit: cupit.

pallidi_|ora ge_|rens, ‖ ex_|horruit _| aequoris _| instar,
quod tremit _| exigu_|a ‖ cum _| summum _| stringitur _| aura.

SHE TRIES TO RECALL HIM TO LIFE

Sed post_|quam remo_|rata ‖ su_|os co_|gnovit a_|mores,
percutit _| indi_|gnos ‖ cla_|ro plan_|gore la_|certos   205
et lani_|ata co_|mas ‖ am_|plexaque _| corpus a_|matum
vulnera _| supple_|vit lacri_|mis ‖ fle_|tumque cru_|ori
miscuit, _| et geli_|dis in _| vultibus _| oscula _| figens,
'Pyrame,' _| clama_|vit, ‖ 'quis _| te mihi _| casus ad_|emit?
Pyrame, _| respon_|de : ‖ tua _| te ca_|rissima _| Thisbe   210
nominat : _| exau_|di, _| vul_|tusqu^e at_|tolle ia_|centes !'
Ad no_|men This_|bes ‖ ocu_|los iam _| morte gra_|vatos
Pyramus _| ere_|xit ‖ vi_|saque re_|condidit _| illa.

HER VOW AND PRAYER

Quae post_|quam ve_|stemque su_|am co_|gnovit ‖ et _| ense
vidit e_|bur vacu_|um, ‖ 'Tua _| te manus,' _| inquit, 'a_|morque   215

exhorruit aequoris īnstar, quod tremit cum summum aurā exiguā stringitur.

Sed postquam remorāta amōrēs suōs cognōvit, lacertōs indīgnōs clārō plangōre percutit, et laniāta comās corpusque amātum amplexa, lacrimīs vulnera eius supplēvit, flētumque cruōrī miscuit, et ōscula gelidīs in vultibus figēns, 'Pȳrame,' clāmāvit, 'quis cāsus tē mihi adēmit? Respondē, Pȳrame : tua Thisbē cārissima tē nōminat : exaudī, vultūsque tuōs attolle iacentēs.' Pȳramus ad nōmen Thisbēs oculōs iam morte gravātōs ērēxit, vīsāque illā recondidit.

Quaeque postquam vestem suam cognōvit et ebur ēnse vacuum

---

202. **īnstar**: sīcut. — 203. **exiguā**: levī.   **stringitur**: impellitur. — 204. **amōrēs**: amantem, 175. — 209. **adēmit**: sustulit, ēripuit. — 211. **attolle**: ērige. — 213. **recondidit**: clausit. — 215. **ebur**: vāgīnam.

perdidit, | infe|lix. ‖ Est | et mihi | fortis in | unum
hoc manus, | est et a|mor ; ‖ dabit | hic in | vulnera | vires.
Persequar | exstinc|tum ‖ le|tique mi|serrima | dicar
causa co|mesque tu|i ; ‖ qui|que a me | morte re|velli
heu so|la pote|ras, ‖ pote|ris nec | morte re|velli.   220
Hoc tamen | ambo|rum ver|bis ‖ es|tote ro|gati,
O mul|tum mise|ri, ‖ meus | illi|usque pa|rentes,
ut quos | certus a|mor, ‖ quos | hora no|vissima | iunxit,
compo|ni tumu|lo ‖ non | invide|atis e|odem.
At tu | quae ra|mis ‖ ar|bor ‖ mise|rabile | corpus   225
nunc tegis | uni|us, ‖ mox | es tec|tura du|orum,
signa te|ne cae|dis ‖ pul|losqu e et | luctibus | aptos
semper ha|be fe|tus, ‖ gemi|ni monu|menta cru|oris.'

HER DEATH

Dixit et | apta|to pec|tus mu|crone sub | imum
incubu|it fer|ro ‖ quod ad|huc a | caede te|pebat.   230

vīdit, 'Tua manus,' inquit, 'amorque, īnfēlīx, tē perdidit. Et
mihi est manus fortis in hōc ūnum, et mihi est amor; hīc vīrēs
in vulnera mihi dabit. Tē exstīnctum persequar, causaque mi-
serrima comesque lētī tuī dīcar; tūque quī ā mē heu morte
sōlā revellī poterās, poteris nec morte revellī. Hōc tamen,
Ō multum miserī parentēs meus illīusque, ambōrum verbīs estōte
rogātī, ut nōs eōdem in tumulō compōnī nōn invideātis quōs
certus amor, quōs hōra novissima iūnxit. At tū, arbor, quae
nunc rāmīs tuīs miserābile corpus ūnīus tegis, mox duōrum corpora es tēctūra, tenē sīgna caedis, fētūsque pullōs et lūctibus
aptōs semper habē, geminī monumenta cruōris.

Tālia dīxit, et mucrōne sub īmum pectus aptātō, ferrō quod

---

219. revellī: sēiungī. — **227. pullōs:** nigrōs, ātrōs, 192. — **228. fētūs:**
frūctūs.

Vota ta|men teti|gere de|os, ‖ teti|gere pa|rentes :
nam color ₁ in po|m° est ‖ ubi | perma|turuit | ater ;
quodque ro|gis super|est ‖ u|na requi|escit in | urna.

adhūc ab illīus caede tepēbat incubuit.   Vōta tamen eōrum
tetigēre deōs, parentēsque tetigēre : nam color in pōmō ubi
permātūruit, est āter ; idque quod rogīs superest ūnā in urnā
requiēscit.

    231. tetigēre: mōvēre, 84. — **233.** requiēscit : compositum est, 224.

AMOR: MARTIN.

III. APOLLO'S UNREQUITED LOVE FOR DAPHNE

CUPID'S BOAST

Prīmus a₁mor Phoe₁bī ‖ Da₁phnē Pe₁nēïa, ₁ quem non
fors i₁gnāra de₁dit, ‖ sed ₁ saeva Cu₁pīdinis ₁ īra.   235
Dēlius ₁ hunc nu₁per ‖ vic₁tō ser₁pente su₁perbus
vīderat ₁ adduc₁tō ‖ flec₁tentem ₁ cornua ₁ nervō,
'Quid'que 'ti₁bi, ‖ la₁scīve pu₁er, ‖ cum ₁ fortibus ₁ armīs?'
dīxerat; ₁ 'ista de₁cent ume₁rōs ge₁stāmina ₁ nostrōs,

Prīmus amor Phoebī erat Daphnē Pēnēïa, quem amōrem nōn
fors ignāra, sed saeva Cupīdinis īra dedit.   Dēlius victō serpente
superbus hunc cornua nervō adductō flectentem nuper vīderat,
dīxeratque, 'Quid est tibi, lascīve puer, cum fortibus armīs?
Ista gestāmina umerōs decent nostrōs, quī ferae (dare), quī

235. ignāra: caeca.—237. cornua: arcum.

qui dare ˌ certa feˌrae, ‖ dare ˌ vulnera ˌ possumus ˌ hosti,   240
qui modo ˌ pestifeˌro ‖ tot ˌ iugera ˌ ventre preˌmentem
stravimus ˌ innumerˌis ‖ tumiˌdum Pyˌthona saˌgittis.
Tu face ˌ nescio ˌ quos ‖ esˌto conˌtentus aˌmores
indaˌgare tuˌa, ‖ nec ˌ laudes ˌ adsere ˌ nostras.'
Filius ˌ huic Veneˌris, ‖ Fiˌgat tuus ˌ omnia, ˌ Phoebe,   245
te meus ˌ arcus ; ‖ aˌit, ‖ quanˌtoqueͤ aniˌmalia ˌ cedunt
cuncta deˌo, ‖ tanˌto minor ˌ est tua ˌ gloria ˌ nostra.'

HE SHOOTS TWO ARROWS. DAPHNE'S AMBITION

Dixit et ˌ eliˌso ‖ perˌcussis ˌ aere ˌ pennis
impiger ˌ umbroˌsa Parˌnasi ˌ constitit ˌ arce
eque saˌgittifeˌra ‖ promˌpsit duo ˌ tela phaˌretra   250
diverˌsorᵘᵐ opeˌrum ; ‖ fugat ˌ hoc, ‖ facit ˌ illud aˌmorem.
Quod facit ˌ hamaˌtᵘᵐ est ‖ et ˌ cuspide ˌ fulget aˌcuta :
quod fugat ˌ obtuˌsᵘᵐ est ‖ et haˌbet sub haˌrundine ˌ plumbum.
Hoc deus ˌ in nymˌpha ‖ Peˌneide ˌ fixit ; at ˌ illo

hostī vulnera certa dare possumus ; quī modo tumidum Pȳthōna
tot iūgera ventre pestiferō prementem innumerīs sagittīs strāvi-
mus. Estō tū contentus face tuā nēsciō quōs amōrēs indāgāre
nec adsere laudēs nostrās.' Huic fīlius Veneris respondit :
'Omnia tuus fīgat, Phoebe,' ait, 'tē meus arcus fīget : quantō-
que cūncta animālia deō cēdunt, tantō minor est tua glōria
nostrā.'

Tālia dīxit Cupīdō, et āēre ēlīsō percussīs pennīs in umbrōsā
Parnāsī arce impiger cōnstitit, ēque sagittiferā pharetrā duo tēla
prōmpsit dīversōrum operum : hōc fugat, facit autem illud amōrem. Id quod amōrem facit est hāmātum et cuspide acūta fulget :
id vērō quod fugat est obtūsum et sub harundine plumbum habet.

---

241. **prementem** : tegentem, 226. — 248. **pennīs** : ālīs. — 249. **impiger** :
celer, 110. — 250. **prōmpsit** : sūmpsit.

laesit A|polline|as ‖ tra|iecta per | ossa ‖ me|dullas.   255

Protinus | alter a|mat ; ‖ fugit | altera | nomen a|mantis,

silva|rum tene|bris ‖ cap|tiva|rumque fe|rarum

exuvi|is gau|dens ‖ in|nuptae|qu° aemula | Phoebes.

Vitta co|erce|bat ‖ posi|tos sine | lege ‖ ca|pillos.

Mult¹ il|lam peti|er°, ‖ il|lᵃ aver|sata pe|tentes   260

impati|ens ‖ ex|persque vi|ri ‖ nemo|rᵘᵐ avia | lustrat

nec quid Hy|men, ‖ quid A|mor, ‖ quid | sint co|nubia, | curat.

Saepe pa|ter di|xit, ‖ 'Gene|rum ‖ mihi, | filia, | debes.'

Saepe pa|ter di|xit, ‖ 'De|bes mihi, | nata, ‖ ne|potes.'

Illa ve|lut cri|men ‖ tae|das ex|osa iu|gales   265

pulchra ve|recun|do ‖ suf|funditur | ora ru|bore,

inque pa|tris blan|dis hae|rens cer|vice la|certis,

'Da mihi | perpetu|a ‖ geni|tor ca|rissime,' | dixit,

'virgini|tate fru|i. ‖ Dedit | hoc pater | ante Di|anae.'

Hōc deus in nymphā Pēnēide fīxit ; at illō per ossa trāiecta Apol-
līneās medullās laesit. Prōtinus alter amat ; fugit altera ipsum
nōmen amantis, silvārum tenebrīs gaudēns, exuviīsque captīvārum
ferārum, innūptaeque aemula Phoebēs. Vitta capillōs ēius sine
lēge positōs coërcēbat. Multī procī illam petiēre, at illa eōs
petentēs āversāta, expers impatiēnsque virī nemorum āvia lūstrat,
nec quid Hymen, quid Amor, quid cōnūbia sint, cūrat. Saepe
pater ēius dīxit, 'Generum mihi, mī fīlia, dēbes.' Saepe pater
ēius dīxit, 'Nepōtēs mihi, Ō nāta, dēbes.' At illa, taedās iugālēs velut crīmen exōsa, pulchra ōra rubōre verēcundō suffunditur,
blandīsque suīs lacertīs in cervīce patris haerēns, dīxit, 'Dā mihi,
Ō genitor cārissime, virginitāte fruī perpetuā. Namque Diānae
pater hōc ante illī dedit.'

---

255. trāiecta : trānsfīxa. — 258. exuviīs : spoliīs. — 259. coërcēbat : reti-
nēbat. — 261. lūstrat : percurrit, 96. — 264. nāta : fīlia, 263. — 265. exōsa :
āversāta, 260. iugālēs : nūptiālēs.

APOLLO'S GREAT LOVE

Ille qui₁dᵉᵐ obsequi₁tur. ‖ Sed ₁ te decor ₁ iste quod ₁ optas   270
esse ve₁tat, ‖ vo₁toque tu₁o tua ₁ forma re₁pugnat.
Phoebus a₁mat, ‖ vi₁saeque cu₁pit co₁nubia ₁ Daphnes,
quodque cu₁pit spe₁rat ; ‖ sua₁quᵉ illᵘᵐ o₁racula ₁ fallunt.
Utque le₁ves stipu₁lae ‖ dem₁ptis ado₁lentur a₁ristis,
ut faci₁bus sae₁pes ar₁dent, ‖ quas ₁ forte vi₁ator   275
vel nimis ₁ admo₁vit ‖ vel ₁ iam sub ₁ luce re₁liquit ;
sic deus ₁ in flam₁mas abi₁it, ‖ sic ₁ pectore ₁ toto
uritur ₁ et steri₁lem ‖ spe₁rando ₁ nutrit a₁morem.
Spectat in₁orna₁tos ‖ col₁lo pen₁dere ca₁pillos,
et ' Quid ₁ si co₁mantur ?' a₁it. ‖ Videt ₁ igne mi₁cantes   280
sideri₁bus simi₁les ocu₁los, ‖ videt ₁ oscula, ₁ quae non
est vi₁disse sa₁tis ; ‖ lau₁dat digi₁tosque ma₁nusque
bracchia₁quᵉ ‖ et nu₁dos medi₁a plus ₁ parte la₁certos :
siqua la₁tent ‖ meli₁ora pu₁tat. ‖ Fugit ₁ ocior ₁ aura
illa le₁vi, ‖ nequᵉ ad ₁ haec revo₁cantis ₁ verba re₁sistit :   285

Ille quidem obsequitur. Sed tē iste decor esse quod optās
vetat, fōrmaque tua tuō vōtō repūgnat. Phoebus amat, cōnūbiaque
cupit Daphnēs vīsae, idque quod cupit spērat : suaque ōrācula
illum fallunt. Utque levēs stipulae aristīs dēmptīs adolentur, utque
ārdent saepēs facibus quās viātor forte vel nimis admōvit vel iam
sub lūce relīquit ; sīc in flammās abiit deus ; sīc ille tōtō in
pectore ūritur, et spērandō sterilem amōrem suum nūtrit. Capillōs
in illīus collō inōrnātōs pendēre spectat, et ' Quid, sī cōmantur ?'
ait. Oculōsque īgne micantēs sīderibus similēs videt, videtque
ōscula, quae vīdisse nōn est satis : digitōsque manūsque laudat,
bracchiaque et lacertōs plūs quam mediā parte nūdōs : et siqua
latent ea meliōra esse putat. Sed illa ōcior aurā levī fugit, neque
ad haec verba deī revocantis resistit :

---

274. **adolentur** : combūruntur.—276. **lūce** : diē.—278. **sterilem** : vānum.
—281. **ōscula** : ōs, 139.—284. **meliōra** : fōrmōsiōra, 52. **ōcior** : celerior, 110.

A GOD'S WOOING

'Nympha, pre₁cor, ‖ Pe₁nei, ‖ ma₁ne ! ‖ non ₁ insequor ₁ hostis:
nympha, ma₁ne ! ‖ sic ₁ agna lu₁pum, ‖ sic ₁ cerva le₁onem,
sic aqui₁lam ‖ pen₁na fugi₁unt trepi₁dante co₁lumbae,
hostes ₁ quaeque su₁os. ‖ Amor ₁ est mihi ₁ causa se₁quendi.
Me mise₁rum ! ‖ ne ₁ prona ca₁das, ‖ in₁dignave ₁ laedi   290
crura no₁tent sen₁tes, ‖ et ₁ sim tibi ₁ causa do₁loris.
Aspera ₁ qua prope₁ras ₁ loca ₁ sunt. ‖ Mode₁ratius, ₁ oro,
curre fu₁gamqueᵉ inhi₁be. ‖ Mode₁ratius ₁ insequar ₁ ipse.
Cui place₁as in₁quire ta₁men. ‖ Non ₁ incola ₁ montis,
non ego ₁ sum pa₁stor, ‖ non ₁ hic ar₁menta gre₁gesque   295
horridus ₁ obser₁vo. ‖ Ne₁scis, ‖ teme₁raria, ₁ nescis
quem fugi₁as, ‖ ide₁oque fu₁gis. ‖ Mihi ₁ Delphica ₁ tellus
et Claros ₁ et Tene₁dos ‖ Pata₁raeaque ₁ regia ₁ servit.
Iuppiter ₁ est geni₁tor. ‖ Per ₁ me quod e₁ritque fu₁itque
estque pa₁tet. ‖ Per ₁ me con₁cordant ₁ carmina ₁ nervis.   300
Certa quidem nostrᵃ est, ‖ nostra tamen una sagitta

'Manē, precor, nympha Pēnēī ! Nōn hostis īnsequor: manē,
nympha !' Sīc agna lupum, sīc cerva leōnem, sīc columbae pennā
trepidante aquilam fugiunt, hostēs suōs quaeque. Mihi sequendī
amor est causa. Mē miserum ! nē cadās sentēsve crūra laedī
indīgna notent, et sim tibi causa dolōris. Aspera sunt loca quā
properās. Curre, igitur, moderātius, ōrō, fugamque inhibē. Īnse-
quar moderātius ipse. Inquīre tamen cui placeās. Nōn incola
montis, nōn pāstor ego sum ; nōn horridus armenta gregēsque hīc
observō. Nēscīs, Ō temerāria puella, nēscīs quem fugis, ideōque
fugis. Mihi enim Delphica tellus et Claros et Tenedos Pataraeaque
rēgia servit. Iuppiter mihi est genitor. Per mē autem patet id
quod fuit estque eritque. Per mē etiam carmina nervīs concor-
dant. Nostra sagitta quidem est certa, certior tamen nostrā est

290. laedī : vulnerārī.—293. inhibē : cohibē.—296. horridus : hīrsūtus.

certior, in vacuo ‖ quae vulnera pectore fecit.

Inventum medicina me^{um} est, ‖ opiferque per orbem

dicor et herbarum ‖ subiecta potentia nobis.

Ei mihi, quod nullis ‖ amor est sanabilis herbis,   305

nec prosunt domino, ‖ quae prosunt omnibus artes!'

A REFUSAL

Plura locuturum ‖ timido Peneia cursu

fugit cumqu^e ipso ‖ verb^a imperfecta reliquit,

tum quoque visa decens. ‖ Nudabant corpora venti

obviaqu^e adversas ‖ vibrabant flamina vestes   310

et levis impulsos ‖ retro dabat aura capillos;

auctaque forma fug^a est. ‖ Sed enim non sustinet ultra

perdere blanditias ‖ iuvenis deus, utque movebat

ips^e amor, admisso ‖ sequitur vestigia passu.

Ut canis in vacuo ‖ leporem cum Gallicus arvo   315

vidit et hic praedam ‖ pedibus petit, ille salutem;

ūna, quae vacuō in pectore meō vulnera fēcit. Medicīna autem
inventum est meum, opiferque per orbem terrārum dīcor, et herbā-
rum potentia subiecta est nōbīs. Ei mihi, quod amor sānābilis est
nūllīs herbīs, nec dominō prōsunt illae artēs quae omnibus prōsunt!'

Quem plūra locūtūrum Pēnēia timidō cursū fūgit, cumque
Apolline ipsō verba ēius imperfecta relīquit, tum quoque vīsa
decēns. Ventī enim corpora ēius nūdābant, obviaque flāmina
vestēs vibrābant adversās, et levis aura capillōs impulsōs retrō
dabat; fōrmaque illīus fugā est aucta. Sed enim iuvenis deus
blanditiās suās perdere nōn ultrā sustinet, utque amor ipse eum
movēbat, admissō passū vestīgia virginis sequitur. Ut cum Gallicus canis vacuō in arvō leporem vīdit, et hīc praedam, ille salūtem

306. prōsunt: iuvant, 27. — 309. decēns: pulchra, 266. — 314. admissō:
celerī, 110.

alter inhaesuro similis ‖ iam iamque tenere
sperat et extento ‖ stringit vestigia rostro;
alter in ambigu° est ‖ an sit comprensus, et ipsis
morsibus eripitur ‖ tangentiaqu^e ora relinquit: 320
sic deus et virg°, ‖ est hic spe celer, illa timore.
Qui tamen insequitur ‖ pennis adiutus amoris
ocior est ‖ requiemque negat ‖ tergoque fugacis
imminet et crinem ‖ sparsum cervicibus adflat.
Viribus absumptis ‖ expalluit illa, ‖ citaeque   325
victa labore fugae ‖ spectans Peneidas undas,
'Fer pater,' inquit, ‖ 'opem! ‖ Tellus,' ‖ ait, 'hisce, ‖ vel istam
quae facit ut laedar ‖ mutando perde figuram.'

DAPHNE BECOMES A LAUREL TREE INSTEAD OF A BRIDE

Vix prece finita ‖ torpor gravis occupat artus,
mollia cinguntur ‖ tenui praecordia libro,   330
in frondem crines, ‖ in ramos bracchia crescunt:

pedibus petit; alter similis canī inhaesūrō iam iamque praedam
suam tenēre spērat, et extentō rōstrō vestīgia ēius stringit; alter
in ambiguō est an iam sit comprēnsus, et ipsīs morsibus ēripitur,
tangentiaque ōra relinquit: sic deus et virgō, hīc spē est celer,
timōre illa. Is tamen quī pennīs amōris adiūtus īnsequitur est
ōcior, requiemque illī negat, imminetque tergō puellae fugācis,
et crīnem illīus cervīcibus sparsum adflat. Illa vīribus absūmptīs
expalluit, victaque labōre citae fugae Pēnēidas undās spectāns,
'Fer opem, pater,' inquit. 'Hīsce, Tellus,' ait, 'vel mūtandō
perde istam figūram, quae facit ut laedar.'

Prece vix fīnītā torpor gravis artūs ēius occupat, atque mollia
praecordia tenuī librō cinguntur; in frondem crīnēs, bracchia ēius
in rāmōs crēscunt; pēs ēius modo tam vēlōx pigrīs rādīcibus in

---

317. **inhaesūrō**: correptūrō.— 320. **ōra**: rictūs, 164.— 325. **absūmptīs**:
haustīs.— 328. **laedar**: offendar.— 330. **praecordia**: vīscera.

pes modo tam velox ‖ pigris radicibus haeret,
ora cacumen obit. ‖ Remanet nitor unus in illa.
Hanc quoque Phoebus amat, ‖ positaqu^e in stipite dextra
sentit adhuc trepidare ‖ novo sub cortice pectus,　　　335
complexusque suis ramos ‖ ut membra ‖ lacertis
oscula dat ligno : ‖ refugit tamen oscula lignum.
Cui deus, ' At quoniam coniunx ‖ mea non potes esse,
arbor eris certe,' ‖ dixit, ‖ ' mea.　Semper habebunt
te coma, te citharae, ‖ te nostrae, laure, pharetrae.　　　340
Tu ducibus Latiis aderis ‖ cum laeta Triumphum
vox canet et visent longas Capitolia pompas.
Postibus Augustis ‖ eadem fidissima custos
ante fores stabis ‖ mediamque tuebere quercum.
Utque me^{um} intonsis ‖ caput est iuvenale capillis,　　　345
tu quoque perpetuos ‖ semper gere frondis honores.'
　　Finierat Paean. ‖ Factis modo laurea ramis
adnuit utque caput ‖ vis^a est agitasse cacumen.

terrā haeret, obitque ōra cacūmen.　Nitor ūnus in illā remanet.
Hanc quoque Phoebus amat, dextrāque suā in stīpite positā pectus
Daphnēs novō sub cortice adhūc trepidāre sentit, complexusque
rāmōs illīus ut membra lacertīs suīs, ōscula līgnō dat : ipsum tamen
līgnum ōscula refugit.　Cui deus dīxit : ' At quoniam coniūnx mea
esse nōn potes, arbor mea certē eris.　Semper tē coma, tē citharae,
tē pharetrae nostrae, laure, habēbunt.　Tū Latiīs ducibus aderis
cum vōx laeta Triumphum canet, et vīsent Capitōlia longās pompās.
Tū eadem postibus Augustīs fīdissima custōs ante forēs stābis, quer-
cumque mediam tuēbere.　Utque meum caput iuvenāle est intōnsīs
capillīs, tū quoque semper gere perpetuōs frondis honōrēs.'
　　Fīnierat Paeān.　Laurea rāmīs modo factīs adnuit, cacūmenque
ut caput agitāsse est vīsa.

---

　　332. pigrīs : sēgnibus. — 333. nitor : splendor. — 344. tuēbere : dēfen-
dēs. — 348. agitāsse : movēre.

IV. HOW PHAËTHON DROVE HIS FATHER'S CHARIOT

THE PALACE OF THE SUN. PHAËTHON IS DAZZLED BY WHAT HE SEES

Regia Solis erat sublimibus alta columnis,
clara micante auro flammasque imitante pyropo,   350
cuius ebur nitidum fastigia summa tegebat;
argenti bifores radiabant lumine valvae.
Materiam superabat opus; nam Mulciber illic
aequora caelarat medias cingentia terras,
terrarumque orbem caelumque, quod imminet orbi.   355
Caeruleos habet unda deos, Tritona canorum,
Proteaque ambiguum, balaenarumque prementem
Aegaeona suis immania terga lacertis,
Doridaque et natas; quarum pars nare videtur,
pars in mole sedens virides siccare capillos,   360
pisce vehi quaedam: facies non omnibus una,
nec diversa tamen; qualem decet esse sororum.

353. opus: ars. — 355. imminet: impositum est. — 360. móle: rúpe, 181.

Terra viros urbesque gerit, silvasque ferasque,
fluminaque et nymphas et cetera numina ruris.
Haec super imposita est caeli fulgentis imago,   365
signaque sex foribus dextris, totidemque sinistris.

Quo simul acclivo Clymeneïa limite proles
venit et intravit dubitati tecta parentis,
protinus ad patrios sua fert vestigia vultus
consistitque procul : neque enim propiora ferebat   370
lumina.   Purpurea velatus veste sedebat
in solio Phoebus claris lucente smaragdis.
A dextra laevaque Dies et Mensis et Annus
Saeculaque et positae spatiis aequalibus Horae,
Verque novum stabat cinctum florente corona ;   375
stabat nuda Aestas et spicea serta gerebat;
stabat et Autumnus calcatis sordidus uvis,
et glacialis Hiems canos hirsuta capillos.

HE VENTURES INTO HIS FATHER'S PRESENCE. A RASH PROMISE

Inde loco medius rerum novitate paventem
sol oculis iuvenem, quibus adspicit omnia, vidit,   380
'Quae'que 'viae tibi causa? quid hac' ait 'arce petisti,
progenies, Phaëthon, haud infitianda parenti?'
Ille refert 'O lux immensi publica mundi,
Phoebe pater, si das huius mihi nominis usum,
nec falsa Clymene culpam sub imagine celat ;   385
pignora da, genitor, per quae tua vera propago
credar, et hunc animis errorem detrahe nostris.'
Dixerat.   At genitor circum caput omne micantes

---

367. **acclīvō līmite**: ardᵘā (411) viā — 369. **fert**: dīrigit. — 376. **serta**:
corōnam, 375. — 378. **hīrsūta**: horrida, 296. — 382. **īnfitianda**: abnegan-
da. — 383. **refert**: respondet, 210. — 386. **propāgō**: fīlius, prōlēs, 367.

deposuit radios, propiusque accedere iussit,
amplexuque dato, ' Nec tu meus esse negari   390
dignus es, et Clymene veros ' ait ' edidit ortus.
Quoque minus dubites, quodvis pete munus, ut illud
me tribuente feras : promissi testis adesto
dis iuranda palus, oculis incognita nostris.'

PHAËTHON'S STARTLING REQUEST

Vix bene desierat, currus rogat ille paternos,   395
inque diem alipedum ius et moderamen equorum.
Paenituit iurasse patrem : qui terque quaterque
concutiens inlustre caput, ' Temeraria ' dixit
' vox mea facta tua est; utinam promissa liceret
non dare ! confiteor, solum hoc tibi, nate, negarem :   400
dissuadere licet.   Non est tua tuta voluntas.
Magna petis, Phaëthon, et quae nec viribus istis
munera conveniant nec tam puerilibus annis.
Sors tua mortalis; non est mortale quod optas.
Plus etiam, quam quod superis contingere fas est,   405
nescius adfectas.   Placeat sibi quisque licebit ;
non tamen ignifero quisquam consistere in axe
me valet excepto.   Vasti quoque rector Olympi,
qui fera terribili iaculatur fulmina dextra,
non agat hos currus : et quid Iove maius habemus?   410

THE DANGERS OF THE STAR ROUTE

Ardua prima via est et qua vix mane recentes
enituntur equi : medio est altissima caelo,

391. ortūs: orīginem, 58. — 395. dēsierat: fīnierat, 347. — 396. moderāmen: regimen. — 398. inlūstre: splendidum. — 403. conveniant: apta sint, 227. — 405. contingere: cōnsequī, 113. — 406. adfectās: cupis, 273.

unde mare et terras ipsi mihi saepe videre
fit timor, et pavida trepidat formidine pectus.
Ultima prona via est et eget moderamine certo :   415
tunc etiam quae me subiectis excipit undis,
ne ferar in praeceps, Tethys solet ipsa vereri.
Adde quod adsidua rapitur vertigine caelum,
sideraque alta trahit celerique volumine torquet.
Nitor in adversum, nec me qui cetera, vincit   420
impetus, et rapido contrarius evehor orbi.
Finge datos currus : quid ages? poterisne rotatis
obvius ire polis, ne te citus auferat axis?
Forsitan et lucos illic urbesque deorum
concipias animo delubraque ditia donis   425
esse? per insidias iter est formasque ferarum.
Utque viam teneas nulloque errore traharis,
per tamen adversi gradieris cornua Tauri
Haemoniosque arcus violentique ora Leonis
saevaque circuitu curvantem bracchia longo   430
Scorpion atque aliter curvantem bracchia Cancrum.
Nec tibi quadrupedes animosos ignibus illis,
quos in pectore habent, quos ore et naribus efflant,
in promptu regere est : vix me patiuntur, ubi acres
incaluere animi cervixque repugnat habenis.   435

"ASK ANYTHING BUT THAT!"

At tu, funesti ne sim tibi muneris auctor,
nate, cave, dum resque sinit, tua corrige vota.

---

415. prōna : dēclīvis. — 418. adsiduā : continuā. — 420. nītor : contendō.
— 422. finge : suppōne. — 425. concipiās : fingās, 422.   dēlūbra : templa,
87. — 434. in prōmptū : facile, 43.

Scilicet ut nostro genitum te sanguine credas,
pignora certa petis? do pignora certa timendo,
et patrio pater esse metu probor. Adspice vultus   440
ecce meos : utinamque oculos in pectora posses
inserere, et patrias intus deprendere curas !
Denique quicquid habet dives, circumspice, mundus,
eque tot ac tantis caeli terraeque marisque
posce bonis aliquid : nullam patiere repulsam.   445
Deprecor hoc unum, quod vero nomine poena,
non honor est: poenam, Phaëthon, pro munere poscis.
Quid mea colla tenes blandis, ignare, lacertis?
Ne dubita, dabitur — Stygias iuravimus undas ! —
quodcumque optaris : sed tu sapientius opta.'   450

THE BOY CANNOT BE DISSUADED.   THE CHARIOT OF THE SUN. FINAL PREPARATIONS

Finierat monitus ; dictis tamen ille repugnat
propositumque premit flagratque cupidine currus.
Ergo qua licuit genitor cunctatus, ad altos
deducit iuvenem, Vulcania munera, currus.
Aureus axis erat, temo aureus, aurea summae   455
curvatura rotae, radiorum argenteus ordo.
Per iuga chrysolithi positaeque ex ordine gemmae
clara repercusso reddebant lumina Phoebo.
Dumque ea magnanimus Phaëthon miratur opusque
perspicit, ecce vigil rutilo patefecit ab ortu   460
purpureas Aurora fores et plena rosarum
atria ; diffugiunt stellae, quarum agmina cogit

---

442. īnserere: immittere. — 446. dēprecor: āvertō. — 452. flagrat: ārdet,
275. — 453. cunctātus: morātus, 102. — 458. repercussō: reflexō.

Lucifer, et caeli statione novissimus exit.

Quem petere ut terras, mundumque rubescere vidit,

cornuaque extremae velut evanescere lunae,　　　　　465

iungere equos Titan velocibus imperat Horis.

Iussa deae celeres peragunt, ignemque vomentes

ambrosiae suco saturos praesaepibus altis

quadrupedes ducunt adduntque sonantia frena.

Tum pater ora sui sacro medicamine nati　　　　　470

contigit et rapidae fecit patientia flammae,

imposuitque comae radios, praesagaque luctus

pectore sollicito repetens suspiria dixit:

DIRECTIONS FOR DRIVING THE FIERY HORSES

'Si potes his saltem monitis parere paternis,

parce, puer, stimulis, et fortius utere loris.　　　　　475

Sponte sua properant; labor est inhibere volentes.

Nec tibi directos placeat via quinque per arcus.

Sectus in obliquum est lato curvamine limes,

zonarumque trium contentus fine, polumque

effugit australem iunctamque aquilonibus Arcton.　　　　480

Hac sit iter: manifesta rotae vestigia cernes.

Utque ferant aequos et caelum et terra calores,

nec preme, nec summum molire per aethera cursum.

Altius egressus caelestia tecta cremabis,

inferius terras: medio tutissimus ibis.　　　　　485

Neu te dexterior tortum declinet ad Anguem,

neve sinisterior pressam rota ducat ad Aram:

---

467. vomentēs: efflantēs, 433.—**468. saturōs**: plēnōs, 461.—**472. prae-
sāga**: praenūntia.—**476. inhibēre**: coërcēre.—**483. preme**: dēprime. **mōlīre**: age, 410.—**487. pressam**: dēpressam.

inter utrumque tene.   Fortunae cetera mando,
quae iuvet et melius quam tu tibi consulat opto.
Dum loquor, Hesperio positas in litore metas   490
umida nox tetigit ; non est mora libera nobis.
Poscimur : effulget tenebris aurora fugatis.
Corripe lora manu ! — vel, si mutabile pectus
est tibi, consiliis, non curribus utere nostris,
dum potes, et solidis etiam nunc sedibus adstas,   495
dumque male optatos nondum premis inscius axes.
Quae tutus spectes, sine me dare lumina terris ! '

THE START.   THE STEEDS BOLT

Occupat ille levem iuvenali corpore currum,
statque super, manibusque datas contingere habenas
gaudet, et invito grates agit inde parenti.   500
Interea volucres Pyrois et Eoüs et Aethon,
solis equi, quartusque Phlegon hinnitibus auras
flammiferis implent pedibusque repagula pulsant.
Quae postquam Tethys, fatorum ignara nepotis,
reppulit, et facta est immensi copia mundi,   505
corripuere viam, pedibusque per aëra motis
obstantes scindunt nebulas, pennisque levati
praetereunt ortos îsdem de partibus Euros.
Sed leve pondus erat, nec quod cognoscere possent
solis equi, solitaque iugum gravitate carebat.   510
Utque labant curvae iusto sine pondere naves
perque mare instabiles nimia levitate feruntur,
sic onere adsueto vacuus dat in aëra saltus,

---

497. **sine**: patere. — 503. **repāgula**: carcerēs, 93. — 505. **reppulit**: re-
mōvit. — 511. **labant**: vacillant.

succutiturque alte similisque est currus inani.
Quod simul ac sensere, ruunt tritumque relinquunt   515
quadriiugi spatium, nec quo prius, ordine currunt.
Ipse pavet; nec qua commissas flectat habenas,
nec scit qua sit iter; nec, si sciat, imperet illis.

DOUBT AND DISMAY

Ut vero summo despexit ab aethere terras
infelix Phaëthon penitus penitusque iacentes,   520
palluit, et subito genua intremuere timore,
suntque oculis tenebrae per tantum lumen obortae.
Et iam mallet equos numquam tetigisse paternos;
iam cognosse genus piget et valuisse rogando :
iam Meropis dici cupiens, ita fertur, ut acta   525
praecipiti pinus borea, cui victa remisit
frena suus rector, quam dis votisque reliquit.
Quid faciat? multum caeli post terga relictum,
ante oculos plus est : animo metitur utrumque.
Et modo quos illi fatum contingere non est,   530
prospicit occasus, interdum respicit ortus.
Quidque agat ignarus stupet, et nec frena remittit,
nec retinere valet, nec nomina novit equorum.
Sparsa quoque in vario passim miracula caelo
vastarumque videt trepidus simulacra ferarum.   535

OFF THE TRACK. HOTTER AND HOTTER

Est locus, in geminos ubi bracchia concavat arcus
Scorpios, et cauda flexisque utrimque lacertis

524. **piget**: paenitet, 397. — 526. **pīnus**: nāvis, 511. — 530. **contingere**: pervenīre, 162. — 535. **simulācra**: imāginēs, 365. — 536. **concavat**: flectit, 237, 537.

porrigit in spatium signorum membra duorum.
Hunc puer ut nigri madidum sudore veneni
vulnera curvata minitantem cuspide vidit,   540
mentis inops gelida formidine lora remisit.
Quae postquam summo tetigere iacentia tergo,
exspatiantur equi, nulloque inhibente per auras
ignotae regionis eunt ; quaque impetus egit,
hac sine lege ruunt, altoque sub aethere fixis   545
incursant stellis, rapiuntque per avia currum.
Et modo summa petunt, modo per declive viasque
praecipites spatio terrae propiore feruntur.
Inferiusque suis fraternos currere Luna
admiratur equos, ambustaque nubila fumant.   550

SOL

Corripitur flammis ut quaeque altissima, tellus,
fissaque agit rimas et sucis aret ademptis.
Pabula canescunt ; cum frondibus uritur arbor,

materiamque suo praebet seges arida damno.
Parva queror : magnae pereunt cum moenibus urbes,   555
cumque suis totas populis incendia gentes
in cinerem vertunt ; silvae cum montibus ardent.
Tum vero Phaëthon cunctis e partibus orbem
adspicit accensum, nec tantos sustinet aestus,
ferventesque auras velut e fornace profunda   560
ore trahit, currusque suos candescere sentit.
Et neque iam cineres eiectatamque favillam
ferre potest, calidoque involvitur undique fumo.
Quoque eat, aut ubi sit, picea caligine tectus
nescit, et arbitrio volucrum raptatur equorum.   565

THE EARTH SUFFERS FROM THE HEAT

Sanguine tunc credunt in corpora summa vocato
Aethiopum populos nigrum traxisse colorem.
Tum facta est Libye raptis umoribus aestu
arida ; tum nymphae passis fontesque lacusque
deflevere comis.   570
Dissilit omne solum, penetratque in Tartara rimis
lumen et infernum terret cum coniuge regem ;
et mare contrahitur, siccaeque est campus harenae
quod modo pontus erat ; quosque altum texerat aequor
exsistunt montes et sparsas Cycladas augent.   575
Ima petunt pisces, nec se super aequora curvi
tollere consuetas audent delphines in auras.
Corpora phocarum summo resupina profundo
exanimata natant ; ipsum quoque Nerea fama est

554. **māteriam**: pābulum. — 563. **involvitur**: circumfunditur. — 564. **pi-**
ceā: obscūrā, 167. — 566. **vocātō**: ēductō. — 567. **trāxisse**: sūmpsisse. —
571. **dissilit**: hiat, agit rīmās, 552. — 578. **resupīna**: inversa.

Doridaque et natas tepidis latuisse sub antris.   580
Ter Neptunus aquis cum torvo bracchia vultu
exserere ausus erat; ter non tulit aëris ignes.
Alma tamen Tellus, ut erat circumdata ponto,
inter aquas pelagi, contractos undique fontes,
qui se condiderant in opacae viscera matris,   585
sustulit oppressos collo tenus arida vultus;
opposuitque manum fronti, magnoque tremore
omnia concutiens paulum subsedit et infra
quam solet esse fuit; sacraque ita voce locuta est:

HER BITTER COMPLAINT

'Si placet hoc, meruique, quid O tua fulmina cessant,   590
summe deum? liceat periturae viribus ignis
igne perire tuo, clademque auctore levare.
Vix equidem fauces haec ipsa in verba resolvo' —
presserat ora vapor — 'tostos en adspice crines,
inque oculis tantum, tantum super ora favillae.   595
Hosne mihi fructus, hunc fertilitatis honorem
officiique refers, quod adunci vulnera aratri
rastrorumque fero totoque exerceor anno,
quod pecori frondes alimentaque mitia, fruges
humano generi, vobis quoque tura ministro?   600
Sed tamen exitium fac me meruisse; quid undae,
quid meruit frater? cur illi tradita sorte
aequora decrescunt et ab aethere longius absunt?
Quod si nec fratris, nec te mea gratia tangit,
at caeli miserere tui! circumspice utrumque: 605

---

580. **tepidīs**: calidīs, 563. — 582. **exserere**: ēmittere. — 592. **clādem**: exitium. — 593. **resolvō**: aperiō.   **faucēs**: ōs, 433. — 597. **aduncī**: curvī, 576. — 600. **ministrō**: praebeō, 554. — 601. **fac**: finge, 422.

fumat uterque polus; quos si vitiaverit ignis,
atria vestra ruent. Atlas en ipse laborat,
vixque suis umeris candentem sustinet axem.
Si freta, si terrae pereunt, si regia caeli,
in chaos antiquum confundimur. Eripe flammis　　610
siquid adhuc superest, et rerum consule summae.'
Dixerat haec Tellus: neque enim tolerare vaporem
ulterius potuit nec dicere plura; suumque
rettulit os in se propioraque manibus antra.

JUPITER TO THE RESCUE

At pater omnipotens, superos testatus et ipsum　　615
qui dederat currus, nisi opem ferat, omnia fato
interitura gravi, summam petit arduus arcem,
unde solet latis nubes inducere terris,
unde movet tonitrus vibrataque fulmina iactat.
Sed neque quas posset terris inducere nubes　　620
tunc habuit nec quos caelo dimitteret imbres.
Intonat et dextra libratum fulmen ab aure
misit in aurigam pariterque animaque rotisque
expulit, et saevis compescuit ignibus ignes.
Consternantur equi et saltu in contraria facto　　625
colla iugo eripiunt abruptaque lora relinquunt.
Illic frena iacent, illic temone revulsus
axis, in hac radii fractarum parte rotarum,
sparsaque sunt late laceri vestigia currus.
At Phaëthon, rutilos flamma populante capillos,　　630
volvitur in praeceps longoque per aëra tractu

607. **ruent**: cadent, 290. — 613. **ulterius**: diūtius, 103. — 623. **mīsit**: iēcit, 116. — 624. **compescuit**: oppressit; cf. 169. — 629. **lacerī**: frāctī, 628. — 630. **rutilōs**: flāvōs.

fertur, ut interdum de caelo stella sereno
etsi non cecidit, potuit cecidisse videri.

THE DEATH OF PHAËTHON. HIS MOTHER'S SORROW

Quem procul a patria diverso maximus orbe
excipit Eridanus fumantiaque abluit ora.   635
Naides Hesperiae trifida fumantia flamma
corpora dant tumulo, signant quoque carmine saxum:
'HIC SITUS EST PHAËTHON, CURRUS AURIGA PATERNI
QUEM SI NON TENUIT MAGNIS TAMEN EXCIDIT AUSIS.'

Nam pater obductos, luctu miserabilis aegro,   640
condiderat vultus: et si modo credimus, unum
isse diem sine sole ferunt; incendia lumen
praebebant, aliquisque malo fuit usus in illo.
At Clymene, postquam dixit quaecumque fuerunt
in tantis dicenda malis, lugubris et amens   645
et laniata sinus totum percensuit orbem:
exanimesque artus primo, mox ossa requirens,
repperit ossa tamen peregrina condita ripa,
incubuitque loco, nomenque in marmore lectum
perfudit lacrimis et aperto pectore fovit.   650

A SONLESS FATHER AND A SUNLESS WORLD

Squalidus interea genitor Phaëthontis et expers
ipse sui decoris, qualis cum deficit orbem
esse solet, lucemque odit seque ipse diemque,
datque animum in luctus et luctibus adicit iram,
officiumque negat mundo. 'Satis' inquit 'ab aevi   655

---

638. situs est: positus est, 490. — 639. excidit: frūstrātus est. — 645. lūgubris: trīstis. — 646. percēnsuit: perlūstrāvit. — 648. peregrīnā: exterā.
— 651. squālidus: horridus, 296.

  sors mea principiis fuit inrequieta, pigetque
actorum sine fine mihi, sine honore laborum.
Quilibet alter agat portantes lumina currus!
Si nemo est, omnesque dei non posse fatentur,
ipse agat; ut saltem, dum nostras temptat habenas, 660
orbatura patres aliquando fulmina ponat.
Tum sciet, ignipedum vires expertus equorum,
non meruisse necem, qui non bene rexerit illos.'

  Talia dicentem circumstant omnia Solem
numina, neve velit tenebras inducere rebus, 665
supplice voce rogant; missos quoque Iuppiter ignes
excusat, precibusque minas regaliter addit.
Conligit amentes et adhuc terrore paventes
Phoebus equos, stimuloque domans et verbere caedit;
saevit enim natumque obiectat et imputat illis. 670

  656. **prīncipiīs:** initiō.—**661.** **orbātūra:** quae prīvent

JUPITER (from a Cameo)

V. ORPHEUS AND EURYDICE

A DISAPPOINTED BRIDEGROOM

Inde per immensum croceo velatus amictu
aethera digreditur Ciconumque Hymenaeus ad oras
tendit, et Orphea nequiquam voce vocatur.
Adfuit ille quidem, sed nec sollemnia verba
nec laetos vultus nec felix attulit omen.   675
Fax quoque quam tenuit lacrimoso stridula fumo
usque fuit, nullosque invenit motibus ignes.
Exitus auspicio gravior.   Nam nupta per herbas
dum nova Naiadum turba comitata vagatur,
occidit in talum serpentis dente recepto.   680

HIS VISIT TO HADES

Quam satis ad superas postquam Rhodopeius auras
deflevit vates, ne non temptaret et umbras,
ad Styga Taenaria est ausus descendere porta,
perque leves populos simulacraque functa sepulcro
Persephonen adiit inamoenaque regna tenentem   685
umbrarum dominum.   Pulsisque ad carmina nervis
sic ait: 'O positi sub terra numina mundi,
in quem recidimus, quicquid mortale creamur,
si licet et falsi positis ambagibus oris,
vera loqui sinitis, non huc, ut opaca viderem   690
Tartara, descendi, nec uti villosa colubris

---

671. amictus, 171.—672. Hymenaeus: Hymen, 262.—673. nēquīquam, 145.—682. vātēs: poēta.—684. fūncta: potīta, 10.—

terna Medusaei vincirem guttura monstri.
Causa viae est coniunx, in quam calcata venenum
vipera diffudit, crescentesque abstulit annos.

THE GUARDIAN OF THE UNDER WORLD

Posse pati volui, nec me temptasse negabo;   695
vicit Amor.   Supera deus hic bene notus in ora est;
an sit et hic, dubito.   Sed et hic tamen auguror esse;
famaque si veteris non est mentita rapinae,
vos quoque iunxit Amor. Per ego haec loca plena timoris,
per Chaos hoc ingens vastique silentia regni,   700
Eurydices, oro, properata retexite fata.
Omnia debentur vobis, paulumque morati
serius aut citius sedem properamus ad unam.
Tendimus huc omnes, haec est domus ultima, vosque
humani generis longissima regna tenetis.   705
Haec quoque, cum iustos matura peregerit annos,
iuris erit vestri; pro munere poscimus usum.
Quod si fata negant veniam pro coniuge, certum est
nolle redire mihi; leto gaudete duorum.'

692. terna: tria.—701. properāta: intempestāta.—706. perēgerit: fīnīverit.—708. veniam: mūnus.

THROUGH THE CHARM OF HIS SONG EURYDICE IS RESTORED

Talia dicentem nervosque ad verba moventem   710
exsangues flebant animae, nec Tantalus undam
captavit refugam, stupuitque Ixionis orbis,
nec carpsere iecur volucres, urnisque vacarunt
Belides, inque tuo sedisti, Sisyphe, saxo.
Tunc primum lacrimis victarum carmine fama est   715
Eumenidum maduisse genas. Nec regia coniunx
sustinet oranti, nec qui regit ima, negare,
Eurydicenque vocant. Umbras erat illa recentes
inter, et incessit passu de vulnere tardo.
Hanc simul et legem Rhodopeius accipit heros,   720
ne flectat retro sua lumina, donec Avernas
exierit valles; aut inrita dona futura.

Carpitur acclivis per muta silentia trames
arduus, obscurus, caligine densus opaca.
Nec procul afuerunt telluris margine summae.   725
Hic, ne deficeret, metuens avidusque videndi
flexit amans oculos; et protinus illa relapsa est.
Bracchiaque intendens prendique et prendere certans

ONLY TO BE LOST AGAIN

nil nisi cedentes infelix adripit auras.
Iamque iterum moriens non est de coniuge quicquam   730
questa suo: quid enim nisi se quereretur amatam?
Supremumque 'vale,' quod iam vix auribus ille
acciperet, dixit revolutaque rursus eodem est.

716. maduisse: *cf.* madidus, 539.—722. inrita: vāna.—723. acclīvis: *cf.* dēclīvis, 547.—732. valē, 146.

ORPHEUS AND EURYDICE

Non aliter stupuit gemina nece coniugis Orpheus,
quam tria qui timidus, medio portante catenas,   735
colla canis vidit.   Quem non pavor ante reliquit
quam natura prior, saxo per corpus oborto;
quique in se crimen traxit voluitque videri
Olenos esse nocens; tuque, O confisa figurae
infelix Lethaea tuae, iunctissima quondam   740
pectora, nunc lapides, quos umida sustinet Ide.
Orantem frustraque iterum transire volentem
portitor arcuerat.   Septem tamen ille diebus

734. nece: lētō, 700.—739. nocēns: 177.

squalidus in ripa Cereris sine munere sedit;
cura dolorque animi lacrimaeque alimenta fuere.   745
Esse deos Erebi crudeles questus, in altam
se recipit Rhodopen pulsumque aquilonibus Haemum.

AFTER THE POET'S CRUEL DEATH ORPHEUS AND EURYDICE ARE REUNITED

Sed tandem in ventos anima exhalata recessit.
Umbra subit terras, et quae loca viderat ante
cuncta recognoscit; quaerensque per arva piorum   750
invenit Eurydicen, cupidisque amplectitur ulnis.
Hic modo coniunctis spatiantur passibus ambo,
nunc praecedentem sequitur, nunc praevius anteit
Eurydicenque suam iam tuto respicit Orpheus.

745. **alimenta:** 99. —751. **ulnīs:** bracchiīs, 581.—752. **spatiantur:** ambulant.

DEATH OF ORPHEUS

THE DRUNKEN SILENUS IN A PROCESSION OF BACCHANALS.

VI. THE TOUCH OF GOLD

KING MIDAS DOES THE GOD A FAVOR

Nec satis hoc Baccho est: ipsos quoque deserit agros,   755
cumque choro meliore sui vineta Timoli
Pactolonque petit — quamvis non aureus illo
tempore nec caris erat invidiosus harenis.
Hunc adsueta cohors satyri bacchaeque frequentant,
at Silenus abest. Titubantem annisque meroque   760
ruricolae cepere Phryges, vinctumque coronis
ad regem duxere Midan, cui Thracius Orpheus
orgia tradiderat cum Cecropio Eumolpo.
Qui simul adgnovit socium comitemque sacrorum,
hospitis adventu festum genialiter egit   765
per bis quinque dies et iunctas ordine noctes.
Et iam stellarum sublime coëgerat agmen
Lucifer undecimus, Lydos cum laetus in agros
rex venit, et iuveni Silenum reddit alumno.

A WONDERFUL GIFT

Huic deus optandi gratum, sed inutile, fecit   770
muneris arbitrium, gaudens altore recepto.
Ille, male usurus donis, ait 'Effice, quicquid
corpore contigero, fulvum vertatur in aurum.'

756. chorō: āgmine, 704. — 758. cārīs: pretiōsīs. — 760. **titubantem:**
labantem, 511. — 761. corōnīs: sertīs, 376.

Adnuit optatis, nocituraque munera solvit
Liber, et indoluit, quod non meliora petisset.   775
Laetus abit gaudetque malo Berecyntius heros :
pollicitique fidem tangendo singula temptat.
Vixque sibi credens, non alta fronde virentem
ilice detraxit virgam : virga aurea facta est ;
tollit humo saxum : saxum quoque palluit auro ;   780
contigit et glebam : contactu gleba potenti
massa fit ; arentes Cereris decerpsit aristas :
aurea messis erat ; demptum tenet arbore pomum :
Hesperidas donasse putes. Si postibus altis
admovit digitos, postes radiare videntur.   785
Ille etiam liquidis palmas ubi laverat undis,
unda fluens palmis Danaën eludere posset.
Vix spes ipse suas animo capit, aurea fingens
omnia. Gaudenti mensas posuere ministri
exstructas dapibus, nec tostae frugis egentes :   790
tum vero, sive ille sua Cerealia dextra
munera contigerat, Cerealia dona rigebant ;
sive dapes avido convellere dente parabat,
lamina fulva dapes, admoto dente, premebat.
Miscuerat puris auctorem muneris undis :   795
fusile per rictus aurum fluitare videres.

MIDAS REPENTS HIS CHOICE, AND THE GILDED CURSE IS REMOVED

Attonitus novitate mali, divesque miserque,
effugere optat opes, et quae modo voverat, odit.

782. **dēcerpsit**: dētrāxit, 779. — 783. **dēmptum**: dēcerptum, 782. —
786. **palmās**: manūs, 215. — 789. **posuēre**: apposuēre. — 790. **exstrūctās**:
congestās. — 796. **fūsile**: liquefactum.

Copia nulla famem relevat: sitis arida guttur
urit, et inviso meritus torquetur ab auro.   800
Ad caelumque manus et splendida bracchia tollens,
'Da veniam, Lenaee pater! peccavimus;' inquit,
'sed miserere, precor, speciosoque eripe damno.'
Mite deum numen Bacchus peccasse fatentem
restituit, factique fide data munera solvit.   805
'Neve male optato maneas circumlitus auro,
vade' ait 'ad magnis vicinum Sardibus amnem,
perque iugum montis labentibus obvius undis
carpe viam, donec venias ad fluminis ortus;
spumigeroque tuum fonti, qua plurimus exit,   810
subde caput, corpusque simul, simul elue crimen.'
Rex iussae succedit aquae. Vis aurea tinxit
flumen, et humano de corpore cessit in amnem.

THE LYRE VERSUS THE PIPES

Ille, perosus opes, silvas et rura colebat,
Panaque montanis habitantem semper in antris.   815
Pingue sed ingenium mansit; nocituraque, ut ante,
rursus erant domino stolidae praecordia mentis.
Nam freta prospiciens late riget arduus alto
Tmolus in ascensu, clivoque extensus utroque
Sardibus hinc, illinc parvis finitur Hypaepis.   820
Pan ibi dum teneris iactat sua carmina nymphis
et leve cerata modulatur harundine carmen,
ausus Apollineos prae se contemnere cantus,
iudice sub Tmolo certamen venit ad impar.
Monte suo senior iudex consedit, et aures   825

799. guttur: fauces, 593.—802. dā veniam: ignōsce, 21.—814. colēbat:
frequentābat, 759.—816. pingue: stolidum.—819. clīvō: colle.

liberat arboribus : quercu coma caerula tantum
cingitur, et pendent circum cava tempora glandes.
Isque deum pecoris spectans, 'In iudice' dixit
'nulla mora est.'   Calamis agrestibus insonat ille :
barbaricoque Midan — aderat nam forte canenti —   830
carmine delenit.   Post hunc sacer ora retorsit
Tmolus ad os Phoebi ; vultum sua silva secuta est.

APOLLO WITH LYRE

Ille, caput flavum lauro Parnaside vinctus,
verrit humum Tyrio saturata murice palla ;
instrictamque fidem gemmis et dentibus Indis   835
sustinet a laeva, tenuit manus altera plectrum :

831. retorsit : convertit.

artificis status ipse fuit. Tum stamina docto
pollice sollicitat, quorum dulcedine captus
Pana iubet Tmolus citharae submittere cannas.

THE KING AGAIN MAKES A BAD CHOICE AND RECEIVES A STRANGE PUNISHMENT

Iudicium sanctique placet sententia montis   840
omnibus. Arguitur tamen atque iniusta vocatur
unius sermone Midae. Nec Delius aures
humanam stolidas patitur retinere figuram ;
sed trahit in spatium, villisque albentibus implet,
instabilesque imas facit et dat posse moveri.   845
Cetera sunt hominis : partem damnatur in unam,
induiturque aures lente gradientis aselli.
Ille quidem celare cupit, turpique pudore
tempora purpureis temptat velare tiaris ;
sed solitus longos ferro resecare capillos   850
viderat hoc famulus. Qui cum nec prodere visum
dedecus auderet, cupiens efferre sub auras,
nec posset reticere tamen, secedit humumque
effodit, et domini quales adspexerit aures
voce refert parva terraeque immurmurat haustae ;   855
indiciumque suae vocis tellure regesta
obruit, et scrobibus tacitus discedit opertis.
Creber harundinibus tremulis ibi surgere lucus
coepit, et, ut primum pleno maturuit anno,
prodidit agricolam : leni nam motus ab austro   860
obruta verba refert, dominique coarguit aures.

845. īmās: ab īnferā parte.—846. damnātur: pūnitur.—847. asellī: asinī.—857. obruit: tegit, 351. scrobibus: fossīs.—859. plēnō: exāctō.—861. coarguit: culpat, 22.

VII. PHILEMON AND BAUCIS

THE AGED COUPLE'S HOME

Tiliae contermina quercus
collibus est Phrygiis, modico circumdata muro.
Haud procul hinc stagnum est, tellus habitabilis olim,
nunc celebres mergis fulicisque palustribus undae.   865
Iuppiter huc specie mortali, cumque parente
venit Atlantiades positis caducifer alis.
Mille domos adiere, locum requiemque petentes:
mille domos clausere serae. Tamen una recepit,
parva quidem, stipulis et canna tecta palustri: 870
sed pia Baucis anus parilique aetate Philemon
illa sunt annis iuncti iuvenalibus, illa
consenuere casa; paupertatemque fatendo
effecere levem nec iniqua mente ferendo.
Nec refert, dominos illic famulosne requiras: 875
tota domus duo sunt, idem parentque iubentque.

863. **modicō**: parvō, 820. — 873. **paupertātem**: inopiam. — 875. **rēfert**: interest.

59

THEIR GENEROUS RECEPTION OF THE STRANGERS

Ergo ubi caelicolae parvos tetigere penates,
submissoque humiles intrarunt vertice postes,
membra senex posito iussit relevare sedili,
quo superiniecit textum rude sedula Baucis;   880
inde foco tepidum cinerem dimovit, et ignes
suscitat hesternos foliisque et cortice sicco
nutrit et ad flammas anima producit anili,
multifidasque faces ramaliaque arida tecto
detulit et minuit, parvoque admovit aëno.   885
Quodque suus coniunx riguo conlegerat horto,
truncat holus foliis. Furca levat ille bicorni
sordida terga suis nigro pendentia tigno;
servatoque diu resecat de tergore partem
exiguam, sectamque domat ferventibus undis.   890

Interea medias fallunt sermonibus horas,
concutiuntque torum de molli fluminis ulva
impositum lecto, sponda pedibusque salignis.
Vestibus hunc velant, quas non nisi tempore festo
sternere consuerant; sed et haec vilisque vetusque   895
vestis erat, lecto non indignanda saligno.

THE DINNER

Accubuere dei. Mensam succincta tremensque
ponit anus: mensae sed erat pes tertius impar:
testa parem fecit. Quae postquam subdita clivum
sustulit, aequatam mentae tersere virentes.   900
Ponitur hic bicolor sincerae baca Minervae,

877. **penātēs**: casam, 873. — 883. **animā**: spīritū. — 899. **subdita**: subiecta, 304.

conditaque in liquida corna autumnalia faece,
intibaque et radix et lactis massa coacti,
ovaque non acri leviter versata favilla,—
omnia fictilibus. Post haec caelatus eodem 905
sistitur argento crater fabricataque fago
pocula, qua cava sunt, flaventibus inlita ceris.

Parva mora est, epulasque foci misere calentes,
nec longae rursus referuntur vina senectae
dantque locum mensis paulum seducta secundis. 910
Hic nux, hic mixta est rugosis carica palmis
prunaque, et in patulis redolentia mala canistris
et de purpureis conlectae vitibus uvae.
Candidus in medio favus est. Super omnia vultus
accessere boni nec iners pauperque voluntas. 915

THE GODS REVEALED. A TRANSFORMATION SCENE

Interea totiens haustum cratera repleri
sponte sua, per seque vident succrescere vina.
Attoniti novitate pavent, manibusque supinis
concipiunt Baucisque preces timidusque Philemon,
et veniam dapibus nullisque paratibus orant. 920

Unicus anser erat, minimae custodia villae,
quem dis hospitibus domini mactare parabant.
Ille celer penna tardos aetate fatigat,
eluditque diu, tandemque est visus ad ipsos
confugisse deos. Superi vetuere necari: 925
'Di'que 'sumus, meritasque luet vicinia poenas
impia,' dixerunt ; 'vobis immunibus huius

---

906. sistitur: pōnitur, 789. fabricāta: facta, 347.— 908. mīsēre: dedēre, 654.— 915. accessēre: sunt additī, 667.— 920. nūllīs: exiguīs, 890.
— 926. luet: dabit.

esse mali dabitur: modo vestra relinquite tecta
ac nostros comitate gradus et in ardua montis
ite simul.'   Parent ambo, baculisque levati   930
nituntur longo vestigia ponere clivo.
Tantum aberant summo, quantum semel ire sagitta
missa potest: flexere oculos et mersa palude
cetera prospiciunt, tantum sua tecta manere.
Dumque ea mirantur, dum deflent fata suorum,   935
illa vetus, dominis etiam casa parva duobus
vertitur in templum: furcas subiere columnae;
stramina flavescunt aurataque tecta videntur,
caelataeque fores, adopertaque marmore tellus.

A PIOUS WISH FULFILLED

Talia tum placido Saturnius edidit ore: 940
'Dicite, iuste senex et femina coniuge iusto
digna, quid optetis.'   Cum Baucide pauca locutus,
iudicium superis aperit commune Philemon:
'Esse sacerdotes delubraque vestra tueri
poscimus; et quoniam concordes egimus annos,   945
auferat hora duos eadem, nec coniugis umquam
busta meae videam, neu sim tumulandus ab illa.'
Vota fides sequitur: templi tutela fuere,
donec vita data est.   Annis aevoque soluti
ante gradus sacros cum starent forte locique   950
narrarent casus, frondere Philemona Baucis,
Baucida conspexit senior frondere Philemon.
Iamque super geminos crescente cacumine vultus

929. **comitāte**: sequiminī, 672. — 934. **tantum**: sōlum. — 944. **tuērī**:
servāre.

mutua, dum licuit, reddebant dicta, 'Vale'que
'O coniunx' dixere simul, simul abdita texit 955
ora frutex.   Ostendit adhuc Thineïus illic
incola de gemino vicinos corpore truncos.
Haec mihi non vani, neque erat cur fallere vellent,
narravere senes: equidem pendentia vidi
serta super ramos, ponensque recentia dixi, 960
'Cura pii dis sunt, et qui coluere, coluntur.'

960. recentia: nova.

MERCURY.

THE DESTRUCTION OF THE CHILDREN OF NIOBE.

VIII. THE IMPIETY AND PUNISHMENT OF NIOBE

NIOBE'S PRIDE

Ecce venit comitum Niobe celeberrima turba,
vestibus intexto Phrygiis spectabilis auro
et, quantum ira sinit, formosa, movensque decoro
cum capite immissos umerum per utrumque capillos.　965
Constitit: utque oculos circumtulit alta superbos,
'Quis furor, auditos' inquit 'praeponere visis
caelestes? aut cur colitur Latona per aras,
numen adhuc sine ture meum est? Mihi Tantalus auctor,
cui licuit soli superorum tangere mensas.　970
Pleïadum soror est genetrix mea; maximus Atlas
est avus, aetherium qui fert cervicibus axem;
Iuppiter alter avus; socero quoque glorior illo.
Me gentes metuunt Phrygiae, me regia Cadmi
sub domina est, fidibusque mei commissa mariti　975
moenia cum populis a meque viroque reguntur.
In quamcumque domus adverti lumina partem,
immensae spectantur opes. Accedit eodem

970. **tangere**: accēdere, 389. — 975. **commissa**: cōnstrūcta.

digna dea facies.   Huc natas adice septem
et totidem iuvenes, et mox generosque nurusque.   980
Quaerite nunc, habeat quam nostra superbia causam!
Sum felix: quis enim neget hoc? felixque manebo:
hoc quoque quis dubitet?   Tutam me copia fecit.
Maior sum, quam cui possit Fortuna nocere;
multaque ut eripiat, multo mihi plura relinquet.   985
Excessere metum mea iam bona.   Fingite demi
huic aliquid populo natorum posse meorum:
non tamen ad numerum redigar spoliata duorum,
Latonae turbam: qua quantum distat ab orba?
Ite, satisque superque sacri, laurumque capillis   990
ponite.'   Deponunt, infectaque sacra relinquunt,
quodque licet, tacito venerantur murmure numen.

LATONA'S RIGHTEOUS INDIGNATION

Indignata dea est; summoque in vertice Cynthi
talibus est dictis gemina cum prole locuta:
'En ego vestra parens, vobis animosa creatis,   995
et, nisi Iunoni, nulli cessura dearum,
an dea sim, dubitor; perque omnia saecula cultis
arceor, O nati, nisi vos succurritis, aris.
Nec dolor hic solus: diro convicia facto
Tantalis adiecit, vosque est postponere natis   1000
ausa suis, et me, quod in ipsam recidat, orbam
dixit, et exhibuit linguam scelerata paternam.'
Adiectura preces erat his Latona relatis:
'Desine!'   Phoebus ait; 'poenae mora longa querella est.'
Dixit idem Phoebe; celerique per aëra lapsu   1005

979. ādice: adde, 667.— 983. cōpia: numerus.— 986. dēmī: subtrahī.
— 991. pōnite: āvellite. —1001. orbam: dēstitūtam.

contigerant tecti Cadmeïda nubibus arcem.
Planus erat lateque patens prope moenia campus,
adsiduis pulsatus equis, ubi turba rotarum
duraque mollierat subiectas ungula glebas.

HER REVENGE. THE DEATH OF ISMENOS AND SIPYLUS

Pars ibi de septem genitis Amphione fortes   1010
conscendunt in equos, Tyrioque rubentia suco
terga premunt, auroque graves moderantur habenas
E quibus Ismenos, qui matri sarcina quondam
prima suae fuerat, dum certum flectit in orbem
quadrupedis cursus, spumantiaque ora coërcet,   1015
'Ei mihi !' conclamat, medioque in pectore fixa
tela gerit, frenisque manu moriente remissis,
in latus a dextro paulatim defluit armo.

Proximus, audito sonitu per inane pharetrae,
frena dabat Sipylus : veluti cum praescius imbris   1020
nube fugit visa, pendentiaque undique rector
carbasa deducit, ne qua levis effluat aura.
Frena dabat : dantem non evitabile telum
consequitur, summaque tremens cervice sagitta
haesit, et exstabat nudum de gutture ferrum.   1025
Ille, ut erat, pronus per crura admissa iubasque
volvitur, et calido tellurem sanguine foedat.

PHAEDIMUS AND TANTALUS SLAIN TOGETHER; THEN ALPHENOR

Phaedimus infelix et aviti nominis heres
Tantalus, ut solito finem imposuere labori,

1016. fīxa : trāiecta, 255. — 1018. dēfluit : dēcidit. — 1019. ināne : āëra,
506. — 1020. dabat : relaxābat. — 1022. carbasa : vēla. — 1027. foedat :
inficit, 37.

transierant ad opus nitidae iuvenile palaestrae :   1030
et iam contulerant arto luctantia nexu
pectora pectoribus, cum tento concita nervo,
sicut erant iuncti, traiecit utrumque sagitta.
Ingemuere simul, simul incurvata dolore
membra solo posuere ; simul suprema iacentes   1035
lumina versarunt ; animam simul exhalarunt.
Adspicit Alphenor, laniataque pectora plangens
advolat, ut gelidos complexibus adlevet artus,
inque pio cadit officio ; nam Delius illi
intima fatifero rupit praecordia ferro.   1040
Quod simul eductum, pars est pulmonis in hamis
eruta, cumque anima cruor est effusus in auras.

THE LAST TWO BROTHERS SLAIN

At non intonsum simplex Damasichthona vulnus
adficit. Ictus erat, qua crus esse incipit, et qua
mollia nervosus facit internodia poples.   1045
Dumque manu temptat trahere exitiabile telum,
altera per iugulum pennis tenus acta sagitta est.
Expulit hanc sanguis, seque eiaculatus in altum
emicat, et longe terebrata prosilit aura.

Ultimus Ilioneus non profectura precando   1050
bracchia sustulerat, ' Di 'que ' O communiter omnes,'
dixerat, ignarus non omnes esse rogandos,
' Parcite ! ' Motus erat, cum iam revocabile telum
non fuit, Arcitenens ; minimo tamen occidit ille
vulnere, non alte percusso corde sagitta.   1055

1032. tentō : adductō, 237. — 1036. versārunt : retorsērunt, 831. —
1046. exitiābile : fātāle. — 1053. parcite : ignōscite, 21.

NIOBE'S PRIDE SURVIVES HER GRIEF

Fama mali populique dolor lacrimaeque suorum
tam subitae matrem certam fecere ruinae
mirantem potuisse, irascentemque quod ausi
hoc essent superi, quod tantum iuris haberent.
Nam pater Amphion ferro per pectus adacto   1060
finierat moriens pariter cum luce dolorem.
Heu quantum haec Niobe Niobe distabat ab illa,
quae modo Latois populum submoverat aris
et mediam tulerat gressus resupina per urbem,
invidiosa suis, at nunc miseranda vel hosti !   1065
Corporibus gelidis incumbit, et ordine nullo
oscula dispensat natos suprema per omnes.
A quibus ad caelum liventia bracchia tollens
' Pascere, crudelis, nostro, Latona, dolore ;
pascere ' ait, ' satiaque meo tua pectora luctu :   1070
corque ferum satia ! ' dixit ; ' per funera septem
efferor : exsulta, victrixque inimica triumpha.
Cur autem victrix? miserae mihi plura supersunt,
quam tibi felici.   Post tot quoque funera vinco.'

HER PUNISHMENT COMPLETE. THE FATE OF HER SEVEN DAUGHTERS. HER OWN LOT

Dixerat, et sonuit contento nervus ab arcu :   1075
qui praeter Nioben unam conterruit omnes.
Illa malo est audax.   Stabant cum vestibus atris
ante toros fratrum demisso crine sorores ;
e quibus una trahens haerentia viscere tela

1063. **submōverat**: arcuerat, 729. — 1064. **resupīna**: superba, 966. —
1075. contentō: tentō, 1032.

imposito fratri moribunda relanguit ore;   1080
altera solari miseram conata parentem
conticuit subito, duplicataque vulnere caeco est:
haec frustra fugiens conlabitur: illa sorori
immoritur; latet haec; illam trepidare videres.

NIOBE

Sexque datis leto diversaque vulnera passis,   1085
ultima restabat; quam toto corpore mater,
tota veste tegens, 'Unam minimamque relinque!
De multis minimam posco' clamavit 'et unam.'
Dumque rogat, pro qua rogat, occidit. Orba resedit
exanimes inter natos natasque virumque,   1090

1080. relanguit: dēfēcit. — 1082. duplicāta: incurvāta, 1034.

deriguitque malis.   Nullos movet aura capillos;
in vultu color est sine sanguine; lumina maestis
stant immota genis: nihil est in imagine vivum.
Ipsa quoque interius cum duro lingua palato
congelat, et venae desistunt posse moveri;   1091
nec flecti cervix nec bracchia reddere motus
nec pes ire .potest: intra quoque viscera saxum est.
Flet tamen, et validi circumdata turbine venti
in patriam rapta est.   Ibi fixa cacumine montis
liquitur, et lacrimas etiam nunc marmora manant.   1100

1091. dēriguit: indūrāta est, 730.

DIANA   APOLLO

IX. THE FLOOD

THE WORLD DOOMED. THE SUMMONING OF THE WATERS

Poena placet diversa, genus mortale sub undis
perdere et ex omni nimbos demittere caelo.
Protinus Aeoliis Aquilonem claudit in antris
et quaecumque fugant inductas flamina nubes,
emittitque Notum.   Madidis Notus evolat alis,   1105
terribilem picea tectus caligine vultum :
barba gravis nimbis, canis fluit unda capillis,
fronte sedent nebulae, rorant pennaeque sinusque.
Utque manu late pendentia nubila pressit,
fit fragor, inclusi funduntur ab aethere nimbi.   1110
Nuntia Iunonis varios induta colores
concipit Iris aquas, alimentaque nubibus adfert.
Sternuntur segetes et deplorata coloni
vota iacent, longique perit labor inritus anni.
Nec caelo contenta suo est Iovis ira, sed illum   1115
caeruleus frater iuvat auxiliaribus undis.
Convocat hic amnes ; qui postquam tecta tyranni
intravere sui, ‘Non est hortamine longo
nunc’ ait ‘utendum ; vires effundite vestras,
sic opus est ; aperite domos, ac mole remota   1120
fluminibus vestris totas immittite habenas.’

1105. **madidīs**: ūmidīs, 491. — 1118. **hortāmine**: hortātiōne, hortandō.

THE DELUGE

Iusserat; hi redeunt, ac fontibus ora relaxant,
et defrenato volvuntur in aequora cursu.
Ipse tridente suo terram percussit; at illa
ıntremuit motuque vias patefecit aquarum.   1125
Exspatiata ruunt per apertos flumina campos,
cumque satis arbusta simul pecudesque virosque
tectaque, cumque suis rapiunt penetralia sacris.
Siqua domus mansit potuitque resistere tanto
indeiecta malo, culmen tamen altior huius   1130
unda tegit, pressaeque latent sub gurgite turres.
Iamque mare et tellus nullum discrimen habebant :
omnia pontus erant; deerant quoque litora ponto.
Occupat hic collem; cymba sedet alter adunca
et ducit remos illic ubi nuper ararat;   1135
ille super segetes aut mersae culmina villae
navigat; hic summa piscem deprendit in ulmo;
figitur in viridi, si fors tulit, ancora prato,
aut subiecta terunt curvae vineta carinae.
Et, modo qua graciles gramen carpsere capellae,   1140
nunc ibi deformes ponunt sua corpora phocae.
Mirantur sub aqua lucos urbesque domosque
Nereïdes; silvasque tenent delphines, et altis
incursant ramis, agitataque robora pulsant.
Nat lupus inter oves, fulvos vehit unda leones,   1145
unda vehit tigres; nec vires fulminis apro,
crura nec ablato prosunt velocia cervo.

1128. **rapiunt**: auferunt, 423.—1130. **culmen**: fastīgia, 351.—1131. **pressae**: submersae.—1135. **dūcit**: movet, 506.—1139. **terunt**: vādunt, 95.—1147. **crūra**: pedēs.

Quaesitisque diu terris, ubi sistere detur,
in mare lassatis volucris vaga decidit alis.
Obruerat tumulos immensa licentia ponti,   1150
pulsabantque novi montana cacumina fluctus.
Maxima pars unda rapitur : quibus unda pepercit,
illos longa domant inopi ieiunia victu.

DEUCALION AND PYRRHA SURVIVE

Separat Aonios Oetaeis Phocis ab arvis,
terra ferax, dum terra fuit : sed tempore in illo   1155
pars maris et latus subitarum campus aquarum.
Mons ibi verticibus petit arduus astra duobus,
nomine Parnasus, superantque cacumina nubes.
Hic ubi Deucalion (nam cetera texerat aequor),
cum consorte tori parva rate vectus adhaesit,   116(
Corycidas nymphas et numina montis adorant,
fatidicamque Themin, quae tunc oracla tenebat.
Non illo melior quisquam nec amantior aequi
vir fuit, aut illa metuentior ulla deorum.

THE WATERS SUBSIDE

Iuppiter ut liquidis stagnare paludibus orbem,   1165
et superesse virum de tot modo milibus unum,
et superesse videt de tot modo milibus unam,
innocuos ambos, cultores numinis ambos,
nubila disiecit, nimbisque aquilone remotis
et caelo terras ostendit et aethera terris.   1170

1148. dētur: liceat, 401. — 1149. lassātīs: dēfessīs. — 1155. ferāx:
fertilis. — 1160. cōnsorte torī: uxōre. — 1165. orbem: mundum, 655. —
1170. ostendit: patefēcit, 1125.

Nec maris ira manet, positoque tricuspide telo
mulcet aquas rector pelagi, supraque profundum
exstantem atque umeros innato murice tectum
caeruleum Tritona vocat, conchaeque sonanti
inspirare iubet, fluctusque et flumina signo   1175
iam revocare dato.

Omnibus audita est telluris et aequoris undis,
et quibus est undis audita, coërcuit omnes.
Flumina subsidunt, collesque exire videntur :
iam mare litus habet ; plenos capit alveus amnes ;   1180
surgit humus ; crescunt loca decrescentibus undis ;
postque diem longam nudata cacumina silvae
ostendunt, limumque tenent in fronde relictum.

THE TWO SURVIVORS CONSULT

Redditus orbis erat : quem postquam vidit inanem
et desolatas agere alta silentia terras,   1185
Deucalion lacrimis ita Pyrrham adfatur obortis :
' O soror, O coniunx, O femina sola superstes,
terrarum, quascumque vident occasus et ortus,
nos duo turba sumus : possedit cetera pontus.
Haec quoque adhuc vitae non est fiducia nostrae   1190
certa satis ; terrent etiam nunc nubila mentem.
Quis tibi, si sine me fatis erepta fuisses,
nunc animus, miseranda, foret? quo sola timorem
ferre modo posses? quo consolante doleres?
Namque ego, crede mihi, si te quoque pontus haberet, 1195
te sequerer, coniunx, et me quoque pontus haberet.

1186. adfātur : adloquitur. — 1187. **superstes** : relīcta, restāns, 1086.

O utinam possem populos reparare paternis
artibus atque animas formatae infundere terrae!
Nunc genus in nobis restat mortale duobus;
sic visum est superis: hominumque exempla manemus.' 1200

AN ORACLE WITH A HIDDEN MEANING

Dixerat, et flebant; placuit caeleste precari
numen, et auxilium per sacras quaerere sortes.
Nulla mora est; adeunt pariter Cephisidas undas,
ut nondum liquidas, sic iam vada nota secantes.
Inde ubi libatos inroravere liquores   1205
vestibus et capiti, flectunt vestigia sanctae
ad delubra deae, quorum fastigia turpi
pallebant musco stabantque sine ignibus arae.
Ut templi tetigere gradus, procumbit uterque
pronus humi, gelidoque pavens dedit oscula saxo.   1210
Atque ita, 'Si precibus' dixerunt 'numina iustis
victa remollescunt, si flectitur ira deorum,
dic, Themi, qua generis damnum reparabile nostri
arte sit, et mersis fer opem, mitissima, rebus.'

Mota dea est sortemque dedit, 'Discedite templo,   1215
et velate caput, cinctasque resolvite vestes,
ossaque post tergum magnae iactate parentis.'
Obstipuere diu, rumpitque silentia voce
Pyrrha prior, iussisque deae parere recusat,
detque sibi veniam, pavido rogat ore, pavetque   1220
laedere iactatis maternas ossibus umbras.

1197. reparāre: renovāre. — 1198. īnfundere: immittere. — 1199. restat: superest, 1166. — 1200. vīsum: placitum, 406. — 1204. vada: al-
veum, 1180. — 1205. inrōrāvēre: īnfūdēre. — 1216. resolvite: discingite.
— 1221. laedere: violāre.

Interea repetunt caecis obscura latebris
verba datae sortis secum, inter seque volutant.

THE WORLD REPEOPLED

Inde Promethiades placidis Epimethida dictis
mulcet et 'Aut fallax' ait 'est sollertia nobis,   1225
aut pia sunt nullumque nefas oracula suadent.
Magna parens Terra est: lapides in corpore terrae
ossa reor dici: iacere hos post terga iubemur.'
Coniugis augurio quamquam Titania mota est,
spes tamen in dubio est: adeo caelestibus ambo   1230
diffidunt monitis : — sed quid temptare nocebit?
Descendunt velantque caput tunicasque recingunt
et iussos lapides sua post vestigia mittunt.
Saxa — quis hoc credat, nisi sit pro teste vetustas? —
ponere duritiem coepere suumque rigorem,   1235
mollirique mora, mollitaque ducere formam.
Mox ubi creverunt, naturaque mitior illis
contigit, ut quaedam, sic non manifesta, videri
forma potest hominis, sed uti de marmore coepto,
non exacta satis rudibusque simillima signis.   1240
Quae tamen ex illis aliquo pars umida suco
et terrena fuit, versa est in corporis usum :
quod solidum est flectique nequit, mutatur in ossa :
quae modo vena fuit, sub eodem nomine mansit ;
inque brevi spatio superorum numine saxa   1245
missa viri manibus faciem traxere virorum,
et de femineo reparata est femina iactu.

1222. repetunt: revolvunt. — 1228. reor: opīnor. — 1232. recingunt:
resolvunt, 1216. — 1234. vetustās: antīquitās. — 1236. dūcere: sūmere. —
1238. contigit: data est. — 1246. trāxēre: induēre, 1111.

X. PERSEUS AND ANDROMEDA

PERSEUS BEARS THE GORGON'S HEAD THROUGH THE AIR

Viperei referens spolium memorabile monstri
aëra carpebat tenerum stridentibus alis;
cumque super Libycas victor penderet harenas,   1250
Gorgonei capitis guttae cecidere cruentae,
quas humus exceptas varios animavit in angues:
unde frequens illa est infestaque terra colubris.

Inde per immensum ventis discordibus actus
nunc huc, nunc illuc, exemplo nubis aquosae   1255
fertur, et ex alto seductas aethere longe
despectat terras totumque supervolat orbem.
Ter gelidas Arctos, ter Cancri bracchia vidit:
saepe sub occasus, saepe est ablatus in ortus.
Iamque cadente die veritus se credere nocti,   1260
constitit Hesperio, regnis Atlantis, in orbe:
exiguamque petit requiem, dum Lucifer ignes
evocet Aurorae, currus Aurora diurnos.

ATLAS GIVES HIM A COLD RECEPTION

Hic hominum cunctos ingenti corpore praestans
Iapetionides Atlas fuit.   Ultima tellus   1265

1248. **spolium**: exuviās, 258. — 1260. **crēdere**: committere, 744. —
1263. **diurnōs**: diē.

rege sub hoc et pontus erat, qui Solis anhelis
aequora subdit equis et fessos excipit axes.
Mille greges illi, totidemque armenta per herbas
errabant ; et humum vicinia nulla premebant.
Arboreae frondes auro radiante virentes   1270
ex auro ramos, ex auro poma tegebant.

PERSEUS

'Hospes,' ait Perseus illi, 'seu gloria tangit
te generis magni, generis mihi Iuppiter auctor ;
sive es mirator rerum, mirabere nostras.
Hospitium requiemque peto.' Memor ille vetustae   1275
sortis erat ; Themis hanc dederat Parnasia sortem :

1275. vetustae: antïquae.

'Tempus, Atla, veniet, tua quo spoliabitur auro
arbor, et hunc praedae titulum Iove natus habebit.'
Id metuens solidis pomaria clauserat Atlas
moenibus et vasto dederat servanda draconi,   1280
arcebatque suis externos finibus omnes.
Huic quoque, 'Vade procul, ne longe gloria rerum,
quam mentiris,' ait 'longe tibi Iuppiter absit;'
vimque minis addit manibusque expellere temptat
cunctantem et placidis miscentem fortia dictis.   1285

AND IS TURNED TO STONE

Viribus inferior — quis enim par esset Atlanti
viribus? — 'At quoniam parvi tibi gratia nostra est,
accipe munus!' ait, laevaque a parte Medusae
ipse retroversus squalentia prodidit ora.
Quantus erat, mons factus Atlas: nam barba comaeque   1290
in silvas abeunt, iuga sunt umerique manusque;
quod caput ante fuit, summo est in monte cacumen;
ossa lapis fiunt.   Tum partes auctus in omnes
crevit in immensum — sic di statuistis — et omne
cum tot sideribus caelum requievit in illo.   1295

THE HERO ESPIES ANDROMEDA

Clauserat Hippotades aeterno carcere ventos,
admonitorque operum caelo clarissimus alto
Lucifer ortus erat.   Pennis ligat ille resumptis
parte ab utraque pedes, teloque accingitur unco,
et liquidum motis talaribus aëra findit.   1300
Gentibus innumeris circumque infraque relictis,

1281. externōs: peregrīnōs, 648.— 1285. fortia: aspera.— 1289. squā-
lentia: horrida, 296.

Aethiopum populos, Cepheaque conspicit **arva**.
Illic immeritam maternae pendere linguae
Andromedan poenas immitis iusserat **Ammon**.
Quam simul ad duras religatam bracchia **cautes**   1305
vidit Abantiades, — nisi quod levis aura capillos
moverat, et tepido manabant lumina fletu,
marmoreum **ratus** esset opus — **trahit** inscius **ignes**
et stupet; et visae correptus imagine formae
paene suas quatere est oblitus in aëre pennas.   1310
Ut stetit, 'O' dixit 'non istis digna catenis,
sed quibus inter se cupidi iunguntur amantes,
pande requirenti nomen terraeque tuumque,
et cur vincla geras.'   Primo silet illa, nec audet
appellare virum virgo; manibusque modestos   1315
celasset vultus, si non religata fuisset.
Lumina, quod potuit, lacrimis implevit obortis.

AN OFF-HAND OFFER OF MARRIAGE

Saepius instanti, sua ne delicta fateri
nolle videretur, nomen terraeque suumque,
quantaque maternae fuerit fiducia formae,   1320
indicat.   Et nondum memoratis omnibus unda
insonuit, veniensque immenso belua ponto
imminet et latum sub pectore possidet aequor.
Conclamat virgo; genitor lugubris et una
mater adest, ambo miseri, sed iustius illa.   1325
Nec secum auxilium, sed dignos tempore fletus

1305. **cautēs**: rūpēs, 181. — 1308. **ratus**: arbitrātus.   **trahit**: concipit, 23. — 1313. **pande**: nārrā, 959. — 1317. **lūmina**: oculōs. — 1322. **immēnsō**: altō, 574. — 1323. **imminet**: appāret.

plangoremque ferunt, vinctoque in corpore adhaerent;
cum sic hospes ait: 'Lacrimarum longa manere
tempora vos poterunt; ad opem brevis hora ferendam est.
Hanc ego si peterem Perseus Iove natus et ille   1330
Gorgonis anguicomae Perseus superator, et alis
aetherias ausus iactatis ire per auras,
praeferrer cunctis certe gener. Addere tantis
dotibus et meritum, faveant modo numina, tempto;
ut mea sit servata mea virtute, paciscor.'   1335
Accipiunt legem — quis enim dubitaret? — et orant,
promittuntque super regnum dotale parentes.

THE DUEL BY THE SEA

Ecce velut navis praefixo concita rostro
sulcat aquas, iuvenum sudantibus acta lacertis,
sic fera dimotis impulsu pectoris undis   1340
tantum aberat scopulis, quantum Balearica torto
funda potest plumbo medii transmittere caeli:
cum subito iuvenis pedibus tellure repulsa
arduus in nubes abiit. Ut in aequore summo
umbra viri visa est, visam fera saevit in umbram.   1345
Utque Iovis praepes, vacuo cum vidit in arvo
praebentem Phoebo liventia terga draconem,
occupat aversum, neu saeva retorqueat ora,
squamigeris avidos figit cervicibus ungues:
sic celer immisso praeceps per inane volatu   1350
terga ferae pressit, dextroque frementis in armo
Inachides ferrum curvo tenus abdidit hamo.

1337. **super**: īnsuper. **dōtāle**: in dōtem, 87. — 1339. **sulcat**: findit,
1300. — 1346. **praepēs**: āles, 28. — 1348. **retorqueat**: reflectat.

Vulnere laesa gravi, modo se sublimis in auras
attollit, modo subdit aquis, modo more ferocis
versat apri, quem turba canum circumsona terret.   1355
Ille avidos morsus velocibus effugit alis :
quaque patent, nunc terga cavis super obsita conchis,
nunc laterum costas, nunc qua tenuissima cauda
desinit in piscem, falcato verberat ense.
Belua puniceo mixtos cum sanguine fluctus   1360
ore vomit : maduere graves aspergine pennae.

PERSEUS VICTORIOUS. THE ORIGIN OF CORAL

Nec bibulis ultra Perseus talaribus ausus
credere, conspexit scopulum, qui vertice summo
stantibus exstat aquis, operitur ab aequore moto.
Nixus eo rupisque tenens iuga prima sinistra   1365
ter quater exegit repetita per ilia ferrum.
Litora cum plausu clamor superasque deorum
implevere domos. Gaudent, generumque salutant
auxiliumque domus servatoremque fatentur
Cassiope Cepheusque pater. Resoluta catenis   1370
incedit virgo, pretiumque et causa laboris.
Ipse manus hausta victrices abluit unda :
anguiferumque caput dura ne laedat harena,
mollit humum foliis, natasque sub aequore virgas
sternit, et imponit Phorcynidos ora Medusae.   1375
Virga recens bibulaque etiamnum viva medulla
vim rapuit monstri, tactuque induruit huius,

1354. subdit: mergitur, 933. — 1357. obsita: tēcta, 351. — 1359. dēsi-
nit: terminātur. falcātō: uncō, 1299. — 1360. pūniceō: purpureō, 913. —
1362. bibulīs: madefactīs, 193. — 1370. resolūta: līberāta. — 1372. hausta:
sūmpta.

percepitque novum ramis et fronde rigorem.
At pelagi nymphae factum mirabile temptant
pluribus in virgis, et idem contingere gaudent,   1380
seminaque ex illis iterant iactata per undas.
Nunc quoque curaliis eadem natura remansit,
duritiam tacto capiant ut ab aëre, quodque
vimen in aequore erat, fiat super aequora saxum.

TO THE VICTOR BELONG THE SPOILS. THE WEDDING FEAST

Dis tribus ille focos totidem de caespite ponit,   1385
laevum Mercurio, dextrum tibi, bellica virgo ;
ara Iovis media est : mactatur vacca Minervae,
Alipedi vitulus, taurus tibi, summe deorum.
Protinus Andromedan et tanti praemia facti
indotata rapit. Taedas Hymenaeus Amorque   1390
praecutiunt ; largis satiantur odoribus ignes,
sertaque dependent tectis, et ubique lyraeque
tibiaque et cantus, animi felicia laeti
argumenta, sonant. Reseratis aurea valvis
atria tota patent, pulchroque instructa paratu   1395
Cepheni proceres ineunt convivia regis.

Postquam epulis functi generosi munere Bacchi
diffudere animos, cultusque genusque locorum
quaerit Lyncides moresque animumque virorum.
Qui simul edocuit ' Nunc, O fortissime,' dixit   1400
' Fare precor, Perseu, quanta virtute, quibusque
artibus abstuleris crinita draconibus ora.'

1380. **contingere**: ēvenīre, accidere. — 1381. **iterant**: renovant. —
1391. **largīs**: multīs. — 1394. **argūmenta**: indicia, 856.   **reserātīs**: pa-
tentibus, 142.

AN AFTER-DINNER SPEECH. THE TAKING OF MEDUSA

Narrat Agenorides gelido sub Atlante iacentem
esse locum solidae tutum munimine molis,
cuius in introitu geminas habitasse sorores   1405
Phorcidas, unius partitas luminis usum :
id se sollerti furtim, dum traditur, astu
subposita cepisse manu ; perque abdita longe
deviaque et silvis horrentia saxa fragosis
Gorgoneas tetigisse domos ; passimque per agros   1410
perque vias vidisse hominum simulacra ferarumque
in silicem ex ipsis visa conversa Medusa :
se tamen horrendae clipei, quod laeva gerebat,
aere repercusso formam adspexisse Medusae ;
dumque gravis somnus colubrasque ipsamque tenebat,   1415
eripuisse caput collo ; pennisque fugacem
Pegason et fratrem matris de sanguine natos.
Addidit et longi non falsa pericula cursus :
quae freta, quas terras sub se vidisset ab alto,
et quae iactatis tetigisset sidera pennis.   1420
Ante expectatum tacuit tamen.

1407. sollertī : callidō, 743.   astū : dolō. — 1409. fragōsīs : sonōrīs. —
1410. tetigisse : subiisse, 731. — 1416. fugācem : celerem.

XI. CADMUS

CADMUS GOES IN SEARCH OF HIS SISTER

Iamque deus posita fallacis imagine tauri
se confessus erat Dictaeaque rura tenebat,
cum pater ignarus Cadmo perquirere raptam
imperat et poenam, si non invenerit, addit   1425
exsilium, facto pius et sceleratus eodem.
Orbe pererrato (quis enim deprendere possit
furta Iovis?) profugus patriamque iramque parentis
vitat Agenorides, Phoebique oracula supplex
consulit et quae sit tellus habitanda requirit.   1430
'Bos tibi,' Phoebus ait, 'solis occurret in arvis,
nullum passa iugum curvique immunis aratri.
Hac duce carpe vias et qua requieverit herba
moenia fac condas Boeotiaque illa vocato.'

AN IMMEDIATE ANSWER

Vix bene Castalio Cadmus descenderat antro,   1435
incustoditam lente videt ire iuvencam
nullum servitii signum cervice gerentem.
Subsequitur pressoque legit vestigia gressu
auctoremque viae Phoebum taciturnus adorat.
Iam vada Cephisi Panopesque evaserat arva;   1440
bos stetit et tollens speciosam cornibus altis
ad caelum frontem mugitibus impulit auras.
Atque ita respiciens comites sua terga sequentes

1428. furta: *cf.* furtim, 1407.—1431. sōlīs: dēsertīs.—1437.
servitiī: iugī.—1441. speciōsam: pulchram.

procubuit teneraque latus submisit in herba.
Cadmus agit grates peregrinaeque oscula terrae   1445
figit et ignotos montes agrosque salutat.

A LUCKLESS SACRIFICE

Sacra Iovi facturus erat; iubet ire ministros
et petere e vivis libandas fontibus undas.
Silva vetus stabat nulla violata securi
et specus in medio virgis ac vimine densus,   1450
efficiens humilem lapidum compagibus arcum,
uberibus fecundus aquis, ubi conditus antro
Martius anguis erat, cristis praesignis et auro.
Igne micant oculi; corpus tumet omne veneno;
tresque vibrant linguae; triplici stant ordine dentes.   1455
Quem postquam Tyria lucum de gente profecti
infausto tetigere gradu, demissaque in undas
urna dedit sonitum, longo caput extulit antro
caeruleus serpens, horrendaque sibila misit.
Effluxere urnae manibus, sanguisque relinquit   1460
corpus et attonitos subitus tremor occupat artus.
Ille volubilibus squamosos nexibus orbes
torquet, et immensos saltu sinuatur in arcus;
ac media plus parte leves erectus in auras
despicit omne nemus, tantoque est corpore quanto,   1465
si totum spectes, geminas qui separat Arctos.
Nec mora.   Phoenicas, sive illi tela parabant
sive fugam, sive ipse timor prohibebat utrumque,
occupat; hos morsu, longis amplexibus illos,
hos necat adflata funesti tabe veneni.   1470

1450. specus: antrum.—1458. longō: profundō.

CADMUS SEEKS HIS ATTENDANTS AND MEETS THE DRAGON

Fecerat exiguas iam sol altissimus umbras;
quae mora sit sociis miratur Agenore natus,
vestigatque viros.   Tegumen direpta leonis
pellis erat, telum splendenti lancea ferro
et iaculum, teloque animus praestantior omni.   1475

Ut nemus intravit letataque corpora vidit,
victoremque supra spatiosi corporis hostem
tristia sanguinea lambentem vulnera lingua,
'Aut ultor vestrae, fidissima corpora, mortis,
aut comes,' inquit, 'ero.'   Dixit, dextraque molarem   1480
sustulit et magnum magno conamine misit.
Illius impulsu cum turribus ardua celsis
moenia mota forent; serpens sine vulnere mansit,
loricaeque modo squamis defensus et atrae
duritia pellis validos cute reppulit ictus.   1485

THE CONFLICT

At non duritia iaculum quoque vicit eadem,
quod medio lentae spinae curvamine fixum
constitit, et totum descendit in ilia ferrum.
Ille dolore ferox caput in sua terga retorsit
vulneraque adspexit fixumque hastile momordit,   1490
idque ubi vi multa partem labefecit in omnem,
vix tergo eripuit; ferrum tamen ossibus haesit.
Tum vero postquam solitas accessit ad iras
causa recens, plenis tumuerunt guttura venis,
spumaque pestiferos circumfluit albida rictus,   1495
terraque rasa sonat squamis, quique halitus exit
ore niger Stygio vitiatas inficit auras.

1473. tegumen: clipeum.   1481. cōnāmine: impetū, 544.—1495.
rictūs: ōra.

Ipse modo immensum spiris facientibus orbem
cingitur, interdum longa trabe rectior exstat;
impete nunc vasto ceu concitus imbribus amnis   1500
fertur, et obstantes proturbat pectore silvas.

SUCCESS AT LAST

Cedit Agenorides paulum, spolioque leonis
sustinet incursus, instantiaque ora retardat
cuspide praetenta.   Furit ille et inania duro
vulnera dat ferro, figitque in acumine dentes.   1505
Iamque venenifero sanguis manare palato
coeperat et virides aspergine tinxerat herbas;
sed leve vulnus erat, quia se retrahebat ab ictu
laesaque colla dabat retro plagamque sedere
cedendo arcebat nec longius ire sinebat,   1510
donec Agenorides coniectum in gutture ferrum
usque sequens pressit, dum retro quercus eunti
obstitit, et fixa est pariter cum robore cervix.
Pondere serpentis curvata est arbor et ima
parte flagellari gemuit sua robora caudae.   1515

THE DRAGON'S TEETH

Dum spatium victor victi considerat hostis,
vox subito audita est.   Neque erat cognoscere promptum
unde, sed audita est: 'Quid, Agenore nate, peremptum
serpentem spectas?   Et tu spectabere serpens.'
Ille diu pavidus pariter cum mente colorem   1520
perdiderat, gelidoque comae terrore rigebant.
Ecce viri fautrix superas delapsa per auras
Pallas adest motaeque iubet supponere terrae

1499.   interdum: modo.   longā: altā —1500.   impete: impetū.

vipereos dentes, populi incrementa futuri.
Paret et ut presso sulcum patefecit aratro,   1525
spargit humi iussos, mortalia semina, dentes.
Inde, fide maius, glebae coepere moveri,
primaque de sulcis acies apparuit hastae;
tegmina mox capitum picto nutantia cono;
mox umeri pectusque onerataque bracchia telis   1530
exsistunt, crescitque seges clipeata virorum.
Sic ubi tolluntur festis aulaea theatris,
surgere signa solent primumque ostendere vultus,
cetera paulatim, placidoque educta tenore
tota patent imoque pedes in margine ponunt.   1535

AN UNEXPECTED BATTLE

Territus hoste novo Cadmus capere arma parabat.
'Ne cape,' de populo quem terra creaverat unus
exclamat, 'nec te civilibus insere bellis.'
Atque ita terrigenis rigido de fratribus unum
comminus ense ferit; iaculo cadit eminus ipse.   1540
Hic quoque qui leto dederat non longius illo
vivit, et exspirat modo quas acceperat auras.
Exemploque pari furit omnis turba, suoque
Marte cadunt subiti per mutua vulnera fratres.
Iamque brevis vitae spatium sortita iuventus   1545
sanguineo tepidam plangebat pectore matrem,
quinque superstitibus, quorum fuit unus Echion.
Is sua iecit humo monitu Tritonidis arma
fraternaeque fidem pacis petiitque deditque.

1528. aciēs: ferrum, 1511.—1534. tenōre: mōtū, 677.—1537.
nē cape: nōlī capere.—1538. nec: neve.—1541. longius: diūtius.
—1544. Mārte: proeliō.

Hos operis comites habuit Sidonius hospes,　　　　1550
cum posuit iussam Phoebeis sortibus urbem.
　　Iam stabant Thebae; poteras iam, Cadme, videri
exsilio felix.　Soceri tibi Marsque Venusque
contigerant; huc adde genus de coniuge tanta,
tot natos natasque et pignora cara nepotes,　　　　1555
hos quoque iam iuvenes.　Sed scilicet ultima semper
exspectanda dies homini, dicique beatus
ante obitum nemo supremaque funera debet.

1551.　Phoebēīs: Phoebī.

CERES

XII. THE FLIGHT OF DAEDALUS

AN EARLY AVIATOR

Daedalus interea Creten longumque perosus
exsilium, tactusque loci natalis amore,   1560
clausus erat pelago. 'Terras licet,' inquit, 'et undas
obstruat, at caelum certe patet; ibimus illac.
Omnia possideat, non possidet aëra Minos.'
Dixit.   Et ignotas animum dimittit in artes,
naturamque novat.   Nam ponit in ordine pennas,   1565
a minima coeptas, longam breviore sequenti,
ut clivo crevisse putes.   Sic rustica quondam
fistula disparibus paulatim surgit avenis.
Tum lino medias et ceris adligat imas,
atque ita compositas parvo curvamine flectit,   1570
ut veras imitetur aves.   Puer Icarus una
stabat et, ignarus sua se tractare pericla,
ore renidenti modo quas vaga moverat aura
captabat plumas, flavam modo pollice ceram
mollibat, lusuque suo mirabile patris   1575
impediebat opus.   Postquam manus ultima coepto
imposita est, geminas opifex libravit in alas
ipse suum corpus, motaque pependit in aura.

ICARUS ALSO TAKES A FLIGHT

Instruit et natum, 'Medio' que 'ut limite curras,
Icare,' ait, 'moneo, ne, si demissior ibis,   1580
unda gravet pennas; si celsior, ignis adurat.
Inter utrumque vola.   Nec te spectare Booten

1578. mōta: pulsa.—1580. dēmissior: *cf*. īnferius, 485.

aut Helicen iubeo strictumque Orionis ensem.
Me duce carpe viam.'   Pariter praecepta volandi
tradit et ignotas umeris accommodat alas.   1585
Inter opus monitusque genae maduere seniles
et patriae tremuere manus.   Dedit oscula nato
non iterum repetenda suo.   Pennisque levatus
ante volat comitique timet, velut ales ab alto
quae teneram prolem produxit in aër nido;   1590
hortaturque sequi damnosasque erudit artes,
et movet ipse suas et nati respicit alas.

BUT DISOBEYS DIRECTIONS AND FALLS

Hos aliquis tremula dum captat harundine pisces,
aut pastor baculo stivave innixus arator
vidit et obstipuit, quique aethera carpere possent   1595
credidit esse deos.   Et iam Iunonia laeva
parte Samos (fuerant Delosque Parosque relictae),
dextra Lebinthos erat fecundaque melle Calymne,
cum puer audaci coepit gaudere volatu,
deseruitque ducem caelique cupidine tractus   1600
altius egit iter.   Rapidi vicinia solis
mollit odoratas, pennarum vincula, ceras.
Tabuerant cerae; nudos quatit ille lacertos,
remigioque carens non ullas percipit auras.
Oraque caerulea patrium clamantia nomen   1605
excipiuntur aqua, quae nomen traxit ab illo.
At pater infelix, nec iam pater, 'Icare,' dixit,
'Icare,' dixit, 'ubi es? qua te regione requiram?'
'Icare,' dicebat, pennas adspexit in undis;
devovitque suas artes, corpusque sepulcro   1610
condidit.   Et tellus a nomine dicta sepulti.

XIII. CERES AND PROSERPINA

(For sight reading)

(In a musical contest with the nine daughters of the Macedonian king
Pierus, the Muses sing of the wanderings of Ceres in search of her daughter.)

Prima Ceres unco glebam dimovit aratro,
prima dedit fruges alimentaque mitia terris,
prima dedit leges; Cereris sunt omnia munus.
Illa canenda mihi est.   Utinam modo dicere possem 1615
carmina digna dea; certe dea carmine digna est.

Vasta giganteis ingesta est insula membris
Trinacris, et magnis subiectum molibus urguet
aetherias ausum sperare Typhoëa sedes.
Nititur ille quidem pugnatque resurgere saepe;   1620
dextra sed Ausonio manus est subiecta Peloro,
laeva, Pachyne, tibi; Lilybaeo crura premuntur;
degravat Aetna caput, sub qua resupinus harenas
eiectat flammamque fero vomit ore Typhoeus.
Saepe remoliri luctatur pondera terrae,   1625
oppidaque et magnos devolvere corpore montes.
Inde tremit tellus, et rex pavet ipse silentum,

1617.   giganteïs membrīs: *i. e.* of Typhoeus, one of the giants who attempted to scale Olympus. ingesta: iniecta. insula Trīnacris: Sicily.
—1618. urguet: premit.—1619. Typhoëa: acc., object of urguet.—
1620. resurgere: cf. surgō, 1181.—1621. Ausoniō Pelōrō, Pachȳne,
Lilybaeō: see map of Sicily. Ausonia was an old name for Southern
Italy.—1623. dēgravat: *holds down* (by its weight).—1625. remōlīrī:
to push off. luctātur, 1031.—1626. dēvolvere: *to roll down*—1627.
rēx silentum (= mortuōrum): Pluto.

ne pateat latoque solum retegatur hiatu,
immissusque dies trepidantes terreat umbras.

Hanc metuens cladem tenebrosa sede tyrannus 1630
exierat, curruque atrorum vectus equorum
ambibat Siculae cautus fundamina terrae.

Postquam exploratum satis est loca nulla labare
depositique metus, videt hunc Erycina vagantem
monte suo residens; natumque amplexa volucrem 1635
'Arma manusque meae, mea, nate, potentia,' dixit,
'illa quibus superas omnes cape tela, Cupido,
inque dei pectus celeres molire sagittas,
cui triplicis cessit fortuna novissima regni.

Tu superos ipsumque Iovem, tu numina ponti 1640
victa domas, ipsumque regit qui numina ponti.
Tartara quid cessant? Cur non matrisque tuumque
imperium profers? Agitur pars tertia mundi.

Et tamen in caelo (quae iam patientia nostra est)
spernimur, ac mecum vires minuuntur Amoris 1645
Pallada nonne vides iaculatricemque Dianam
abscessisse mihi? Cereris quoque filia virgo,
si patiemur, erit; nam spes adfectat easdem.

At tu pro socio (siqua est ea gratia) regno,

1628. retegātur: *uncover.* hiātū: ōre.—1629. immissus: admissus.
—1630. tenebrōsā: cf. tenebrae, 160.—1632. ambībat: *inspected.* Siculae: *Sicilian.* fundāmina: *foundations.*—1633. explōrātum: *proved.*
labāre: cf. 511.—1634. Erycīna: a local name for Venus, who had a
temple on Mt. Eryx.—1638. mōlīre: cf. 483.—1639. triplicis: *i. e.* the
threefold division of the world among Jupiter, Neptune, and Pluto. Cf.
602 and note.—1642. cessant: cf. 590.—1643. prōfers: *extend.* agitur:
is at stake.—1644. quae: tanta.—1645. spernimur: *we are scorned.*
—1646. Pallada: Pallas (Minerva). iaculātrīcem: *huntress.*—1647. abscessisse (abscēdō): *deserted.*—1649. sociō: *i. e.* which we share.

iunge deam patruo.' Dixit Venus; ille pharetram 1650
solvit et arbitrio matris de mille sagittis
unam seposuit, sed qua nec acutior ulla
nec minus incerta est nec quae magis audiat arcus.
Oppositoque genu curvavit flexile cornu
inque cor hamata percussit harundine Ditem.   1655
    Haud procul Hennaeis lacus est a moenibus altae,
nomine Pergus, aquae.   Non illo plura Caystros
carmina cycnorum labentibus audit in undis.
Silva coronat aquas cingens latus omne, suisque
frondibus ut velo Phoebeos submovet ignes.   1660
Frigora dant rami, Tyrios humus umida flores:
perpetuum ver est.   Quo dum Proserpina luco
ludit et aut violas aut candida lilia carpit,
dumque puellari studio calathosque sinumque
implet et aequales certat superare legendo,   1665
paene simul visa est dilectaque raptaque Diti;
usque adeo est properatus amor.   Dea territa maesto
et matrem et comites, sed matrem saepius, ore
clamat; et ut summa vestem laniarat ab ora,
conlecti flores tunicis cecidere remissis.   1670
    Tantaque simplicitas puerilibus adfuit annis,

1650. deam: Cereris filiam, 1647. patruō: *uncle* (father's brother).—
1652. sēposuit: *set aside.*—1653. audiat: *heed*; subjunctive of characteristic.—1654. flexile: *pliant.*—1655. hāmātā: 252. Dītem: Plutōnem.
—1656. Hennaeīs: *of Henna,* a city of Sicily.—1656. Caystros: a river
of Asia Minor famous for its swans (cycnōrum).—1659. corōnat: *in-
closes.*—1660. Phoebēōs: Phoebī.—1661. frīgora: *coolness.*   ūmida:
moist.—1663. lūdit: *sports.*   violās: *violets.*—1664. studiō: *eagerness.*
calathōs: *baskets.*—1665. aequālēs: *playmates.*   certat: *strives.*—1666.
dīlēcta: amāta. Dītī: dat. of agent.—1667. ūsque adeō: *to suck a
degree.*—1669. ōrā: *edge.*—1671. simplicitās: *simpleness.*

haec quoque virgineum movit iactura dolorem.
Raptor agit currus et nomine quemque vocatos
exhortatur equos, quorum per colla iubasque
excutit obscura tinctas ferrugine habenas.   1675
    Est medium Cyanes et Pisaeae Arethusae
quod coit angustis inclusum cornibus aequor.
Hic fuit, a cuius stagnum quoque nomine dictum est,
inter Sicelidas Cyane celeberrima nymphas.
Gurgite quae medio summa tenus exstitit alvo,   1680
adgnovitque deam; 'Nec longius ibitis,' inquit;
'non potes invitae Cereris gener esse; roganda,
non rapienda fuit.   Quod si componere magnis
parva mihi fas est, et me dilexit Anapis;
exorata tamen, nec, ut haec, exterrita nupsi.'   1685
Dixit, et in partes diversas bracchia tendens
obstitit.   Haud ultra tenuit Saturnius iram,
terribilesque hortatus equos in gurgitis ima
contortum valido sceptrum regale lacerto
condidit.   Icta viam tellus in Tartara fecit   1690
et pronos currus medio cratere recepit.

1672. iactūra: *loss.*—1673. raptor: *abductor.*—1674. exhortātur:
urges. iubās: 1026.—1675. excutit: *shakes out.* fērrūgine: *rust color.*—
1676. Cyanēs, Pīsaeae Arethūsae: a spring and fountain near Syracuse.
The waters of Arethusa were said to flow underground from Elis (hence
Pisaean) to Ortygia, where they reappeared on the surface.—1677.
angustīs: *narrow.* aequor: the Great Harbor.—1679. Sīcelidās:
Siculās, 1632. celeberrima: cf. 865, 962.—1680. exstitit: 575. alvō:
waist.—1681. adgnōvit (adgnōscō): *recognized.*—1683. compōnere: *compare.*—1684. Anāpis: a river in Sicily.—1685. exōrāta: *won by entreaty.*
exterrita: perterrita.—1688. hortātus: cf. exhortātur, 1674.—1689.
contortum (contorqueō): *brandished.* scēptrum rēgāle: *royal staff.*—
1690. icta: 1044.

At Cyane raptamque deam contemptaque fontis
iura sui maerens, inconsolabile vulnus
mente gerit tacita lacrimisque absumitur omnis;
et quarum fuerat magnum modo numen, in illas   1695
extenuatur aquas.   Molliri membra videres,
ossa pati flexus, ungues posuisse rigorem,
primaque de tota tenuissima quaeque liquescunt,
caerulei crines digitique et crura pedesque;
nam brevis in gelidas membris exilibus undas   1700
transitus est.   Post haec umeri tergusque latusque
pectoraque in tenues abeunt evanida rivos.
Denique pro vivo vitiatas sanguine venas
lympha subit, restatque nihil quod prendere possis.

Interea pavidae nequiquam filia matri   1705
omnibus est terris, omni quaesita profundo.
Illam non udis veniens Aurora capillis
cessantem vidit, non Hesperus.   Illa duabus
flammiferas pinus manibus succendit ab Aetna
perque pruinosas tulit inrequieta tenebras.   1710
Rursus ubi alma dies hebetarat sidera, natam
solis ab occasu solis quaerebat ad ortus.

Quas dea per terras et quas erraverit undas,
dicere longa mora est.   Quaerenti defuit orbis.

1693. incōnsōlābile: *that cannot be healed.*—1696. extenuātur: *pines away.* vidērēs: past potential, *you might have seen.*—1697. flexūs: *bending, softening.* posuisse: dēposuisse.—1698. quaeque tenuissima: *all the slightest parts.* liquēscunt: *melt away.*—1700. exīlibus: *thin.*—1702. ēvānida: *vanishing away.* rīvōs: *brooks.*—1704. lympha: aqua. prendere: *grasp.*—1705. mātrī: dat. of agent.—1707. ūdīs: ūmidīs. 1661.—1708. Hesperus: the evening star.—1709. succendit: *kindles*—1710. pruīnōsās: 149.—1711. hebetārat: *had dulled* (by its light).

Sicaniam repetit; dumque omnia lustrat eundo,   1715
venit et ad Cyanen.   Ea ni mutata fuisset,
omnia narrasset; sed et os et lingua volenti
dicere non aderant, nec quo loqueretur habebat.
Signa tamen manifesta dedit, natamque parenti
illo forte loco delapsam in gurgite sacro   1720
Persephones zonam summis ostendit in undis.
Quam simul adgnovit, tamquam tunc denique raptam
scisset, inornatos laniavit diva capillos,
et repetita suis percussit pectora palmis.
Nescit adhuc ubi sit; terras tamen increpat omnes,   1725
ingratasque vocat nec frugum munere dignas,
Trinacriam ante alias, in qua vestigia damni
repperit.   Ergo illic saeva vertentia glaebas
fregit aratra manu, parilique irata colonos
ruricolasque boves leto dedit arvaque iussit   1730
fallere depositum vitiataque semina fecit.
Fertilitas terrae latum vulgata per orbem
falsa iacet.   Primis segetes moriuntur in herbis,
et modo sol nimius, nimius modo corripit imber;
sideraque ventique nocent, avidaeque volucres   1735
semina iacta legunt.   Lolium tribulique fatigant
triticeas messes et inexpugnabile gramen.

1715. Sīcaniam: *Sicily*. lūstrat: 261.—**1716.** nī: nisi.—**1720.** dēlāp-
sam: *fallen*.—**1721.** Persephonēs: Greek name of Prosperina.—**1722.**
tamquam: *as if*. tunc dēnique: *then for the first time*.—**1723.** dīva:
dea.—**1724.** repetīta: *repeatedly* (what literally?).—**1725.** increpat:
chides.—**1727.** Trīnacriam: cf. 1618.—**1729.** parilī: cf. 871.—**1730.**
rūricolās: used as adj.; cf. 761.—**1731.** fallere dēpositum: *betray their
trust*.—**1732.** vulgāta: *famed*.—**1736.** lolium: *darnel, tares*. tribulī:
thistles.—**1737.** trīticeās: *of wheat* (trīticum.)

Tum caput Eleis Alpheias extulit undis
rorantesque comas a fronte removit ad aures
atque ait, 'O toto quaesitae virginis orbe   1740
et frugum genetrix, immensos siste labores,
neve tibi fidae violenta irascere terrae!
Terra nihil meruit, patuitque invita rapinae.
Nec sum pro patria supplex; huc hospita veni.
Pisa mihi patria est, et ab Elide ducimus ortus;   1745
Sicaniam peregrina colo.   Sed gratior omni
haec mihi terra solo est. Hos nunc Arethusa Penates,
hanc habeo sedem; quam tu, mitissima, serva.
Mota loco cur sim tantique per aequoris undas
advehar Ortygiam, veniet narratibus hora   1750
tempestiva meis, cum tu curaque levata
et vultus melioris eris.   Mihi pervia tellus
praebet iter, subterque imas ablata cavernas
hic caput attollo desuetaque sidera cerno.
Ergo dum Stygio sub terris gurgite labor,   1755
visa tua est oculis illic Proserpina nostris;
illa quidem tristis neque adhuc interrita vultu,
sed regina tamen, sed opaci maxima mundi,
sed tamen inferni pollens matrona tyranni.'

　　Mater ad auditas stupuit ceu saxea voces,   1760
attonitaeque diu similis fuit.   Utque dolore

1738. Alphēias: Arethusa, loved by the Elean river god, Alpheus.—
1741. genetrīx: cf. genitor. siste: *stay*.—1743. rapīnae: *kidnaping*.—
1744. hospita: *from a foreign land*.—1750. advehar: *am borne to*. nār-
rātibus: *narration*.—1751. tempestīva: *fitting*.—1752. pervia: *passable*
—1753. subter: *underneath*.—1754. dēsuēta: *unaccustomed*, from her
long journey under the earth.—1757. trīstis: maesta.—1759. pollēns
mātrōna: *powerful wife*.—1760. saxea: *of stone, i. e.* turned to marble.

pulsa gravi gravis est amentia, curribus auras
exit in aetherias.   Ibi toto nubila vultu
ante Iovem passis stetit invidiosa capillis,
'Pro' que 'meo veni supplex tibi, Iuppiter,' inquit,   1765
'sanguine proque tuo.   Si nulla est gratia matris,
nata patrem moveat.   Neu sit tibi cura, precamur,
vilior illius, quod nostro est edita partu.
En quaesita diu tandem mihi nata reperta est:
si reperire vocas amittere certius, aut si   1770
scire ubi sit, reperire vocas.   Quod rapta, feremus,
dum modo reddat eam.   Neque enim praedone marito
filia digna tua est, si iam mea filia non est.'
Iuppiter excepit, 'Commune est pignus onusque
nata mihi tecum; sed si modo nomina rebus   1775
addere vera placet, non hoc iniuria factum,
verum amor est.   Neque erit nobis gener ille pudori,
tu modo, diva, velis.   Ut desint cetera, quantum est
esse Iovis fratrem!   Quid quod nec cetera desunt,
nec cedit nisi sorte mihi?   Sed tanta cupido   1780
si tibi discidii est, repetet Proserpina caelum,
lege tamen certa, si nullos contigit illic
ore cibos; nam sic Parcarum foedere cautum est.'

1762. āmentia: cf. āmēns, 645.—1763. nūbila: *gloomy.*—1764. invi-
diōsa: *full of bitterness*; but cf. 758.—1768. nostrō ēdita partū: *born of
me, my daughter.*—1770. āmittere: object of vocās, while reperīre is
pred., *you call it finding to lose more surely.*—1771. quod rapta: *that she
has been stolen.*—1772. praedōne: *robber.*—1774. excēpit: respondit.—
1776. iniūria: *wrong.*—1777. vērum: vērō. pudōrī (848): *to be ashamed
of*; dat. of service.—1778. modo: cf. 1334. ut: *though.*—1779. quid
quod: cf. 57-59.—1781. discidiī: *separation.*—1783. cibōs: *food.* **Par-
cārum:** *of the Fates.*

Dixerat.   At Cereri certum est educere **natam**.
Non ita fata sinunt, quoniam ieiunia virgo   1785
solverat; et cultis dum simplex errat in hortis,
puniceum curva decerpserat arbore pomum,
sumptaque pallenti septem de cortice grana
presserat ore suo.

At medius fratrisque sui maestaeque sororis   1790
Iuppiter ex aequo volventem dividit annum.
Nunc dea, regnorum numen commune duorum,
cum matre est totidem, totidem cum coniuge menses.

1785. iēiūnia: 1153.—1786. simplex: *artlessly*.—1787. pūniceum
pōmum: *pomegranate*.—1788. sūmpta (sūmō): *taken* from the sheath
grāna: *seeds*.—1790. medius: *i. e.* as mediator.

XIV. JASON AND MEDEA

(Aeson, King of Iolcus in Thessaly, entrusted the throne to his brother
Pelias, until his son Jason should grow to manhood. When Jason appeared
to claim his right, Pelias promised to resign the kingdom, provided he
brought the Golden Fleece from Colchis. Accordingly Jason with a band
of heroes and demigods undertook the task and set sail in the ship Argo.)

Iamque fretum Minyae Pagasaea puppe secabant,

perpetuaque trahens inopem sub nocte senectam   1795

Phineus visus erat, iuvenesque Aquilone creati

virgineas volucres miseri senis ore fugarant,

multaque perpessi claro sub Iasone tandem

contigerant rapidas limosi Phasidis undas.

Dumque adeunt regem Phrixeaque vellera poscunt, 1800

Iexque datur Minyis magnorum horrenda laborum,

concipit interea validos Aeetias ignes,

et luctata diu postquam ratione furorem

vincere non poterat, 'Frustra, Medea, repugnas;

nescio quis deus obstat,' ait. 'Mirumque, nisi hoc est   1805

aut aliquid certe simile huic quod amare vocatur.

Nam cur iussa patris nimium mihi dura videntur?

1794. **Minyae:** a mythical race of Greece; the Argonauts. **Pagasaeā
puppe** (= nāvī): the Argo, built in Pagasae, a Thessalian city.—**1796.**
Phīneus: a blind king of Thrace: he had been tormented by the Harpies
—birds with maiden's faces—who were driven away by the sons of the
North wind, Zetes and Calais, who were among the Argonauts. **creātī:**
995.—**1798. perpessī:** *i.e.* the Minyae *having endured* (perpetior).—
1799. līmōsī Phāsidis: *the muddy Phasis*, a river of Colchis.—**1800.**
rēgem: Aeetes, king of Colchis, in whose possession was the Golden
Fleece. **Phrixēa:** of Phrixus, son of Athamas and Nephele. Read the
story of the Fleece in the *Age of Fable* or Lowell's *Jason's Quest.*—
1802. Aeētias: *daughter of Aeetes* (Medea).—**1803. ratiōne:** *reason.*—
1807. nimium: cf. nimis, 276.

Sunt quoque dura nimis. Cur quem modo denique vidi,
ne pereat timeo? Quae tanti causa timoris?

'Excute virgineo conceptas pectore flammas,   1810
si potes, infelix. Si possem, sanior essem.
Sed gravat invitam nova vis; aliudque cupido,
mens aliud suadet. Video meliora proboque,
deteriora sequor. Quid in hospite, regia virgo,
ureris et thalamos alieni concipis orbis?   1815
Haec quoque terra potest quod ames dare. Vivat an ille
occidat, in dis est. Vivat tamen; idque precari
vel sine amore licet. Quid enim commisit Iason?
Quem nisi crudelem non tangat Iasonis aetas
et genus et virtus? Quem non, ut cetera desint,   1820
ore movere potest? Certe mea pectora movit.
At nisi opem tulero, taurorum adflabitur ore
concurretque suae segetis tellure creatis
hostibus, aut avido dabitur fera praeda draconi.
Hoc ego si patiar, tum me de tigride natam,   1825
tum ferrum et scopulos gestare in corde fatebor.
Cur non et specto pereuntem, oculosque videndo
conscelero? Cur non tauros exhortor in illum
terrigenasque feros insopitumque draconem?

1808. modo dēnique: *only just now.*—1810. excute: *cast out.*—
1811. sānior: *more sensible.* Compare this whole passage with the speech
of Atalanta, 52-76.—1812. invītam: sc. mē. nova: cf. 1151.—1813.
mēns: ratiō. probō: *approve.*—1814. dēteriōra: *the worse* (course).
rēgia: *royal.*—1815. aliēnī orbis: *i.e.* in another world.—1816. quod
amēs: *something to love.*—1818. vel: 1065. commīsit: *has done.*—1820.
ut: as in 1238.—1823. concurret: pugnābit. suae segetis: *i.e.* of his
own planting. Modifies hostibus.—1826. gestāre: *carry.*—1828.
cōnscelerō: *pollute.* exhortor: 1674.—1829. terrigenās: *earthborn.*
īnsōpītum: *sleepless.*

'Di meliora velint. Quamquam non ista precanda,   1830
sed facienda mihi.   Prodamne ego regna parentis,
atque ope nescio quis servabitur advena nostra,
ut per me sospes sine me det lintea ventis,
virque sit alterius, poenae Medea relinquar?
Si facere hoc aliamve potest praeponere nobis,   1835
occidat ingratus.   Sed non is vultus in illo,
non ea nobilitas animo est, ea gratia formae,
ut timeam fraudem meritique oblivia nostri.
Et dabit ante fidem; cogamque in foedera testis
esse deos.   Quin tuta times.   Accingere et omnem   1840
pelle moram.   Tibi se semper debebit Iason,
te face sollemni iunget sibi, perque Pelasgas
servatrix urbes matrum celebrabere turba.

'Ergo ego germanam fratremque patremque deosque
et natale solum ventis ablata relinquam?   1845
Nempe pater saevus, nempe est mea barbara tellus,
frater adhuc infans; stant mecum vota sororis;
maximus intra me deus est.   Non magna relinquam,
magna sequar: titulum servatae pubis Achivae,
notitiamque loci melioris, et oppida quorum   1850
hic quoque fama viget, cultusque artisque locorum;

1830. quamquam: *and yet.*—1831. prōdam: for it had been foretold
that Aeetes should lose his throne when he gave up the Golden Fleece.
—1832. advena: *stranger.*—1833. sōspes: *saved.*   lintea: vēla.—
1835. praepōnere: 967.—1836. ix, ea: *such.*—1837. grātia: *charm.*—
1838. oblīvia: *forgetfulness.*—1840. quīn: *nay but.*   accingere: imperative, with reflexive force.—1842. face sollemnī: *i. e.* with solemn
rites of wedlock.   Pelasgās: Graecās.—1843. servātrīx: cf. servātor,
1369.   celebrābere: cf. 962.—1844. germānam: *sister.*—1845. nātāle:
of my birth.—1848. deus: Cupid.—1849. servātae: *of having saved* the
Grecian youth.—1851. viget: *flourishes.*

quemque ego cum rebus quas totus possidet orbis
Aesoniden mutasse velim, quo coniuge felix
et dis cara ferar et vertice sidera tangam.

'Quid, quod nescio qui mediis incurrere in undis 1855
dicuntur montes; ratibusque inimica Charybdis
nunc sorbere fretum, nunc reddere; cinctaque saevis
Scylla rapax canibus Siculo latrare profundo?
Nempe tenens quod amo, gremioque in Iasonis haerens
per freta longa ferar. Nihil illum amplexa verebor; 1860
aut, si quid metuam, metuam de coniuge solo.
Coniugiumne putas, speciosaque nomina culpae
imponis, Medea, tuae? Quin adspice quantum
adgrediare nefas, et dum licet, effuge crimen.'
Dixit. Et ante oculos rectum pietasque pudorque 1865
constiterant, et victa dabat iam terga Cupido.

Ibat ad antiquas Hecates Perseidos aras,
quas nemus umbrosum secretaque silva tegebat.
Et iam fortis erat pulsusque resederat ardor,
cum videt Aesoniden, exstinctaque flamma reluxit. 1870
Erubuere genae, totoque recanduit ore.

1853. **Aesonidēn:** *son of Aeson.*—1854. **vertice:** cf. 878.—1855. **quid,
quod:** 57. **incurrere:** *run against* the traveler. The **montēs** mentioned
are the Symplegades, which were supposed to come together and crush
ships that attempted to pass through.—1856. **Charybdis:** a dangerous
whirlpool on the Italian side of the Straits of Messina. The Sicilian side
was guarded by Scylla, a monster with six heads, who seized and de-
voured sailors from passing ships.—1857. **sorbēre:** *suck in.*—1858.
rapāx: *greedy.* **lātrāre:** *bark.*—1859. **gremiō in:** *on the bosom.*—1862.
speciōsa: 803.—1864. **adgrediāre:** *you are attempting.*—1865. **rēctum:**
right. **pietās:** *filial duty.*—1867. **Hecatēs Persēïdos:** *Hecate, daughter of
Perses,* goddess of magic, identified with Diana and Luna, hence
represented with three forms.—1870. **relūxit** (relūceō): *revived.*—1871.
ērubuēre: *flushed.* **recanduit** (recandēscō): *grew hot again.*

Utque solet ventis alimenta adsumere, quaeque
parva sub inducta latuit scintilla favilla,
crescere et in veteres agitata resurgere vires;
sic iam lentus amor, iam quem languere putares,   1875
ut vidit iuvenem, specie praesentis inarsit.

Et casu solito formiosior Aesone natus
illa luce fuit.   Posses ignoscere amanti.
Spectat et in vultu veluti tum denique viso
lumina fixa tenet, nec se mortalia demens   1880
ora videre putat, nec se declinat ab illo.
Ut vero coepitque loqui, dextramque prehendit
hospes, et auxilium submissa voce rogavit,
promisitque torum, lacrimis ait illa profusis:
'Quid faciam video; nec me ignorantia veri   1885
decipiet, sed amor.   Servabere munere nostro:
servatus promissa dato.'   Per sacra triformis
ille deae, lucoque foret quod numen in illo,
perque patrem soceri cernentem cuncta futuri,
eventusque suos et tanta pericula iurat.   1890
Creditus accepit cantatas protinus herbas,
edidicitque usum, laetusque in tecta recessit.

1872. **alimenta:** 1112. **adsūmere:** *take on.* **-que** connects adsūmere
and crēscere.—1873. **scintilla:** *spark,* subj. of solet.—1874. **resurgere:**
rise again, increase.—1875. **lentus:** *sluggish.* **languēre:** *grow faint.*—
1876. **speciē:** 866. **praesentis:** (of the youth) *present before her.* **inārsit**
(inārdēscō): *blazed up.*—1877. **cāsū:** *by chance.* **solitō:** *than usual.*
Aesone nātus: Aesonidēs.—1882. **prehendit:** *seized.*—1884. **torum:** coniugium. **profūsīs** (profundō): *pouring forth.*—1885. **vērī:** used as a noun.
—1886. **dēcipiet:** *shall deceive.*—1887. **servātus:** conditional.   **tri-**
fōrmis: see note to 1867.—1889. **cernentem cūncta:** cf. 380. The Sun-
god was father of Aeetes.—1890. **ēventūs:** 41.—1891. **cantātās:** *magic.*
—1892. **ēdidicit** (ēdiscō): *taught.*

Postera depulerat stellas aurora micantes;
conveniunt populi sacrum Mavortis in arvum
consistuntque iugis.   Medio rex ipse resedit   1895
agmine purpureus sceptroque insignis eburno.
Ecce adamanteis Vulcanum naribus efflant
aeripedes tauri, tactaeque vaporibus herbae
ardent.   Utque solent pleni resonare camini,
aut ubi terrena silices fornace soluti   1900
concipiunt ignem liquidarum aspergine aquarum;
pectora sic intus clausas volventia flammas
gutturaque usta sonant.   Tamen illis Aesone natus
obvius it.   Vertere truces venientis ad ora
terribiles vultus praefixaque cornua ferro,   1905
pulvereumque solum pede pulsavere bisulco,
fumificisque locum mugitibus impleverunt.

Deriguere metu Minyae.   Subit ille nec ignes
sentit anhelatos (tantum medicamina possunt),
pendulaque audaci mulcet palearia dextra,   1910
suppositosque iugo pondus grave cogit aratri ·
ducere et insuetum ferro proscindere campum.
Mirantur Colchi; Minyae clamoribus augent
adiciuntque animos.   Galea tum sumit aëna

1893. dēpulerat   (dēpellō):   *had   driven   away.*—1894. Māvortis:
Mavors, an old form of Mars.—1896. purpureus: *i. e.* robed in purple.
insīgnis: *distinguished.*—1897. adamantēīs: *of adamant,* hard as steel.
Vulcānum: īgnem.—1898. aeripedēs: *bronze-hoofed.*—1899. camīnī:
furnaces, forges.—1900. solūtī: *softened* into lime.—1904. trucēs (trux):
the savage beasts, subj. of vertēre.—1906. pulvereum: cf. pulvere, 173;
bisulcō: cf. sulcō, 1339.—1907. fūmificīs mūgītibus: *smoky bellowing.*
a spondaic line.—1908. dēriguēre: 1091. subit: *advances.*—1909.
anhēlātōs: *breathed forth.*—1910. pendula paleāria: *hanging dewlaps.*—
1912. īnsuētum: *unaccustomed.*   prōscindere: *to cleave.*—1914. galeā:
helmet.   sūmit: 1788.

vipereos dentes et aratos spargit in agros.   1915
Semina mollit humus valido praetincta veneno,
et crescunt fiuntque sati nova corpora dentes.

Quos ubi viderunt praeacutae cuspidis hastas
in caput Haemonii iuvenis torquere parantes,
demisere metu vultumque animumque Pelasgi. 1920
Ipsa quoque extimuit, quae tutum fecerat illum;
utque peti vidit iuvenem tot ab hostibus unum,
palluit et subito sine sanguine frigida sedit;
neve parum valeant a se data gramina, carmen
auxiliare canit secretasque advocat artes.   1925
Ille gravem medios silicem iaculatus in hostes
a se depulsum Martem convertit in ipsos.
Terrigenae pereunt per mutua vulnera fratres,
civilique cadunt acie. Gratantur Achivi
victoremque tenent avidisque amplexibus haerent. 1930

Pervigilem superest herbis sopire draconem,
qui crista linguisque tribus praesignis et uncis
dentibus horrendus custos erat arietis aureae.
Hunc postquam sparsit Lethaei gramine suci
verbaque ter dixit placidos facientia somnos, 1935
quae mare turbatum, quae concita flumina sistunt,

1915. **vīpereōs**: 1248; these were some of the teeth of the dragon slain
by Cadmus.—1916. **praetincta**: *steeped beforehand.*—1917. **satī**: from
serō, *sow.*—1918. **praeacūtae**: *sharpened.*—1920. **dēmīsēre**: *let sink*; cf.
1078.—1921. **extimuit** (extimēscō): *feared greatly.*—1923. **frīgida**:
chilled.—1924. **parum**: *too little.* **grāmina**: herbae.—1925. **advocat**:
summons to her aid.—1927. **dēpulsum** (dēpellō): *averted.* **Mārtem**: pug-
nam.—1929. **cīvīlī aciē**: *civil strife.* **grātantur**: *rejoice.* **Achīvī**: Pelasgī.—
1931. **pervigilem**: *ever watchful.* **sōpīre**: *lull to sleep.*—1932. **cristā**: *crest*
praesīgnis: īnsīgnis.—1933. **arietis**: *ram.*—1934. **Lethaeī**: *of Lethe,*
i. e. able to produce sleep.—1936. **turbātum**: *troubled.* **sistunt**: *stay,*
check.

somnus in ignotos oculos sibi venit, et auro
heros Aesonius potitur; spolioque superbus
muneris auctorem secum, spolia altera, portans
victor Iolciacos tetigit cum coniuge portus.   1940
Haemoniae matres pro natis dona receptis
grandaevique ferunt patres, congestaque flamma
tura liquefaciunt, inductaque cornibus aurum
victima vota cadit.   Sed abest gratantibus Aeson
iam propior leto, fessusque senilibus annis;   1945
cum sic Aesonides: 'O cui debere salutem
confiteor, coniunx, quamquam mihi cuncta dedisti,
excessitque fidem meritorum summa tuorum,
si tamen hoc possunt (quid enim non carmina possint?)
deme meis annis, et demptos adde parenti;'   1950
nec tenuit lacrimas.   Mota est pietate rogantis,
dissimilemque animum subiit Aeeta relictus.

  Nec tamen adfectus tales confessa, 'Quod' inquit
'excidit ore pio, coniunx, scelus?   Ergo ego cuiquam
posse tuae videor spatium transcribere vitae?   1955
Nec sinat hoc Hecate, nec tu petis aequa.   Sed isto
quod petis experiar maius dare munus, Iason.
Arte mea soceri longum temptabimus aevum,
non annis revocare tuis; modo diva triformis
adiuvet et praesens ingentibus adnuat ausis.'   1960
  Tres aberant noctes, ut cornua tota coirent
efficerentque orbem.   Postquam plenissima fulsit

1938. Aesonius: Aesonidēs.—**1940.** Iolciacōs: *of Iolcus,* in Thessaly.
—**1942. congesta** (congerō): *heaped up.*—**1943. liquēfaciunt:** *dissolve.*
inducta aurum: *gilded.*—**1945.** senīlibus: senectae.—**1948. summa:**
total.—**1952. dissimilem:** *unlike* his.   Aeēta: *i. e.* the thought of Aeetes
left behind.—**1953. adfectūs:** *feelings.*—**1955. trānscrībere:** *transfer.*

ac solida terra spectavit imagine luna,
egreditur tectis vestes induta recinctas,
nuda pedem, nudos umeris infusa capillos,   1965
fertque vagos mediae per muta silentia noctis
incomitata gradus. Homines volucresque ferasque
solverat alta quies; nullo cum murmure saepes;
immotaeque silent frondes; silet umidus aër;
sidera sola micant. Ad quae sua bracchia tendens   1970
ter se convertit, ter sumptis flumine crinem
inroravit aquis, ternisque ululatibus ora
solvit; et in dura submisso poplite terra,
'Nox,' ait, 'arcanis fidissima, quaeque diurnis
aurea cum luna succeditis ignibus, astra,   1975
tuque triceps Hecate, quae coeptis conscia nostris
adiutrixque venis, cantusque artesque magorum
quaeque magos, Tellus, pollentibus instruis herbis,
auraeque et venti montesque amnesque lacusque,
dique omnes nemorum, dique omnes noctis, adeste, 1980
quorum ope, cum volui, ripis mirantibus amnes
in fontes rediere suos, concussaque sisto,
stantia concutio cantu freta, nubila pello
nubilaque induco, ventos abigoque vocoque,
vipereas rumpo verbis et carmine fauces   1985

1964. recīnctās: 1232.—1965. nūdōs: *unbound.* īnfūsa (īnfundō):
spread upon.—1966. vagōs: 1149. mūta: *still.*—1967. incomitāta: sōla.
—1968. quiēs: silentium. saepēs: 275.—1972. inrōrāvit: 1205. ter-
nīs: *threefold.*—1974. arcānīs: *secrets.* diurnīs: 1263.—1976. trīceps:
trifōrmis. coeptīs: ausīs.—1977 adiūtrīx: *helper.* magōrum: an order
of priests among the Medes, connected especially with astrology and
enchantment.—1978: pollentibus: 1759. īnstruis: cf. 1395.—1982.
concussa: agrees with freta. Cf. the description of Dido's priestess in
Aen. IV. 487-491.—1984. abigō: dīsiciō, 1169.

vivaque saxa, sua convulsaque robora terra
et silvas moveo, iubeoque tremescere montes
et mugire solum manesque exire sepulchris.

'Tē quōque, Luna, traho, quamvis Temesaea labores
aera tuos minuant, currus quoque carmine nostro   1990
pallet avi, pallet nostris Aurora venenis;
vos mihi taurorum flammas hebetastis et unco
impatiens oneris collum pressistis aratro.
Vos serpentigenis in se fera bella dedistis;
custodemque rudem somni sopistis et aurum   1995
vindice decepto Graias misistis in urbes.

'Nunc opus est sucis, per quos renovata senectus
in florem redeat primosque recolligat annos. ·
Et dabitis; neque enim micuerunt sidera frustra,
nec frustra volucrum tractus cervice draconum   2000
currus adest.'   Aderat demissus ab aethere currus.

Quo simul ascendit frenataque colla draconum
permulsit manibusque leves agitavit habenas.
Sublimis rapitur subiectaque Thessala Tempe
despicit et Threces regionibus applicat angues;   2005
et quas Ossa tulit, quas altum Pelion herbas,

1987. tremēscere: tremere.—1988. sepulchrīs: *tombs.*—1989. quamvīs: 757. Temesaea: *Temesaean,* a name taken perhaps from the copper
mines of Tamassus in Cyprus. Bronze vessels (aera) were beaten during
an eclipse (labōrēs) to break the magic spell.—1991. pallet: 1208.—1992.
hebetāstis: 1711.—1994. serpentigenīs: *dragon-born.*—1995. rudem: cf.
77.—1996. vindice: *guardian.* Grāiās: *Greek.*—1997. opus: 6, 1120. re-
novāta: *restored.* senectūs: senecta, 909.—1998. recolligat: *gather
again.*—2002. ascendit: cf. ascēnsus, 819. frēnāta: cf. frēnum, 469.—
2003. permulsit: 1910.—2004. Thessala Tempē: the famous valley of
North Thessaly, between Mt. Olympus and Mt. Ossa.—2005. Thrēcēs:
of Thrace. applicat: *drives toward.*

Othrys quas Pindusque et Pindo maior Olympus,
perspicit et placitas partim radice revellit,
partim succidit curvamine falcis aënae.

Et iam nona dies curru pennisque draconum　　2010
nonaque nox omnes lustrantem viderat agros,
cum rediit; neque erant tacti nisi odore dracones,
et tamen annosae pellem posuere senectae.

Constitit adveniens citra limenque foresque,
et tantum caelo tegitur refugitque viriles　　2015
contactus; statuitque aras e cespite binas,
dexteriore Hecates, ast laeva parte Iuventae.

Has ubi verbenis silvaque incinxit agresti,
haud procul egesta scrobibus tellure duabus
sacra facit cultrosque in guttera velleris atri　　2020
conicit et patulas perfundit sanguine fossas.

Tum super invergens liquidi carchesia Bacchi
aeneaque invergens tepidi carchesia lactis
verba simul fudit terrenaque numina civit
umbrarumque rogat rapta cum coniuge regem　　2025
ne properent artus anima fraudare senili.

Quos ubi placavit precibusque et murmure longo,

2006-2007. Pēlion, Othrys: mountains of Thessaly.—**2008. partim:** *some.*—**2009. succīdit:** *cut off.* **falcis,** from falx: *sickle.*—**2010. nōna:** *ninth.*—**2011. lūstrantem:** 261.—**2013. annōsae:** *full of years.* **pellem:** *skin.*—**2014. adveniēns:** cf. adventus, 765. **līmen:** *threshold.*—**2015. tantum:** cf. 934. **virīlēs:** *of her husband.*—**2016. cespite:** *turf.* **bīnās:** *two.*—**2017. ast:** at. **Iuventae:** *Youth.*—**2018. verbēnīs:** *with sacred boughs.* **incīnxit:** cf. cingō, 375, 827.—**2019. ēgesta (ēgerō):** *cast out, removed.*—**2020. cultrōs:** *knives.*—**2021. patulās:** 912. **fossās:** *scrobēs.*—**2022. invergēns:** *pouring upon.* **carchēsia:** *goblets.* **Bacchī:** vīnī.—**2024. cīvit (cieō):** *summoned.*—**2025. raptā coniuge:** Proserpina —**2026. fraudāre:** cf. fraudem, 1838.—**2027. plācāvit:** *appeased.*

Aesonis effoetum proferri corpus ad auras
iussit et in plenos resolutum carmine somnos
exanimi similem stratis porrexit in herbis.   2030
Hinc procul Aesoniden, procul hinc iubet ire ministros,
et monet arcanis oculos removere profanos
Diffugiunt iussi; passis Medea capillis
bacchantum ritu flagrantes circuit aras;
multifidasque faces in fossa sanguinis atra   2035
tinguit et intinctas geminis accendit in aris;
terque senem flamma, ter aqua, ter sulfure lustrat.
    Interea validum posito medicamen aëno
fervet et exsultat spumisque tumentibus albet.
Illic Haemonia radices valle resectas   2040
seminaque floresque et sucos incoquit acres.
Adicit extremo lapides Oriente petitos
et quas Oceani refluum mare lavit harenas.
Addit et exceptas luna pernocte pruinas
et strigis infames ipsis cum carnibus alas   2045
inque virum soliti vultus mutare ferinos
ambigui prosecta lupi; nec defuit illic
squamea Cinyphii tenuis membrana chelydri

2028. effoetum: *worn out.* pröferrï: *to be brought out.*—2029. reso-
lütum: (resolvö):*relaxed.*—2030. strātïs (sternö): 1375. porrēxit: 538.—
2032. arcānïs: 1974. profānōs: *unholy.*—2034. bacchāntum rïtū: *after
the manner of Bacchantes.* circuit: *walks about.*—2035. multifidās: 884.
—2036. intinctās: *dipped in* the blood.—2039. fervet: cf. 890. exsultat:
boils over. spümïs: *foam.* tumentibus: tumidïs, 242.—2041. incoquit:
boils in.—2043. refluum: *flowing back, i. e.* the tides of the Ocean.—
2044. pernocte: *full* moon. pruïnās: cf. pruïnōsās, 149.—2045. strigis:
(strix): *screech owl.* īnfāmēs: *ill-omened.* carnibus: *flesh.*—2046.
ferïnōs: ferae.—2047. prōsecta: *the parts cut off* for an offering. lupï:
the werewolf.—2048. *The scaly membranes of the Libyan water snake.*

vivacisque iecur cervi, quibus insuper addit
ora caputque novem cornicis saecula passae. 2050

His et mille aliis postquam sine nomine rebus
propositum instruxit remorari Tartara munus,
arenti ramo iam pridem mitis olivae
omnia confudit summisque immiscuit ima.
Ecce vetus calido versatus stipes aëno 2055
fit viridis primo, nec longo tempore frondes
induit, et subito gravidis oneratur olivis.
At quacumque cavo spumas eiecit aëno
ignis et in terram guttae cecidere calentes,
vernat humus floresque et mollia pabula surgunt. 2060

Quae simul ac vidit, stricto Medea recludit
ense senis iugulum veteremque exire cruorem
passa replet sucis. Quos postquam combibit Aeson
aut ore acceptos aut vulnere, barba comaeque
canitie posita nigrum rapuere colorem; 2065
pulsa fugit macies, abeunt pallorque situsque,
adiectoque cavae supplentur corpore rugae,
membraque luxuriant. Aeson miratur et olim
ante quater denos hunc se reminiscitur annos.

2049. iecur: *liver.* **insuper:** *in addition.*—**2050. novem:** *nine.* **cornicis:** *crow.*—**2052. propositum:** *undertaking.* **Tartara:** mortem.—
2053. iam pridem: *now for a long time*; modifies ārentī.—**2054. immiscuit:** *blended.*—**2055. stipes:** *stick.*—**2057. gravidīs:** *ripening.* **oneratur:** cf. onus.—**2058. quācumque:** *wherever.* **eiecit:** cf. ēiectō, 562.—**2059. calentēs:** 908.—**2060. vērnat:** *blooms.*—**2061. reclūdit:** *unsheathes.*—**2062. iugulum:** *throat.*—**2063. combibit:** *has swallowed.*—**2065. cānitiē:** *whiteness.*—**2066. maciēs:** *leanness.* **situs:** *decay* of age.—**2067. corpore:** *i. e. flesh.* **rūgae:** cf. rūgōsus, 911.—**2068. lūxuriant:** *fill out.*—**2069. dēnōs:** ten. **hunc:** tālem. **reminīscitur:** *remembers.*

Epilogue to the Metamorphoses

Iamque opus exegi,—quod nec Iovis ira nec ignis 2070
nec poterit ferrum nec edax abolere vetustas.
cum volet, illa dies quae nil nisi corporis huius
ius habet incerti spatium mihi finiat aevi;
parte tamen meliore mei super alta perennis
astra ferar nomenque erit indelebile nostrum. 2075
Quaque patet domitis Romana potentia terris
ore legar populi perque omnia saecula fama,
si quid habent veri vatum praesagia, vivam.

2070. exēgī: 1240.—2071. edāx: *devouring.* abolēre: *to destroy.*—
2074. perennis: *everlasting.*—2075. indēlēbile: *eternal.*—2078. praesā-
gia: cf. praesāgus, 472.

ABBREVIATIONS

abl.	ablative.	*intens.*	intensitive.
absol.	absolute.	*interj.*	interjection.
acc.	accusative.	*interrog.*	interrogative.
adj.	adjective.	*loc.*	locative.
adv.	adverb.	*m.*	masculine.
cf. (*confer*)	compare.	*n.*	neuter.
comp.	comparative.	*nom.*	nominative.
conj.	conjunction.	*num.*	numeral.
dat.	dative.	*p.*	participle.
dem.	demonstrative.	*pass.*	passive.
dim.	diminutive.	*pl.*	plural.
etc.	*et cetera.*	*poss.*	possessive.
f.	feminine.	*pred.*	predicate.
freq.	frequentative.	*prep.*	preposition.
gen.	genitive.	*pron.*	pronoun.
i.e. (*id est*)	that is.	*pronom.*	pronominal.
imper.	imperative.	*reflex.*	reflexive.
impers.	impersonal.	*sc.* (*scilicet*)	supply.
inch.	inchoative.	*superl.*	superlative.
indecl.	indeclinable.	*rel.*	relative.
indef.	indefinite.	*sing.*	singular.
infin.	infinitive.	*w.*	with.

A dash (—) shows that a form is lacking.

A form is inclosed in parentheses to show that it is used only in other cases, or, if a verb, to indicate that the present system is not used.

A numeral after the first form of a verb shows the conjugation to which it belongs.

In proper names a reference is given only to the first line where the word occurs. In words occurring six or more times the first three references are noted, followed by "etc."

BOOKS OF REFERENCE: Bulfinch, *Age of Fable.* Revised by J. L. Scott. Philadelphia: D. McKay.

Cox's *Tales of Ancient Greece.* Chicago: Jansen McClurg & Co.

Guerber's *Myths of Greece and Rome.* American Book Company.

Seeman's *Mythology of Greece and Rome.* Edited by G. H. Bianchi. New York: Harper & Bros.

NOTES

H. = Harkness' Complete Latin Grammar, 1898, references to Harkness' Standard Grammar being inclosed in parentheses. M. = Lane and Morgan. A. = Allen and Greenough. G. = Gildersleeve. B. = Bennett.

The Poet. — Publius Ovidius Naso was the last of the great writers of the so-called Augustan age. Sallust, who belonged rather to the Republic, died when the poet was but nine years old; but Vergil (70–19 B.C.) and Horace (65–8 B.C.) were still at their best when he reached the age of manhood, while the life of the historian Livy (59 B.C.–17 A.D.) was almost parallel with that of the poet. On March 20, 43 B.C., at almost the closing hour of the Roman Republic, Ovid was born in Sulmo, a fine old town in the district of Peligni, north of Rome. His parents were of high rank, but not wealthy, so that Ovid and his elder brother were early sent to Rome to be educated for the law. The younger brother found this course little to his liking, and though he kept to his studies diligently, even at that time devoted his spare moments to writing verses. In his nineteenth year his brother died, so that it was no longer necessary for him to depend upon the practice of law for his living. He resolved, nevertheless, to continue his studies, and after working with the best teachers of Rome, went to Athens, and in company with his life-long friend, the poet Macer, visited the Greek cities of Asia Minor. Then he went to Sicily, where he spent a year, probably the happiest of his life. On his return to Rome he held various minor offices, and was evidently considered a man of importance in judicial matters, but after a few years gave up all thought of a public career, and settled down to the quiet life of a literary gentleman of moderate means. Early in his life he was twice married, but the venture in both instances proved unhappy, and a separation followed. A third marriage, in middle life, was happier; and Ovid's letters to his wife, during his exile, contain many proofs of his affection for her. Ovid was banished by the Emperor Augustus in 9 A.D., ostensibly for endangering the public morals by something that he had written ten years earlier, but probably in reality for some secret reason of the Emperor's. The place of his exile was Tomi, a little town on the Black Sea, a cold, bleak region, quite different from his fertile and sunny home in Italy. Here in lonely retirement ne passed the rest of his days, until his death in 18 A.D, writing many pathetic letters to his friends, and hoping constantly for the imperial decree which never came to end his banishment.

The poem which would have afforded the best means of comparison with Vergil, Ovid's tragedy of *Medea*, unfortunately has been lost.   In general, however, it is agreed that his style is easier and more fluent than Vergil's, and in fact than that of any other Latin writer.   While he does not rise often to the grandeur of the *Aeneid*, his poetry does not show the mechanical difficulties and harsh effects which one meets at times in Vergil.   His verses flow of themselves without any visible effort, so easily that in places they seem a little careless and slipshod.   But he is usually interesting and always charming; and as a spinner of yarns, a maker of light verses to be read before the fashion and beauty of Rome, he had no equal.   Much, however, that he wrote, especially in the years at Tomi, was really noble; and if a good part of his earlier work was unrefined, and some of it even immoral, it was quite in keeping with the social standards of polite society at that time.

The Poem. — The *Metamorphoses*, or *Transfigurations*, or *Changes*, as they might have been called, were the Wonder Book or Fairy Tales of the Romans.   The poems were in an unfinished state when Ovid was banished, and, with other manuscripts, were committed to the flames on his departure. Several copies of the verses, which had been given to friends of the poet, were left, luckily; and it is likely that he finished and revised the whole work during his banishment.   In this work, Ovid has collected all the well-known legends of Greek mythology, connecting them by a slight and frequently invisible thread which runs through the whole fabric.   Beginning with the description of Chaos, the Creation of the World, the Four Ages, and the Flood, one story suggests another until, in a rambling, offhand sort of way, we have passed through, in a single narrative, the whole range of fairyland, — gods, nymphs, heroes, and even favored men included, — ending finally with the deification of Caesar.   The book receives its name from the number of instances related in which human beings are turned, as in our own fairy stories, into animals and objects of various kinds, though the charm of the poem lies rather in the incidents which lead to the different transformations, than in the changes themselves.

The subject matter of the poem is divided into fifteen books of about eight hundred lines each, the principal topics of which are as follows: —

I.   Chaos, the Creation; the Four Ages; the Guilt of Lycaon; the Flood; Apollo's Love for Daphne; Jupiter and Io.

II.   Phaëthon's Misadventure; Callisto; a number of minor incidents, the best known of which is the Abduction of Europa.

III.   Cadmus and the Dragon; the Founding of Thebes; Actaeon; the Birth of Bacchus; Tiresias; Echo and Narcissus; a Miracle of Bacchus.

IV. Pyramus and Thisbe; Leucothoe and the Sun; Clytie; Salmacis; Ino; Perseus and Andromeda.

V. A Quarrel settled by Perseus and the Gorgon's Head; the Muses and the Pierian Nymphs; the Battle of the Giants; many transformations of the gods; Ceres and Proserpina; Arethusa.

VI. Arachne; Niobe's Pride and Punishment; Tereus, Procus, and Philomela.

VII. Jason's Quest and its Sequels; Theseus; Minos.

VIII. Theseus and Ariadne; Daedalus and Icarus; Meleager; Philemon and Baucis; Proteus.

IX. The Centaurs; Hercules.

X. Orpheus; Hyacinthus; Pygmalion; Myrrha; Adonis; Atalanta.

XI. The Death of Orpheus; Midas; Thetis; Ceyx and Alcyone; Morpheus.

XII. The Gathering before Troy; Cygnus; the Battle of the Lapithae and Centaurs; the Death of Achilles; the Rivalry of Ajax and Ulysses.

XIII. Ajax and Ulysses; Hecuba; the Voyage of Aeneas; Galatea; Polyphemus; Glaucus.

XIV. Scylla; Sibylla; Circe; Aeneas at Latium; the Foundation of Rome and Deification of Romulus.

XV. Numa and Pythagoras and the Transmigration of the Soul; Various Changes in and on the Earth; Aesculapius; Julius Caesar.

Other Works of Ovid. — Beside the *Metamorphoses*, Ovid was the author of a comparatively large number of other poems. His earliest important work was the *Heroides*, consisting of twenty-one letters in elegiac verse, assumed to have been written by the famous women of antiquity — as Penelope, Medea, Ariadne, etc. — to absent husbands or friends. The *Fasti* was a Roman calendar or almanac, only six of whose twelve books were finished — a collection of the good old stories and legends connected with the holy days and festivals of the Roman year. The *Amores* consisted of three books of elegies, on various topics, containing several poems of a very high order, but for the most part of an amatory nature. The *Ars Amoris* and *Remedium Amoris* were amatory compositions of a not particularly nice character; such, indeed, that in the author's preface he advises decent people not to read the book. The authorship of these poems was the reason given officially for the poet's banishment. The *Tristia*, in five books, and *Epistulae ex Ponto*, in four books, were letters in elegiac form, written during Ovid's exile, mainly on personal topics, including nearly all that we know of the poet's own life. Besides the works mentioned, there were several unimportant poems or fragments of a miscellaneous nature.

I. ATALANTA'S LAST RACE

In a song given before a spellbound audience of forest trees and animals, Orpheus tells among other things of the love of Venus for Adonis. In the song Venus relates to Adonis the story of the beautiful daughter of the Boeotian Schoeneus, a maiden who so excelled in swiftness of foot that she offered her hand as a prize to any one who could outrun her, the price of defeat being death. A Boeotian youth among the spectators fell in love with the maiden one day, and challenged her to a race. She accepted, and was defeated through the intervention of Venus, who supplied the youth with three golden apples, which he threw down upon the course and thus distracted the attention of Atalanta.

1. **audieris:** H. 552 (485); M. 717, 718; A. 447a, and note; G. 257-59; B. 280.

   aliquam: puellam.

3. **non dicere posses:** *and you could not have told.* H. 555 (485, N. 3); M. 720; A. 447, 2; G. 257; B. 280.

4. **laude, bono:** abl. of specification. H. 480 (424); M. 650; A. 418; G. 397; B. 226, 1. Render, *in the swiftness of her feet or her surpassing beauty.* But what literally?

   -ne: really introduces a double question, with the interrogative word omitted in the first member.

5. **deus:** what god, probably, is meant?

   coniuge: H. 477, III (414, IV); M. 646; A. 411; G. 406; B. 218, 2.

6. **coniugis usum:** *the marriage tie.*

7. **effugies:** observe the force of the compound, as well as the tense of the verb.

   teque ipsa viva carebis: notice that **ipsa** and **viva** are not in the same case, and for the ablative see H. 462 (414, I); M. 601; A. 401; G. 405; B. 214, 1, c. Translate, *while living you will be deprived of yourself, i. e.* of your human form. Read in some book of mythology how this prophecy came true.

9. **violenta:** find out by scansion the case, and so the agreement of this word.

10. **nec: et non**, of which the negative belongs to **sum potiunda**, while the connective joins **inquit** with the preceding clause.

11. **pedibus: cursu.** Why abl.?

12. **praemia:** in apposition with **coniunx** and **thalami.**

15. **venit: ut veniret** would be expected here.

17. **cuiquam:** H. 431, 6 (388, 4); M. 545; A. 375, a; G. 354; B. 189, 3.

19. **ut . . . posito . . . velamine vidit:** *but when her outer garment was laid aside and he saw.*

20. **quale:** *like,* but see prose order.
    meum: *i. e.* of Venus.
    tuum: of Adonis, to whom Venus was telling the story.
23. **peteretis:** informal indirect discourse. H. 649, I (528, 1); M. 1029; A. 592, N.; G. 508, 3; B. 323.
24. **ne currat:** this does double duty as a negative clause after **optat** and positive with **timet.**
25. **invidia:** abl. of cause. H. 475 (416); M. 612; A. 404; G. 408; B. 219.
26. **mihi:** cf. cuiquam, l. 17.
27. **audentes . . . :** something like our "Fortune favors the brave." What god is meant by **deus ipse?**
28. **passu:** abl. of maner. H. 473, 3 (419, III); M. 635; A. 412; G. 399; B. 220, I.
29. **quae:** do not say *who although she.*
    Scythica: the Scythians were famous for their strength and skill in archery.
30. **Aonio:** see l. 46.
31. **facit:** *creates, adds to.*
32. **ablata:** take with **talaria.**
33. **quaeque:** see prose order.
34. **picto limbo:** descriptive abl. H. 473, 2 (419, II); M. 643; A. 415; G. 400; B. 224. Modifies **genualia.**
35. **puellari candore:** descriptive abl.
37. **candida:** *i. e.* of white marble.
40. **ex foedere:** *demanded by the compact.*
45. **fecerit:** future perfect, *if fortune shall prove me the better.*
48. **seu:** correlative with **seu** in l. 44.
49. **Hippomene victo:** abl. absolute, but how best rendered?
50. **Schoeneia:** Atalanta was the daughter of Schoeneus, king of Boeotia.
52. **formosis:** *"the beautiful";* for the case see H. 434 (391, I); M. 536; A. 384; G. 359; B. 192, 1.
53. **discrimine:** H. 476 (420); M. 645; A. 409, c; G. 401; B. 218.
54. **hoc:** *i. e. with me.*
    me iudice: abl. absolute.
    tanti: gen. of value. H. 448, 1 (404, N. 1); M. 576; A. 417; G. 380; B. 203, 3.
57. **quid, quod:** *what (matter) that.* The **quod** clause is a substantive clause in apposition with **quid.** Cf. a similar sentence in Cicero in Catilinam, I, viii, 19: Quid, quod tu te ipse in custodiam dedisti?
    leti: gen. of specification, *undaunted at the thought of death.* H. 452 (399, III); M. 575; A. 349, d; G. 374; B. 204.
58. **ab aequorea origine: ab rege aquarum,** l. 47.

59. **tanti:** cf. tanti, l. 54.

 nostra: meum, l. 62; cf. hoc, l. 54.

60. **illi:** indirect object.

61. **cruentos:** *i. e.* which involves a risk of life.

62. **nulla nolet:** *no maiden will refuse.*

63. **potes:** *thou may'st.*

64. **tui:** objective gen., *for thee.*

 tot: tot procis, l. 9, 65.

65. **viderit:** perfect subjunctive, but **intereat** is present.

69. **non erit:** see prose order.

 invidiae: pred. gen. of description. H. 440, 3 (396, V); M. 558; A. 345; G. 365; B. 203.

70. **velles:** notice the form of the wish as shown by the tense. H. 558, 1 (483, 2); M. 712; A. 441; G. 261; B. 279, 2.

73. **nollem visa fuissem:** equivalent to an optative subjunctive. H. 558, 4; A. 442, b; G. 261, R.

 tibi: H. 431, 2 and 6 (384, 1; 388, 4); M. 544, 545; A. 375 and a; G. 354; B. 189, 2 and 3.

74. **vivere:** a Greek construction used only in poetry. H. 608, 4, N. 1 (533, II, 3); M. 952; A. 535, f, N. 2; G. 552, R. 2; B. 333. The prose construction would be **qui viveres.**

 essem . . . eras: H. 581, 1 (511, 1); M. 940; A. 517, b; G. 597, R. 3; B. 304, 3. *"Thou wert (the only) one with whom I willingly would share my life."*

76. **vellem:** H. 591, 5 (503, II, 1); M. 836; A. 535; G. 631, 1; B. 283, 1.

78. **quid facit:** what would this be in prose? H. 649, II, 6 (529, II, 7); M. 810, 817; A. 575, c; B. 300, 6.

85. **nomine:** H. 480 (424); M. 650; A. 253; G. 397; B. 226, 1.

87. **dotem:** in apposition with **hanc.**

89. **comam:** acc. of specification, a common Greek construction. H. 416 (378); M. 510; A. 397, b; G. 338, B. 180.

 {**ramis crepitantibus:** abl. abs. of description or descriptive abl.

90. **hinc:** take with **decerpta.**

 mea: what word does this modify?

91. **nulli:** dat. of agent. H. 431 (388); M. 544; A. 374; G. 355; B. 189, 1.

93. **carcere:** probably a rope or "tape" stretched across the track to insure an equal start.

95. **putes:** potential. H. 552, 554, 1; 555 (485, 486); M. 717; A. 417, 2; G. 257-259; B. 280.

99. **utere:** not infinitive. What case follows **utor?**

101. **gaudeat:** see prose order, and cf. **esset** in l. 4.

 his dictis: abl. of cause. H. 475 (416); M. 612; A. 404; G. 408; B. 219.

102. **cum iam**: *just when.*
    morata est: notice the gender of the participle, and remember that the
    verb is deponent.
110. **cessata tempora . . . corrigit**: *makes up for lost time.*
113. **cursus**: genitive.
115. **quo**: ut eo, *that so.* H. 568, 7 (497, II, 2); M. 908; A. 531, a; G. 545, 2;
    B. 282, a.
118. **sublato**: (from **tollo**), *when she had taken it up.*
120. **cursu**: H. 471 (417); M. 615; A. 406; G. 398; B. 217.
121. **duxit sua praemia victor**: but forgot to pay his vows to the goddess who
    had helped him. So she caused the lovers to offend Cybele, who trans-
    formed them into a lion and lioness, and harnessed them to her chariot.

TABLE I. — THE DESCENT OF ATALANTA

Aeolus (see Table VI)
|
Athamas
(Themisto)
|
Schoeneus
|
Atalanta

BOOKS OF REFERENCE. — Atalanta: Guerber, pp. 276–278; *Age of Fable,*
pp. 174–177; Landor's *Hippomenes and Atalanta.* Venus and Adonis: *Age
of Fable,* pp. 83–85; Guerber, 108–110; Seeman, p. 66.

II. PYRAMUS AND THISBE

This story is told by one of the Minyeides, three Theban sisters who refused
to worship the god Bacchus, but remained at home, devoting themselves to
domestic occupations, and lightening their toil by repeating in turn some
legendary tale. In the story, two young people of Babylon plan to elope from
their homes, and arrange a meeting at the tomb of Ninus outside the city.
Thisbe precedes her lover to the rendezvous, and is frightened away by the
sight of a lion. A little later, Pyramus finds the tracks of the lion, and sees
Thisbe's mantle torn and bloody. Imagining that she is slain, he kills himself.
Then Thisbe emerges from her hiding place, finds her lover's corpse, and stabs
herself with the same sword. In token of the double death, a mulberry tree,
whose white berries were stained with the lovers' blood, bears ever afterward
dark red berries.

123. puellis: dat. [H. 429 (386); M. 534; A. 370; G. 347; B. 187, III], but render **praelata** surpassing.

124. tenuere: the form of the perfect in **ēre** is very common in poetry, and must not be confounded with the present active infinitive. What would be the infinitive of this verb?

125. coctilibus: because there were no quarries in the vicinity.

Semiramis: a half mythical Assyrian queen, noted for her executive and military ability. According to some accounts, she murdered her husband, King Ninus, whose splendid tomb is mentioned a few lines later.

urbem: Babylon, famous for its high walls and buildings.

126. gradus: *i.e.* ad amorem.

127. tempore: *as time went on.*

taedae: an allusion to the **conferratio,** or most solemn form of marriage among the Romans. In this ceremony, the bride was escorted from her parents' home to the house of the bridegroom by her relatives and friends, bearing pine torches in honor of Ceres. Also the bridegroom presented the bride with symbolical gifts of fire and water. From this custom, **taedae** came to be used as **taedae iugales,** *i.e. marriage.*

coissent: the apodosis of a past unreal condition. But notice the real assertion which takes the place of the protasis.

128. quod: the antecedent of **quod** is the fact of the following line.

129. captis mentibus: abl. abs.

131. quoque: not from **quisque.** -que connects **tegitur** with the verb of the preceding sentence, while **quo** is correlative with an omitted **eo** with **aestuat:** *the more . . . the more.*

134. nulli: dat. Cf. nulli, l. 91.

136. vocis iter: *a passage for your voices.*

141. quantum erat: *how great (a favor) would it be,* i.e. *it would be very little,* the subject of **erat** being the substantive clause of result: **ut sineres.** For the mood of **erat,** see H. 583 (511, N. 3); M. 940; A. 522, a, N. 1.; B. 271, b.

144. quod: *(the fact) that.*

145. diversa: hinc, illinc, l. 138.

146. dixere, dedere: cf. tenuere, l. 124.

147. quisque: in partitive apposition with the subject of **dedere.**

152. custodes: especially **parentes;** cf. l. 128.

foribus: in poetry the preposition with the abl. of place, *from which,* and acc. of place, *to which* (end of motion), is often omitted. H. 419, 3, 466 (380, II, 3, 412, II, 2); M. 518; A. 428, g; G. 337, N. 1, 391, N. 3; B. 182, 4.

154. spatiantibus: in agreement with **illis;** to be supplied as dat. of agent with **errandum:** *and that they may not (be obliged to) miss each other.*

155. **conveniant**: in the same construction as **relinquant** and **temptent**.
  busta: see the derivation of this word in the vocabulary. This was a splendid tomb of great size, which Semiramis built, in honor of her husband, at some distance from the city.

157. **fonti**: H. 434 (391, I); M. 536; A. 384; G. 359; B. 192, 1.

158. **lux**: *daylight*.
  visa: *i.e.* to the lovers.

159. **praecipitatur aquis**: *sinks into the waters* [H. 428, 1 (380, II, 4); M. 540; A. 363, 3; G. 358; B. 193]; *sets in the ocean*.
  nox surgit: cf. *Aeneid*, II, 250, Ruit Oceano nox.

161. **suos**: custodes, l. 152.
  vultum: acc. of specification, a Greek construction: H. 416 (378); M. 510; A. 397, b; G. 338; B. 180.

162. **sedit**: note the change in tense.

164. **caede**: abl. of means. Render *with the blood of freshly slain cattle*, but translate also literally.
  oblita: from oblino; *oblīta* would be from obliviscor.
  rictus: acc. pl. For the case, cf. **vultum**, l. 161.

165. **depositura**: the future participle is a favorite Greek construction to express purpose.

168. **dum fugit**: observe the tense with **dum** here and in l. 170, and see H. 533, 4 (467, III, 4); M. 917; A. 556; G. 570; B. 293.

170. **sine ipsa**: *without its owner*.

172. **serius**: *later than* Thisbe, or, perhaps *too late* to keep his appointment.

173. **ore**: abl. of place, like **foribus**, l. 152.

176. **longa dignissima vita**: see how the quantity of the final **a** decides the agreement of the two adjectives. For the case of **vita**, see H. 481 (421, III); M. 654; A. 418, b; G. 397, N. 2; B. 226, 2.

177. **nostra nocens anima est**: *my soul is*, i.e. *I am, the guilty one*.

178. **metus**: periculi.
  venires: for ut **venires**, a substantive clause of purpose instead of the prose infinitive. What common verb of ordering requires the subjunctive?

179. **nostrum**: meum.

182. **timidi (est)**: predicate gen. H. 447 (402); M. 556; A. 343, b; G. 366; B. 198, 3: *it is the part of a faint heart (merely) to wish for death.*
  Thisbes: a Greek form of gen.

186. **quoque**: cf. quoque in l. 131, and see prose order.

187. **nec mora**: *and without hesitating*.

188. **humo**: humi, locative abl., instead of the regular locative.

189. **non aliter quam cum**: a homely, but apt figure.

189. **vitiato plumbo**: abl. abs., to be rendered *from a flaw in the lead*. Cf. **vitium**, l. 134.

190. **scinditur**: with the force of a Greek middle voice: *bursts*. **foramine**: see note on **foribus**, l. 152.

192. **arborei fetus**: **mora**, l. 194; cf. l. 156.

196. **oculis animoque**: *with all her senses*.

197. **vitarit**: indirect question.

198. **ut . . . sic**: *though . . . yet*. **visa in arbore formam**: *the shape of the tree previously seen*.

199. **an haec sit**: (*in doubt*) *whether this is the one*.

202. **gerens**, like the Greek participle ἔχων, often best rendered *with*. Cf. *Aeneid*, I, 315, virginis os habitumque gerens. **instar**: really an indeclinable noun, and followed by the gen. H. 446, 4 (398, 4); A. 359, b; G. 373; B. 198, 2.

204. **remorata**: i.e. *an instant later*. **amores**: amantem.

205. **indignos**: *too beautiful for such treatment*.

206. **comas**: cf. rictus, l. 164.

207. **cruori**: dat. H. 474, 2, N. 2; 427 (385, II, 3); A. 413, a, N.; G. 348, R.; B. 358, 3.

209. **mihi**: *from me*. H. 427 (385, II, 2); M. 539; A. 381; G. 345, R. 1; B. 188, 2, d.

212. **Thisbes**: what case? Cf. l. 182. For syntax, see H. 440, 4 (396, vi); M. 569; A. 343, d; G. 361; B. 202.

213. **visa illa**: abl. abs.: *after looking at her*.

214. **-que**: connects **cognovit** with the preceding verb. **ense**: abl. with **vacuum**. H. 465 (414, III); M. 604; A. 402, a; G. 390, 3; B. 214, d.

216. **est et mihi**: *I, too, have*. **in**: of purpose, *for* this one thing, *i.e.* destroying herself. So **in** the next line, **in vulnera**.

221. **hoc estote rogati**: a most awkward phrase: *be ye asked this*. Some verbs of asking and teaching take, in the active, two accusatives, as **vos hoc rogamus**, *we ask you this* (instead of **hoc a vobis**, the common phrase). In changing to the passive, one accusative becomes the subject, here the other accusative being retained. A construction like this is bad enough at best, but, in the imperative, reaches the height of awkwardness.

222. **meus**: used rarely for the regular vocative, **mi**.

223. **ut**: introducing **non invideatis** = **patiamini**, *to allow* (literally, *not grudge*), a substantive clause in apposition with **hoc**, l. 221.

224. **tumulo**: abl. of place. See **foribus**, l. 152.

225. **arbor**: incorporated in the relative clause.
230. **incubuit ferro**: the *fell on his sword* of the Old Testament.
232. **ater**: *dark*, not *black*.
233. **rogis**: H. 429 (386); M. 532; A. 370; G. 347; B. 187, III.

BOOKS OF REFERENCE.—Guerber, pp. 117–118; Shakespeare, *Midsummer Night's Dream*.

———◆———

III. APOLLO'S UNREQUITED LOVE FOR DAPHNE

After the flood (see Selection IX), the softened surface of the earth gave birth to a number of strange creatures, among them the serpent Python, which Apollo met and slew. Elated by his success, he ridiculed the childish weapons of Cupid, who, in revenge, shot a dart at the god and another at the nymph, Daphne. In consequence of this, Apollo was filled with love for Daphne, and she with the opposite emotion. The love-smitten god pursued the nymph, but just as he was on the point of overtaking her she was transformed by divine interposition into a laurel tree.

235. **Cupidinis**: compare this prank of the son of Venus with that described in the first book of the *Aeneid*, where, for his mother's sake, he inspired Dido with her fatal love for Aeneas.
236. **hunc**: **Cupidinem**.
    serpente: **Pythone**, ll. 241–242.
237. **cornua**: **arcum**.
238. **quidque tibi (est)**: *what have you to do?* Que connects **dixerat** and **viderat**.
242. **stravimus**: from sterno.
    tumidum: *i.e.* **veneno**.
    Pythona: see introductory sketch. It was to celebrate Apollo's victory over the Python that the Pythian games were instituted.
243. **face**: not from **facio**.
    nescio quos: *some*.
245. **figat**: potential subjunctive. H. 552 (485); M. 717; A. 446; G. 257–59; B. 280.
246. **quanto . . . tanto**: take the second clause first and render, *as much (smaller) . . . as*.
    cedunt: *are inferior (to)*, about the same idea as **minor est** of the next line.
247. **deo**: indirect object.
248. **percussis pennis**: *by the beating of his wings*.

249. **arce**: cf. **tumulo**, l. 224.

251. **operum**: *purposes,* descriptive gen.; H. 440, 3 (396, V); M. **558**; A. 345; G. 365; B. 203.

255. **Apollineas**: **Apollinis**; cf. **proles Neptunia**, l. 80. A derivative adjective is often found in Latin, where in English a possessive is used.

257. **tenebris, exuviis**: abl. of *place;* cf. H. 476, 3 (425, II, 1, N.); M. 629; A. 431; G. 401, N. 6; B. 218, 3.

258. **Phoebes**: cf. **Thisbes**, l. 182; for case see H. 435, 4 (399); M. 573; A. 3˚5, c; G. 359, R. 1; cf. B. 204, 3.

PHOEBE

259. **vitta**: a band, or fillet, worn by unmarried girls.

260. **illam petiere**: *sought her hand.*

261. **impatiens viri**: *hating the very thought of marriage:* cf. **fugit nomen amantis**, above.

   expers viri: *unmarried.*

265. **taedas**: see l. 127.

266. **ora**: cf. **comas**, l. 206.

269. **virginitate**: abl. after **frui**.

   frui: in prose, **ut fruar**.

270. **quod optas esse**: **innupta**.

271. **voto**: H. 426, 1 (385, I); M. 531; A. 367; G. 346; B. 187, II.

   repugnat: because her beauty would bring her many suitors.

272. **visae**: render by a relative clause, as in l. 198.

   Daphnes: objective gen. with **conubia**.

273. **fallunt**: *mislead, i.e.* give empty promises of success with Daphne.

275. **facibus**: abl. of source or cause.

276. **nimis admovit**: *kindled too near.*

   iam sub luce: *when already it was growing light.* Ovid uses the same figure in the *Fasti* (Book IV, 139-140): Semiustamque facem vigilata nocte viator Ponet. The hunter's neglect to extinguish his camp fire is the cause of many a forest fire in the North and West to-day.

277. **pectore toto**: cf. **toto ore**, l. 173.

278. **uritur**: with the force of a Greek middle voice, like **scinditur**, l. 190.

280. **igne**: *with light.*

282. **vidisse**: the subject of **est**.

283. **media plus parte**: like **pectore toto** in l. 277, but with **quam** omitted after the comparative **plus**. Render *more than half exposed*. What, literally?

284. **siqua latent meliora putat**: *"hidden charms he pictures all the fairer"* Translate also literally.

   aura: H. 471 (417); M. 615; A. 406; G. 398; B. 217.

285. **ad**: *for*.

289. **mihi**: dat. of reference; cf. H. 425, 1 and 4 (384, II, 1 and 4); M. 537; A. 376; G. 352; B. 188, 2.

290. **me miserum**: accusative in exclamations. H. 421 (381); M. 512; A. 397, d; G. 343, 1; B. 183.

ne cadas, notent, sim: optative subjunctive; *I hope you may not*, etc.

indignave laedi: a Greek construction for the regular **indignave ut** (or quae) **laedantur**. Find a similar meaning of **indignus** in Pyramus and Thisbe.

293. **moderatius insequar ipse**: truly a very handsome offer.

294. **cui placeas, etc.**: *i.e. stop a bit and find out who it is whose fancy you have taken.*

295. **hic**: adv.

297. **Delphica tellus**: the regions about Delphi in Phocis, where were Apollo's most famous temple and oracle.

298. **Claros, Tenedos, Pataraea regia**: all well-known temples and shrines of Apollo.

301. **nostra**: sc. **sagitta**. Note the case, and cf. **aura**, l. 284.

304. **nobis**, cf. **nostra**, l. 177, **nostrum**, l. 179, etc. Lines 297–304 make a good memory passage, as they define Apollo's divine origin, the chief places of his worship, and his attributes as god of prophecy, of music, of archery, and of medicine.

305. **ei**: not from **is**.

mihi: dat. of reference; cf. **mihi**, l. 289.

herbis: abl. of means after the verbal idea in **sanabilis**.

308. **cumque ipso**: abl. of accompaniment, *Apollo and his unfinished words.*

309. **visa decens**: **decens visu**, but what literally? Cf. **visae**, l. 272.

310. **obviaque**: *and the gusts fluttered her resisting garments as she met them.* What is the exact construction of **obvia**?

311. **impulsos**: *streaming.*

312. **sed enim**: an ellipsis, as in *Aeneid*, I, 19, usually supplied in some such way as this: *but the young god kept on, for*, etc.

315. **vacuo**: *i.e.* an open field without cover in which the hare might hide.

317. **inhaesuro similis**: *like one who is on the point of seizing.*

319. **an sit comprensus**: *whether he is already taken.* Cf. **an haec sit**, in l. 199.

320. **morsibus**: dat. H. 427 (385, II, 2); M. 539; A. 381; G. 345, R. 1; B. 188, 2, d.

eripitur: cf. **uritur**, l. 278.

323. **tergo**: H. 429 (386); M. 532; A. 370; G. 347; B. 187, III.

324. **cervicibus**: loc. abl. Find another example in this story.

332. **radicibus**: abl. of means.

333. **ora**: object.
    nitor: a reference to the beautiful glossy leaves of the laurel.
337. **oscula**: see the derivation of this word, and cf. its meaning in l. 281.
339. **arbor mea**: various trees were considered sacred to different gods, as the oak to Jupiter, the olive to Minerva, etc.
340. **te coma**: see the figure of Apollo on p. 57.
341. **ducibus**: cf. **tergo**, l. 323.
    Triumphum: the public recognition of a general's services on his return from a successful campaign. The hero usually marched in solemn procession from the Campus Martius to the Capitol, escorted by his victorious legions, and followed by long trains of captives and the spoils of battle (here **longas pompas** in l. 342). The victor wore upon his brow a wreath of laurel.
343. **postibus**: dat. of reference.
344. **ante fores**: a reference to the two laurel trees before the palace gate of Augustus, supporting, as it were, the civic crown of oak leaves suspended over the gateway. This was a wreath presented to the emperor by the senate, and inscribed, " EX. S. C. ob Civis Servatos."
345. **intonsis capillis**: descriptive abl.
347. **Paean**: different derivations are assigned to this epithet given to Apollo: by the Greeks it is said to mean the Archer (παίων, *striking*), or the Healer (παύων, *soothing*), or by some it is said to owe its origin to the exclamation ἴε, παῖ (*strike, my son*), with which his mother urged him to kill the Python.

BOOKS OF REFERENCE. — Apollo: *Age of Fable*, pp. 30–33; Cox, pp. 4–6; Guerber, pp. 61–91; Homer's *Hymn to Apollo* (Shelley's translation); Keats's *Hymn to Apollo*. Apollo and Daphne: Lowell's travesty in *Fable for Critics;* Guerber, pp. 68–70. Cupid: Guerber, p. 107; Seeman, pp. 90–93. Python: *Age of Fable*, p. 29; Guerber, p. 67; Milton's *Paradise Lost*, 10, 531; Shelley s *Adonais*.

———◆———

IV. HOW PHAËTHON DROVE HIS FATHER'S CHARIOT

The Egyptian Epaphus (the son of Jupiter and Io) denied, once upon a time, that Phaëthon was the son of Apollo and Clymene, but asserted that he was, on the contrary, the child of Merops, king of Ethiopia, his mother's husband. The boy resented the allegation and wished to secure proofs of his parentage from the Sun himself. He was kindly received by the Sun, and asked the use of his father's chariot as a proof of his paternity. Apollo consented with reluctance,

and after many warnings and instructions the boy set out. Soon, however,
he lost all control of the fiery horses and set the world on fire. Jupiter stopped
his mad course by a thunderbolt, and quenched the flames. At first the Sun
from grief refused to light the world again, but finally collected and pacified
the scattered horses, and all went on as before.

349. **sublimibus columnis**: *in its lofty columns.* H. 480 (424); M. 650;
       A. 418; G. 397; B. 226, 1. So also **auro** and **pyropo**.

350. **pyropo**: an alloy of copper and gold in the proportion of three parts to
       one (Pliny, XXXIV, 94). The word itself is Greek, and means really
       flammis imitante.

351. **tegebat**: the subject is **ebur**. The reference may be to ivory statues
       standing upon the roof. Take **cuius** with **fastigia**.

352. **argenti**: modifies **lumine**.

353. **Mulciber**: a name of Vulcan, said by the Romans to be derived from
       mulcere, *soften*, and **ferrum**.

       illic: in valvis.

356. **caeruleos**: a standing epithet of sea gods taken from the color of the
       waves, but see its derivation.

       Tritona canorum: cf. l. 1174, where, too, he is called **caeruleus**. He
       was the son of Neptune and Amphitrite, and was the herald of the sea.

357. **Proteaque ambiguum**: Vergil makes his home in Carpathos (G. IV,
       388), Homer in Pharos, near Egypt (*Od.* IV, 355). He was the son of
       Neptune and Amphitrite (see Table III), or, some say, of Oceanus
       and Thetis, and could change himself at will into any shape. In the
       Odyssey (IV, 455–459): "The old man did not forget his crafty wiles:
       for first he turned into a bearded lion, then to a dragon, leopard, and
       huge boar; he turned into liquid water, into a branching tree; still
       we held firm with patient hearts." (Palmer.)

358. **Aegaeona**: here a sea monster, son of Pontus and Terra, but in Homer
       (*Il.* I, 404) a giant: —

           " The hundred-handed, whom the immortal gods
             Have named Briareus, but the sons of men
             Aegeon, mightier than his sire in strength." (Bryant.)

359. **Dorida**: a sea nymph, daughter of Oceanus and Tethys; wife of Nereus,
       and mother of fifty daughters called the Nereids. The names of all
       the Nereids are given in the *Theogony* of Hesiod (ll. 240–264), but
       the best known are Galatea, Thetis, and Amphitrite.

360. **virides**: like **caeruleus**, used of the color of the sea. Mermaids are still
       represented in song as sitting on the shore combing their sea-green
       hair.

361. **quaedam**: pars.

361. **omnibus**: dat. of possession with **est** to be supplied.

362. **qualem**: supply **sed talis**; **qualem** agrees with **faciem**, the omitted
     subject of **esse**. Cf. H. 302, 1; M. 972; A. 455, a; G. 535, 422,
     N. 4; B. 330.

363. **terra**: *i.e.* represented on the doors.

366. **signa sex . . . totidem**: the twelve signs of the Zodiac.
     foribus: in foribus. H 485, 3 (425, II, N. 3); M. 627; A. 429, 4;
     G. 385, N.; B. 228, d.

367. **simul**: simulac, as often in poetry.
     Clymeneia proles: used intentionally of Phaëthon, as doubt had been
     cast upon his paternity by Epaphus.

368. **dubitati**: see introductory note.

370. **ferebat**: ferre poterat.

371. **lumina**: the singular for the plural, a very common occurrence in poetry.

373. **Dies, Mensis, Annus**, etc.: not divinities, but allegorical figures repre-
     senting the divisions of time, in attendance upon the Sun.

374. **Horae**: not, as usual in poetry, the seasons, which are mentioned in
     the following lines, but the hours, as again in l. 466.

375. **novum**: because the beginning of a new year. It would be difficult to
     find four better personifications than these
     figures of the four seasons.

376. **nuda**: as compared with spring, which is clothed
     with blossoms and green leaves.

377. **calcatis**: see a representation of this operation
     in the illustration.

378. **capillos**: a Greek accusative. H. 416 (378);
     M. 510; A. 397, b; G. 338; B. 180.

379. **loco medius**: medio in loco. Loco is abl. of
     specification.

TREADING OUT THE
GRAPES

     novitate: expresses cause.
     The prose order: Inde Sol loco medius oculis quibus omnia adspicit
     iuvenem novitate rerum paventem vidit.

380. **oculis quibus adspicit omnia**: in another place (*Met.* IV, 172), Ovid
     says: Vidit hic deus omnia primus.

381. **que**: belongs really with **ait**.
     tibi: poss. dat.
     hac arce: like foribus, l. 366.

382. **parenti**: dat. of agent. Cf. nulli, l. 91.

387. **animis**: dat., like morsibus, l. 320.
     nostris: meis.

390. **negari**: see note to vivere dignus, l. 74.

392. **quŏque**: (not quŏque) *and that.*

394. **dis**: like **parenti**, l. 382.

    palus: the Styx, the sluggish river of the under world. Cf. *Odyssey*,
    V, 185, "The downflowing water of the Styx, which is the strongest
    and most dreadful oath among the blessed gods" (Palmer), and
    Aeneid, VI, 323, Stygiamque paludem, Di cuius iuvare timent et
    fallere numen.

    oculis incognita: *i.e.* unvisited by the sun.

395. **rogat**: sc. **cum**.

396. **alipedum equorum**: objective gen.

397. **paenituit iurasse patrem**: what is a literal translation?

399. **vox mea . . . tuā (voce)**: *my promise has been proved rash by your
    request.*

400. **negarem**: the apodosis of an unreal present condition, whose protasis
    is to be supplied from **liceret**.

402. **quae**: *such as*, hence followed by a subjunctive of characteristic. H. 591,
    2 (500, I); M. 836; A. 537, 2; G. 631; B. 284, 2.

    viribus: A. 228; H. 429.

403. **munera**: belongs with both **magna** and **quae**.

404. **quod**: id quod. So in l. 405.

406. **placeat**: sc. **ut**. That is, each of the other gods may have as high an
    opinion of his own powers as he pleases.

407. **axe**: by synecdoche for **curru**.

409. **fera**: modifies which word? Determine by scansion the quantities of
    final **a** in this line.

410. **agat**: potential subjunctive. H. 552 (485); M. 717; A. 446; a; G.
    257-259; B. 280.

411. **prima**: like **imus, summus**, and some other superlatives, often denotes,
    as here, not *the first*, but *the first part of*. So **ultima**, in l. 415.

    qua: abl. of the way by which.

413. Render: unde saepe mihi ipsi mare et terras videre fit (= est) timor.
    The real subject of **fit** is **videre**, while **timor** is pred. nom.

415. **moderamine certo**: *a firm rein*. **Eget** usually takes the abl. For
    gen., see H. 458,2 (410, V, 1); M. 594, 603; A. 356; G. 383;
    B. 212, 1.

416. Order: Tunc etiam Tethys ipsa, quae me, etc. Tethys was the greatest
    of the sea goddesses, the wife of Oceanus, mother of Clymene, grand-
    mother of Phaëthon. See Table III.

418. **quod**: *the fact that.*

420. **in adversum**: *i.e.* the sun is moving constantly from east to west, while
    the heavens, with all the stars, are whirling constantly from west to
    east. **Nitor** shows the difficulty of the Sun's course, which is directly
    opposed to the movement of the heavens.

423. axis: this is sometimes taken, as in l. 407, for the chariot of the Sun, but more probably refers to the swift motion of the heavens.

425. concipias: cf. audieris, l. 1.

426. formasque ferarum: *i.e.* some of the constellations, or perhaps the signs of the Zodiac, eight of which are animals.

427. ut: *granted that, though.*

428. adversi: pointing toward the east. In his anxiety to dissuade Phaëthon from his perilous undertaking, the Sun is describing, not a single day's journey, which Phaëthon had in mind, but his course in a whole year. He does not, on any given day, come in contact with all the creatures mentioned below.

429. Haemoniosque arcus: by metonymy for the archer himself, or Sagittarius. A number of writers besides Ovid consider this the Centaur Chiron, a Haemonian, *i.e.* a Thessalian. A good account of Chiron will be found in Mr. D. O. S. Lowell's *Jason's Quest.*

Leonis: said to be the Nemaean lion, killed by Hercules and raised to a place among the stars by Jupiter.

431. aliter: *i.e.* the Scorpion faces the east, while the Crab points to the west.

432. tibi: dat. with **in promptu**, which practically = **facile.** Cf. H. 434, 2 (391); M. 536; A. 383; G. 359; B. 192, 1.

ignibus: abl. of specification, modifying **animosos.**

435. habenis: H. 426 (385, I); M. 531; A. 367; G. 346; B. 187, II.

436–437. Order: At tu, nate, cave ne funesti muneris sim tibi auctor, votaque tua corrige dum res sinit. Notice the odd position of -que in l. 437. What does it connect?

438. sanguine: take with **genitum.** H. 469, 2 (415); M. 609; A. 403, a; G. 395; B. 215.

440. pater esse probor: me esse patrem probo.

444. eque tot ac tantis: bring up **bonis** from the line below. **-Que** connects **posce** with **circumspice.**

445. patiere: not an infinitive.

446. vero nomine: abl. of specification.

449. ne dubita: in prose ne dubitaveris.

undas: per undas. In poetry the acc. is found with verbs of swearing, in reality a Greek construction.

451. dictis: like habenis, l. 435.

452. currus: objective gen.

453. qua: quoad, *as long as.*

454. Vulcania: an adjective, as common in poetry, instead of a gen. See l. 50.

457. gemmae: *i.e.* other gems besides the topazes.

458. repercusso Phoebo: abl. absol., *reflecting the Sun.*

459. **magnanimus**: with probably a reference to his too great a display of spirit in the present instance.

460. **rutilo . . . purpureas . . . rosarum**: so in Homer it is "rosy-fingered Dawn, daughter of the morning," who heralds the approaching day (*Od.* IX, 437). Notice the other details of this beautiful description of the coming of morning.

461. **rosarum**: *i.e.* of rosy light.

463. **Lucifer**: the morning star, probably Venus.

466. **Titan**: the sun god, so called because descended from Hyperion or Coeus, one of the Titans.

Horis: cf. l. 374.

467. **celeres**: celeriter.

ignem vomentes: see above, ll. 432–433.

468. **ambrosiae**: the food of the gods, as nectar was their drink. In Homer, also (*Il.* V, 777), ambrosia is spoken of as the food of the horses of the gods.

suco: abl. with **saturos**. H. 477, II (421, II); M. 651; A. 409, a; G. 405, N. 3; B. 218, 8.

praesaepibus: cf. statione, l. 463.

471. **flammae**: with **patientia**. H. 451, 3 (399, II); M. 574; A. 349, b, N. 1; G. 375; B. 204, a.

472. **comae**: dat. H. 429 (386); M. 534; A. 370; G. 347; B. 187, III.

luctus: like currus, l. 452.

474. **monitis, stimulis, loris**: the first two datives [H. 426 (385, I); M. 531; A. 367; G. 346; B. 187, II], the last ablative [H. 477, I (421, I); M. 646; A. 410; G. 407; B. 218, 1].

476. **volentes**: properare volentes.

477. **directos arcus**: the five great circles; *straight across*, as opposed to **obliquum**, in the following line.

478. **limes**: the Ecliptic, which lies within the limits of the Torrid and the two Temperate Zones, the **trium zonarum** of l. 479.

480. **Arcton**: the constellation of the Bear placed near the North Pole. This is said to have been Callisto, the daughter of Lycaön, changed by Juno into a bear, and afterward numbered by Jupiter among the stars.

481. **hac**: sc. **via**, *i.e.* along the Ecliptic.

483. **nec preme**: cf. ne dubita, l. 449.

484. **altius egressus**: conditional, *if you go* (out of the proper path) *too high.*

486. **dexterior**: dextera; so also **sinisterior** for **sinistra**. Construe both with **rota**.

Anguem: the Hydra placed as a guard over the apples of Hesperides, and slain by Hercules. Juno placed it in the heavens extended between the two Bears, hence in the north.

487. pressam Aram: a constellation toward the South Pole, not far from the tail of Scorpio. Here the Titans were said to have formed their league against the gods. It is called "sunken" because nearly out of sight, and in fact, in northern latitudes, is never seen above the horizon.

489. quae iuvet: sc. **ut**, as in l. 406; *who I hope* (**opto**) *may aid you.*

490. Hesperio in litore: not a definite place, but the shores of the Western or Atlantic Ocean, the goal which both Day and Night reach in their daily journey. This point Night has reached (**tetigit**), finishing her course, so that now it is time for the Sun to begin his course.

495. solidis sedibus: **terra firma.** For case, cf. **foribus**, l. 366.

497. Order: sine me lumina terris dare, quae (lumina) tutus spectes (relative clause of purpose).

sine: not the preposition.

499. contingere: the infinitive, depending on **gaudet**, where in prose a causal clause would be expected.

500. grates: a more formal expression than the familiar **gratias.**

inde: from his commanding position on the chariot.

501. Notice the appropriateness of the names of the Sun's horses, derived from Greek words, meaning respectively *fire, dawn, blaze*, and *flame.* They might be rendered, perhaps, *Firebrand, Sunrise, Blazer*, and *Scorcher.*

504. Tethys: as the Sun rises apparently from the sea, it is a sea divinity who unbars the way for the start.

nepotis: see note to l. 416.

505. facta est copia mundi: cf. our phrase, "the freedom of the city was given."

508. isdem de partibus: *i.e.* from the east.

509. quod cognoscere possent: subjunctive of characteristic. H. 591, 1 (503, I); M. 836; A. 535; G. 631, 2; B. 283. Render *such as they could feel.* Not that Phaëthon was particularly light, but divine bodies were greater than human, in weight as well as size.

510. iugum: standing, like **axes** in l. 496, for **currus.**

512. levitate: abl. of cause.

513. onere: abl. of separation. H. 465 (414, III); M. 604; A. 402, a; G. 390, 3; B. 214, 1, d.

514. currus: subject of **dat** and **succutitur**, as well as of **est.**

516. quo prius: sc. **currebant.**

518. nec si sciat, imperet: a condition in the form of a vague future supposition, where in prose a past unreal (pluperfect subjunctive), or perhaps a present unreal (imperfect subjunctive), would be required, as the preceding verbs are historical presents. The present subjunctive implies that the supposition is still possible. Cf. l. 523, where the imperfect is used.

521. timore: like **levitate,** l. 512.

523. mallet: an apodosis of some suppressed present unreal condition, like *if it were not too late* or *if it were possible.*

525. Meropis: sc. filius. Merops, it will be remembered, was Clymene's husband, and was considered Phaëthon's father. From his present height the lot of a living mortal seemed much more attractive to the young man than that of a dead divinity. A living mouse is better than a dead lion.

526. Order: ut pinus borea praecipiti acta, cui rector suus frena victa remisit.

527. frena: the metaphor is taken from a chariot.

528. faciat: a deliberative subjunctive, *what is he to do?* H. 559, 4 (484, V); M. 723; A. 444; G. 265, 446; B. 277.

530. illi fatum contingere non est: *he is not permitted to reach,* but translate also according to the construction.

534. vario: *diversified* (with constellations).

538. porrigit, etc.: in early astronomy, Scorpio occupied at first the space of two signs; later, the constellation Libra was given the space taken up by the claws.

541. gelida: *chilling.*
   formidine: cf. **levitate,** l. 512.

545. hac: sc. **via,** correlative with **qua.**

548. spatio: locative abl.

549. suis: sc. **equis,** abl. of comparison with **inferius.**
   Luna: Diana, sister of Apollo, who is represented as driving a chariot corresponding to the Sun's. In another place (*Tristia,* I, 3, 28), Ovid says, Lunaque nocturnos alta regebat equos.

551. ut quaeque altissima: *in proportion as each (part) is highest, i.e.* in the order of its height.

552. sucis ademptis: abl. absol.

554. damno: dat. of end. H. 425, 3 (384, II, 1, 3); M. 548; A. 382; G. 356; B. 191.

555. moenibus: *i.e.* tectis.

561. ore trahit: *breathes in, inhales.*

564. picea caligine: a good illustration of what is meant by "pitchy darkness"; the smoke is so dense that the very chariot itself which gives light to the world cannot make itself seen.

566. sanguine vocato: abl. absol.
   credunt: *i.e. it is thought.*

569. fontesque lacusque: acc.

572. coniuge: Proserpina.
   regem: Pluto, ruler of the under world.

575. Cycladas: used here for islands in general.   Observe the short final **as**, and see Helps to Scansion.   Cf. **delphines**, l. 577.

577. consuetas: *i.e.* as they were accustomed to do.

579. Nerea: son of Pontus and Terra, the prophetic Old Man of the Sea, wise, just, and truthful to a fault.   His general abode was in the Aegean Sea.   See also note to l. 359, and Table III.

583. ut erat circumdata: *surrounded as she was.*   Cf. l. 354.

584. fontes: in apposition with **aquas.**

585. viscera: acc. from the idea of motion in **condiderant.**
matris: **Telluris.**

586. collo: take with **tenus**; *raised as far as the neck.*   Order: Tellus . . . arida vultus oppressos collo tenus sustulit.

588. infra: **inferius**, l. 549.

590. si placet hoc: sc. **tibi.**

591. liceat: subjunctive of appeal.
periturae: (*if I am*) *destined to perish.*

592. auctore: *i.e.* by thinking of you as its author, rather than the stripling who drove the chariot.

594. crines: the foliage of the forests.

596. hunc fertilitatis honorem: *is this the reward for* (objective gen.) *my fertileness?*   Mark the emphatic position of **hunc.**

598. exerceor: with the double meaning of *worked* and *worried* or *vexed.*

599. alimenta mitia: as compared with **frondes**, the food of the lower animals.

600. vobis: *i.e.* Jupiter and the other gods, as compared with **humano generi.**

602. frater: Neptunus.
illi tradita: when Saturnus allotted to him the rule of the sea, the heavens to Jupiter, and the infernal regions to Pluto.

604. mea: equivalent to an objective gen. like **fratris**, = in me, in fratrem.

605. caeli tui: gen. with **miserere.**

607. Atlas ipse: who supported the heavens on his shoulders.   This is really an anachronism, as Atlas had not yet been transformed into a mountain.   See Selection **X**, and read the story in some book of mythology.

ATLAS
(Naples Museum)

610. in chaos antiquum: as existing before the creation.

611. rerum summae: *the general welfare, the whole universe.*

615. ipsum: Apollinem.

617. summam arcem: *the very highest part of heaven,* as in *Aeneid,* I, 225: Sic vertice caeli Constitit.

arduus: predicate.

620. posset: a relative clause of purpose.

622. ab aure: *i.e.* drawing back the bolt in order to hurl it with his full strength.

624. expulit: a double use quite common in Latin authors: he *deprived* him of life and *hurled* him from the chariot. The same use of a word is sometimes found in English, in similar cases; as, "he lost his balance and his life."

625. in contraria: sc. loca.

633. potuit: *may.* This is what is called a gnomic perfect. H. 538, 5 (471, II, 5); 744; A. 475; G. 236, N.; B. 262, B, I.

634. patria: Ethiopia.

diverso orbe: *a different,* i.e. *far away, part of the earth,* probably toward the west or north.

635. Eridanus: a mythical river, placed by the oldest writers somewhere near the "ends of the earth." Later writers identify it with the Rhine or, with Ovid himself (*Met.* I, 370), with the Padus or Po.

636. Hesperiae: see l. 490. These naiads were Phaëthon's sisters. See Table III.

639. excidit: a mild pun. Cf. **expulit,** l. 624.

640. pater: Apollo.

646. laniata sinus: *tearing her bosom* (*i.e.* of her garment); literally, *torn in respect to her garment.* Cf. **capillos,** l. 378, and find other instances in what you have read.

648. tamen: *indeed.*

652. deficit orbem: *fails the world,* i.e. *is eclipsed.*

655. officium: *i.e.* lighting the world.

aevi: gen. modifying **principiis;** *from the beginning of time.*

657. actorum: note the gen. usual with **piget** and similar verbs [H. 457 (409, III); M. 585; A. 354, b; G. 377; B. 209, I], but the acc. of the person is omitted.

mihi: dat. of agent, limiting **actorum.**

659. posse: the subject se is omitted.

660. ipse: *i.e.* Jupiter.

661. orbatura patres: in bitter irony, as if this were the usual function of the thunderbolt.

663. meruisse: sc. se as the subject, the antecedent of **qui.**

665. rebus: orbi terrarum.

670. natum: *i.e.* mortem nati.

obiectat: cf. our phrase, "cast in one's teeth."

TABLE II. — THE DESCENT OF PHAËTHON

(See also next Table)

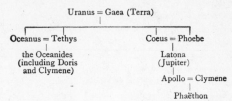

TABLE III. — THE SEA DIVINITIES

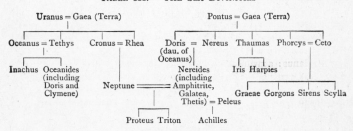

BOOKS OF REFERENCE. — Phaëthon: *Age of Fable*, pp. 50–59; Cox; Guerber, pp. 83–88. Aurora: *Age of Fable*, p. 35; Guerber, p. 85; Seeman, p. 108.

———◆———

V. ORPHEUS AND EURYDICE

The marriage of Orpheus and Eurydice is attended by portents of ill omen. Disaster follows almost immediately, for Eurydice is bitten by a serpent and dies. Orpheus follows her to Hades and by his music charms the divinities below and obtains the release of Eurydice, but loses her again just as he reaches the upper world.

671. **Inde:** from Crete, whither Hymen had been called to bring about the marriage of Iphis and Ianthe. Hymen is often represented by the poets as here, clad in a yellow robe, his perfumed locks wreathed with marjoram, and in his hand a nuptial torch.

672. **Ciconum ad oras:** in Thrace, the home of Orpheus.

673. **nequiquam:** because of Eurydice's untimely death.

676. **fax stridula:** the spluttering, smoky flame was considered an unlucky omen.

678. **nupta nova:** i.e. the bride.

681. **Rhodopeius:** Thracius.

      satis: i.e. *to the full.*

682. **ne non umbras:** *in order to try the shades also.* **Ne** introduces as usual a negative clause of purpose, while **non** negatives the meaning of **temptaret,** i.e. *not to leave untried.* This use of two negatives is called *litotes.*

683. **Taenaria porta:** a grotto in southern Laconia, where tradition placed an entrance to Hades.

684. **leves populos:** umbras.

      sepulcro: for case cf. **viribus,** 99. In the Aeneid (VI. 316) Charon sternly keeps away from the Stygian waters the inops inhumataque turba.

            Nec ripas datur horrendas et rauca fluenta
            transportare prius quam sedibus ossa quierunt.

686. **nervis:** i.e. of his wondrous lyre.

688. **quicquid:** i.e. *whoever of us.*

692. **Medusaei monstri:** Cerberus, whose necks were bound with his mother's snakes.

      vincirem: as Hercules was said to have done.

694. **crescentes:** *budding,* i.e. of her youth.

697. **et hic:** *here as well.*

      et hic: *even here.* What is the subject of **esse?**

699. **vos:** Orpheus is addressing **Persephonen** (685) and **umbrarum dominum** (686).

706. **haec:** Eurydice.

      matura: *of ripe age,* i.e. in time

707. **iuris:** for case cf. **timidi,** 182.

      pro: *instead of, as.*

708. **pro:** *for.*

      certum est mihi: *I am resolved.*

711. Ixion was stretched upon a revolving wheel.

                  "Proud Ixion, doomed to feel
                  the tortures of the eternal wheel."—Sophocles.

712. Notice the curious punishments of these ancient sinners: Tantalus (hence our *tantalize*) parched with thirst stood in a pool, his chin level with the water, which receded whenever he stooped to drink. Over his head hung branches with luscious fruits, which kept always beyond his reach.

713. **iecur:** i.e. of Tityus, the giant whose body covered nine acres. His liver, torn daily by a great vulture, was constantly renewed.

714. **Belides:** the fifty daughters of Danaus, who were condemned to draw water in sieves or porous jars.

Sisyphe: his task was to roll a huge stone to the top of a hill, whence it immediately rushed headlong down again.

716. **Eumenides:** by euphemism for the Furies, Tisiphone, Alecto and Megaera, three sisters who sprang from the blood of Uranus. They were attendants of Proserpina (Persephone) and their chief duty was to visit with remorse those who escaped justice.

719. **passu tardo:** i.e. her shade still limped from the wound received in life.

BACCHANTE

721. **ne flectat retro sua lumina:** compare with this the Bible story of Lot's wife.

725. **margine:** a margine.

726. **hic:** i.e. at the very end of the upward journey.

ne deficeret (sc. **eam**): take with **metuens**.

731. **quereretur:** for mood cf. **posses**, 3.

732. **supremum:** neuter, agreeing with **vale** used as an indeclinable noun.

733. **acciperet·** for mood cf. **possent**, 535.

735. **qui timidus** a man who is said to have been turned to stone at the sight of Cerberus led off in chains by Hercules.

739. **Olenos** was turned into stone, though innocent of crime himself, in order to share the punishment of his wife who was changed to stone on account of her pride.

741. **Ide:** Mount Ida.

742. **orantem:** sc. **vatem.**

portitor: Virgil's portitor horrendus—terribili squalore Charon, the navita tristis of the Styx.

744. **Cereris munere:** in 792 Cerealia dona, *food.*

748. After the death of Eurydice the singer forsook the society of women and the haunts of men, and retired to the solitudes, to sing and sorrow among the forest trees. This act roused

the indignation of the Thracian Bacchantes, who pursued
Orpheus, and tore him in pieces. As punishment for this mad
deed, they were turned into trees by Bacchus. The remains
of the poet were carried down the Hebrus River to Lesbos,
while his spirit, at length, in the shade land rejoined his lost
Eurydice, to be no more parted from her.

749. **umbra**: i.e. Orphei.
750. **arva piorum**: the *Elysian fields*, the home of the blest.
753. **praecedentem**: sc. eam or illam.
754. **iam tuto**: not as in 727, where elapsa est.

BOOKS OF REFERENCE—Orpheus: *Age of Fable*, pp. 234-238; Browning, *Orpheus and Eurydice;* Cox: Guerber, pp. 75-80; Lowell, *Eurydice;* Pope, *Ode for St. Cecilia's Day;* Saxe, *Travesty of Orpheus and Eurydice;* Shelley fragment, *Orpheus;* Seeman, p. 301; Wordsworth, *The Power of Music*. Bacchantes: Guerber, p. 176.

VI. THE TOUCH OF GOLD

Indignant at the treatment of his bard, Bacchus abandoned Thrace for
Phrygia, losing Silenus, the wayward satyr, on the journey. The satyr was
restored to his friends by King Midas, who was allowed to choose his own
reward. He foolishly asked that everything that he touched might be turned
into gold. This power soon became a nuisance and, by the god's favor, was
transferred to the river Pactolus. Midas betook himself to the woods, where
he became an admirer of the god Pan, whom he backed in an unfortunate
musical contest with Apollo. As a reward for his bad judgment, he received
a pair of ass's ears. These he tried to conceal, but his servant whispered
the secret to the earth, from which reeds sprang up, and by their rustling
exposed the whole affair.

755. **hoc**: the punishment of the women described in ll. 737-754.
    ipsos agros: *i.e.* the region where Orpheus had been killed.
756. **Timoli**: Mt. Tmolus in Lydia, famous for its vineyards, so a favorite
    haunt of Bacchus, and called **sui** in this line. There is another interesting allusion to this region in *Metamorphoses*, V, 15-16:—

    Deseruere sui nymphi vineta Timoli,
    deseruere suae nymphae Pactolidas undas.

757. **Pactolon**: a river which rises on the slopes of Mt. Tmolus, famous in
    later times (quamquam non aurea illo tempore) for its golden sands.

758. harenis: abl. of cause. So also **annisque meroque**, in l. 760, and **adventu**, l. 765.

759. hunc: Bacchus, not Pactolus.

760. Silenus: read an account of this interesting personage in some book of mythology.

SILENUS

762. Midan: a mythical king of Phrygia, whose character will be understood by the story which follows.

763. Cecropis: see Jebb's *Primer of Greek Literature*, p. 18.

767. coëgerat agmen: cf. l. 462.

768. undecimus: as, in the determination of time, the point of departure is reckoned in as one of the series, **undecimus** here is the tenth, and not the eleventh, day.

769. iuveni: here an adjective, *the (ever) youthful*.

772. effice: sc. **ut** with **vertatur**.

775. Liber: a Latin name of Bacchus, similar in meaning to the Greek epithet **Lyaeus**.

petisset: subjunctive because the reason is given on the authority of the person described, not on the writer's authority.

776. Berecyntius: as in l. 686.

heros: because the son of Cybele, according to some accounts.

777. polliciti: usually deponent, but here passive.

fidem: *the reality* of the (thing) promise(d).

778. vixque sibi credens: our "scarcely believing his eyes." Prose order: virgam fronde virentem ab ilice detraxit. **Fronde** is abl. of specification.

782. Cereris: used for *grain*, as **Bacchus** often for *wine* (cf. l. 795, **auctorem muneris**), and **Vulcanus** for *fire*.

784. Hesperidas: the daughters of Atlas who had charge of the tree with golden apples which sprang up in honor of the wedding of Jupiter and Juno. Poetry in all lands and languages abounds in allusions to this golden fruit. See Hawthorne's *Wonder Book*.

putes: cf. **putes**, l. 95.

787. eludere possit: *might have deceived*. Danaë was the daughter of Acrisius, king of Argos. She was imprisoned in a dungeon or, some say, in a tower of brass, to avoid the possibility of a marriage which might prove her father's ruin; but Jupiter fell in love with her, and visited her in the form of a shower of gold, called by Ovid **aureus ignis in** *Metamorphoses*, V, 113 (aureus ut Danaen Asopida luserit ignis).

789. **gaudenti**: (sc. **ei**), dat. of reference.   H. 425, 2 & 4 (384, II, 1 & 4);
M. 537; A. 376; G. 353; B. 188, 2.   This line and the following
remind one a little of Dido's banquet in *Aeneid*, I, 701–706.

790. **tostae**: it was the custom of the ancients to parch grain before bruising
or grinding it.   Cf. also *Aeneid*, I, 179: et torrere parant flammis et
frangere saxo.

791. **sive**: *if . . . or if* (l. 793).

795. **auctorem muneris**: a rather artificial expression for **vinum**.   See l. 782.

796. **videres**: potential.   Cf. posses, l. 3.

800. **meritus**: with force of an adverb.

ab auro: not, as it may at first sight appear, an abl. of agent, but an abl.
of source, instead of the more usual construction of means.   This is
not rare in Ovid.

801. **splendida**: showing that the strange gift was beginning to show its
effect on his person.

802. **Lenaee**: another name for Bacchus, from the Greek, meaning *of the
wine press.*

803. **eripe**: sc. **me**.

804. **mite**: belongs to **numen**, which is in apposition to **Bacchus**.

deum: a contracted gen. plur.   The whole phrase is equivalent to **mitis
deus**.

805. **restituit**: a legal term, *to restore* to his former estate.

munera solvit: observe that the meaning here is exactly opposite to
that in l. 774, although the fundamental idea in both cases is the same,
to loose.   In the former instance the god released himself from obliga-
tion by giving the gift, here he releases Midas by annulling it.   Perhaps a more exact expression would have been: eum datis muneribus
solvit.   Render *and as proof of the deed he
canceled the gift which he had given.*

807. **Sardibus**: Sardis was north of Mt. Tmolus.

808. **undis**: dat. with **obvius** following a verb of
motion, as if a verb compounded with **ob**.

811. **crimen**: because it was the result of his guilty
folly.

812. **iussae**: *i.e. as bidden.*

815. Pan is represented in pictures as a curious being, half god, half goat.   His worship was connected with that of Bacchus and the nymphs.

PAN
(From an Ancient Vase)

817. **praecordia mentis**: **mens**.

820. **hinc, illinc**: Sardis was situated to the north
of Mt. Tmolus, Hypaepa to the south.   Arachne, in *Metamorphoses,*
V, 13, parvis habitabat Hypaepis.

821. **nymphis**: dative.

822. **cerata**: like Daedalus' wings, Pan's pipes were fastened together with wax.

823. **se**: *i.e.* **suis** (**cantibus**).

824. **sub**: *under*, i.e. *before*.

impar: inasmuch as Apollo was the god of music.

825. **monte**: locative abl.

iudex: the god of the mountain.

826. **liberat**: just as a modern musician pushes back his hair from his ears, presumably to hear better.

caerula: the effect of the dark green of the trees tempered by hazy distance.

830. **barbarico**: not necessarily *harsh*, but *non-Hellenic, Phrygian*, so that it appealed particularly to the patriotic ears of the Phrygian king.

canenti: *when he played*. What is the syntax of this word?

831. **sacer**: *sacred*, as belonging to Bacchus. See l. 756.

833. **caput**: cf. **pectora**, l. 674.

836. **a laeva**: *i.e. in his left hand*.

837. **artificis**, etc.: "his very posture suggested the musician."

838. **pollice sollicitat**: read this line aloud and see the musical effect of the dactyls.

839. **submittere**: *rank below*.

842. **Delius**: cf. l. 236.

844. **trahit in spatium**: in other words:—

> "The god of wit, to show his grudge,
> Clapt asses' ears upon the judge;
> A goodly pair, erect and wide,
> Which he could neither gild nor hide." (Swift.)

It was particularly fitting that Midas should bear this peculiar badge of disgrace, as his ears had been the means of his unfortunate blunder.

845. **dat posse moveri**: *gave them the power of motion*. This is a poetical construction.

847. **induitur**: used like a Greek middle form, *puts on (himself), assumes*. What verb in the preceding selection is similarly used?

848. **turpi pudore**: abl. of cause.

849. **tiaris**: a Persian cap, covering both ears and fastened under the chin.

850. Prose order: sed famulus capillos longos ferro resecare solitus hoc viderat.

855. **terrae haustae**: *i.e.* the place from which the earth had been removed.

859. **pleno anno**: *in the fullness of the year, i.e.* when the proper time had elapsed.

860. **agricolam**: *the planter*.

TABLE IV. — THE DESCENT OF BACCHUS

```
          Inachus (see Table III)
        /
   Io = Jupiter
    |
 Epaphus
    |
   Libya = Neptune
       |
     Agenor    Mars = Venus
       |            |
    Cadmus = Haemonia
           |
        Semele = Jupiter
             |
          Bacchus
```

BOOKS OF REFERENCE. — Bacchus: *Age of Fable*, p. 204; Guerber, pp. 174–182; Seeman, pp. 134–138.   Midas: *Age of Fable*, pp. 60–62; Guerber, pp. 74, 75, 177–179; John Lyly, the play of *Midas*; Saxe, *The Choice of King Midas*; Seeman, p. 149; Swift, *The Fable of Midas*; *Wonder Book*.   Pan: *Age of Fable*, pp. 211, 212; Guerber, pp. 74, 300, 301; Seeman, pp. 149–152.   Silenus: Guerber, p. 300; Landor, *Silenus*; Seeman, pp. 148, 149.

———◆———

VII. PHILEMON AND BAUCIS

Among the stories with which the river god Achelous entertained Theseus and a party of friends were several in which some of the nymphs were changed to various objects. Pirithous, the son of Ixion, who was present, took exception to the veracity of the stories; whereupon, to silence the unbeliever, Lelex, king of the Locrians, as a proof that the gods could in very truth change the forms of men, related the following incident, the truth of which was undoubted. Jupiter and Mercury, traveling in disguise through a Phrygian town, went from house to house asking hospitality, but found none to take them in until they reached the cabin of two aged peasants. Here they were treated to the best that the house afforded, and after the modest entertainment revealed themselves as gods. The village with its inhospitable inhabitants was submerged in a broad lake, while the peasants' hut was turned into a stately temple, of which the pious couple were made attendants until too old to perform its duties, when they were transformed into trees before the temple door. This is rightly considered one of the finest passages in Ovid.

862. **tiliae**: what case?

863. **collibus**: abl. of place.

867. **Atlantiades**: Hermes or Mercury, son of Jupiter and Maia, the daughter of Atlas.

   caducifer: in his capacity as messenger to the gods, but now he had put aside his **caduceus** with his wings, on assuming a mortal disguise.

872. **illa**: notice the case, and cf. **collibus**, l. 863.

874. **nec iniqua**: et aequa.

875. **nec refert**: not from **refero**, but perhaps for **resfert**; render *it makes no difference whether*, etc., followed by an indirect question.

877. **penates**: *household gods*, so *household* or *house*.

878. **submisso vertice**: *stooping*.

880. **quo**: in quod.

881. **foco**: abl. of separation. One could not wish for a more perfect word picture than this homely little sketch of Baucis at the fireside.

883. **anili**: *i.e. feeble*.

886. Prose order: holusque, quod coniunx suus riguo ex horto conlegerat, foliis truncat.

887. **foliis**: abl. of separation.

888. **sordida**: with the smoke in which it hangs. The **tigno** is **nigro** for the same reason.

   suis: not from **suus**.

891. **medias horas**: *i.e.* while the bacon is being softened and cooked.

892. **de**: here with the ablative of material.

893. **tecto**: dat., but **sponda pedibusque**, descriptive abls. Here **lecto** refers to the couch as a whole, **torum, sponda**, and **pedibus** to the various parts.

895. **et**: *even*.

896. **non indignanda**: *i.e. quite in keeping with*. **Lecto** is dat. of agent, as the use of **indignanda** strictly implies a personification.

897. **accubuere**: Ovid is perhaps introducing here the more luxurious customs of his own times, rather than the simple habits of the earlier period.

898. **tertius pes**: the fact that the table had three legs was in itself a sign of poverty. In Ovid's time the rich had tables with one large central leg.

901. **bicolor**: green and black, or perhaps dark green. This Phrygian dinner was a regulation Roman banquet on a small scale, though quite simple as compared with most Roman ménus. First fruit and herbs, then the solid viands, and lastly the dessert.

904. **non acri**: *no longer glowing*.

905. **fictilibus**: in fictilibus.

906. **eodem argento**: descriptive abl., *of the same kind of plate*, *i.e.* **fictilibus**.

907. pocula qua . . .: *smeared with yellow wax on the inside.* What literally? This was done to make a smooth surface, and to a certain extent to keep the "silver" from being dissolved by acids.

908. calentes: take with **epulas** (the boiled bacon and vegetables mentioned above).

909. nec longae senectae: because cheap; new wine only would be within the means of the poor.

rursus: the wine had been brought in apparently after the first course, and was now presented a second time with the second course, and set aside to make room for the dessert, as the table was too small to hold so many things at the same time.

911. hic: *i.e. in the dessert.*

913. purpureis vitibus: the epithet *purple* belongs in reality to **uvae,** though it goes grammatically with **vitibus.** This is a form of enallage.

915. nec iners pauperque: by litotes *both active and generous.*

916. cratera: a Greek form of acc. With this incident cf. the miracle in I Kings xviii. 16, where "the barrel of meal wasted not, neither did the cruse of oil fail."

920. nullis paratibus: *lack of preparation.* **Paratibus** is a rare form.

921. custodia: for the concrete **custos,** as **tutela** in l. 948. In general the Romans valued geese for their watchfulness, since the time when the cackling of the sacred geese saved Rome. Elsewhere (*Met.* XI, 598) Ovid says: —

> Nec voce silentia rumpit,
> sollicitive canes canibusve sagacior anser.

923. ille: anser.

aetate: abl. of cause with **tardos.**

927. immunibus: dat. to agree with **vobis** by attraction, as common in the case of **licet.** It might have been **immunes: vobis esse dabitur huius mali (vos) esse immunes.**

931. nituntur longo vestigia: notice how the slow, hard climb of the old people is shown by the spondees.

932. summo: a summo clivo.

semel missa: *at a single flight.*

933. mersa: sc. esse. Cf. the tense with that of **manere.**

936. Prose order: illa casa vetus, parva etiam duobus dominis, in templum vertitur.

dominis: dat. of reference.

937. furcas: forked or Y-shaped timbers which supported the roof.

939. tellus: solum.

946. auferat, videam, sim: optative subjunctive. H. 558 (484, I); M. 710, 711; A. 441; G. 260; B. 279.

947. **ab illa**: the dat. would be more common.
951. **casus loci**: *i.e.* the events which had taken place there.
955. **abdita**: *so that they were hidden,* a rather common proleptic use of the
     participle, several cases of which have been pointed out before.
957. **de gemino corpore**: *made from the two bodies.*
     truncos: cf. the opening lines of this story.
961. **cura pii dis sunt**: cf. 1 Samuel ii. 30, "For them that honor me I will
     honor, and they that despise me shall be lightly esteemed."

BOOKS OF REFERENCE. — Philemon and Baucis: *Age of Fable,* pp. 62–65;
Guerber, pp. 43, 44; Swift, travesty on *Philemon and Baucis; Wonder Book.*

———◆———

VIII. THE IMPIETY AND PUNISHMENT OF NIOBE

As a result of her boasting herself superior to Minerva in weaving, the
maiden Arachne had been changed by the goddess into a spider. But Niobe,
daughter of Tantalus, not warned by the fate of Arachne, acted in a similar
manner, elated over her happy lot as the mother of seven sons and seven
daughters, while the goddess Latona had only two, Accordingly she endeav-
ored to have her own name honored above that of the goddess. The injured
divinity called to her aid her two children, Apollo and Diana, who in a single
day put to death, the one all her sons, the other all her daughters. In the
midst of her sudden grief, Niobe became a marble fountain of unceasing tears.

963. **vestibus**: from her Phrygian garments, interwoven with gold. The
     Phrygians at this time had brought weaving to a high degree of per-
     fection. Strictly, **auro** is the abl. of cause, while **vestibus** is a dat.
     depending upon it.
966. **alta**: *i.e. haughty, erect.*
967. **auditos**: *i.e. merely heard of.*
969. **Tantalus**: a king of Phrygia, son of Jupiter. Read the account of his
     sin and punishment in some book of mythology.
970. **soli**: dat. This statement of Niobe was not strictly true, as there are
     a number of other instances where the same favor was granted.
971. **Pleiadum soror**: the Hyades were daughters of Atlas and sisters of the
     Pleiades.
973. **avus, socero**: Jupiter was father of Tantalus as well as of Amphion,
     Niobe's husband. See Table V.
974. **me**: abl. in apposition with **domina**, instead of the reverse, **sub me
     domina**. Niobe claims as hers the honor due both her father and her
     husband.

974. **regni Cadmi**: Cadmus was the founder of the citadel of Thebes, though Amphion built the city itself and was its ruler.

975. **fidibus**: read in some book of reference the story of Amphion.

978. **accedit**: the same use of the word occurred in l. 915.

979. **digna dea**: not in the same case. How does scansion aid in determining the cases?

982. **neget, dubitet**: deliberative subjunctive. H. 559, 4 (484, V); M. **723**; A. 444; G. 466; B. 277.

984. **quam cui possit**: (subjunctive of characteristic) **quam ut mihi.**

986. **excessere**: *have gone beyond,* i.e. *cut off all chance of.*

987. **huic populo**: dat. of separation with **demi**. H. 427 (385, II, 2); M. 539; A. 381; G. 345, R. 1; B. 188, 2, d.

    natorum: appositional gen.

989. **turbam**: used in scorn.

    qua quantum . . . orba: *how much does she differ from a childless woman?* That is, she might as well have no children at all as to have two only.

991. **ponite: deponite.**

992. **quodque licet**: *i.e.* the only thing that they could after Niobe's sweeping prohibition.

995. **vobis animosa creatis**: *proud in having borne you.* Cf. *Aeneid,* I, 502: Latonae tacitum pertemptant gaudia pectus, as she sees Diana moving like a queen amid her attendant nymphs.

996. **cessura**: *disposed to yield.*

997. **dubitor**: *i.e. it is doubted, doubts are felt* (concerning me). Cf. a similar use of **probo** in l. 440.

1000. **adiecit**: as we say, "added insult to injury."

1002. **linguam paternam**: like her father, she seemed to be unable to control her unruly member.

1004. **longa**: belongs with **querella**: **longa querella est mora poenae.**

1006. **Cadmeida arcem**: see l. 974.

1008. **adsiduis pulsatus equis**: **adsiduo pulsatus equis**: *continually beaten by horses.*

1009. **mollierat**: *i.e.* into dust.

1010. **genitis Amphione**: *sons of Amphion.* H. 469, 2 (415, II); M. 609; A. 403, a; G. 395; B. 215.

1011. **suco**: the purple dye for which the Tyrians were famous, made from a kind of shellfish.

1013. **qui . . . fuerat**: *who had been the firstborn of his mother.*

1018. **armo**: *i.e.* of the horse.

1019. **audito sonitu**: cf. *Iliad*, I, 49, "Terrible was heard the clang of that resplendent bow." (Bryant.)

1021. **pendentia**: from the yards.
    rector: sc. **navis**.
1022. **qua**: **qua parte**.
1026. **ut erat**: *just as he was.*
1029. **solito labori**: *their daily practice* in riding.
1030. **nitidae**: used of the wrestling place, but belonging properly to the wrestlers, whose bodies are anointed with oil.
1035. **suprema lumina**: *their dying eyes,* or *their eyes for the last time.*
1036. **exhalarunt**: a double spondee, making a spondaic line. Compare the effect of the slow movement here, as the brothers draw their last breath, with the galloping dactyls of ll. 1008 and 1009.
1037. **laniata**: cf. **abdita**, l. 955.
1039. **illi**: dat. of reference.
1043. Prose order: at vulnus non simplex intonsum Damasichthona adficit.
    intonsum: *i.e. youthful.*
1047. **pennis**: with **tenus**. Remark how **tenus** follows its case.
1050. **profectura**: cf. the use of the future participle in ll. 816 and 996.
1052. **non omnes**: only Latona and her children needed to be propitiated.
1057. **certam fecere**: **certiorem fecerunt.**
1058. **mirantem (deos superos hoc) potuisse**: *wondering that the gods had been able to do this.*
1059. **essent, haberent**: informal indirect discourse. H. 588, II (516, II); M. 851; A. 540, 2; G. 539; B. 286, I.
1061. **luce**: **vita**.
1062. **heu quantum**: cf. l. 989. Notice the arrangement of words here.
1064. **resupina**: observe that the meaning differs from that in ll. 188 and 578.
1065. **suis**: dat. with **invidiosa**; but **hosti** is dat. of agent.
1068. **liventia**: the effect of beating herself as an expression of grief.
1069. **pascere**: imperative.
1072. **efferor**: literally, *I am carried out* (to the grave), the regular word in connection with funerals. The meaning is clearly, *I die seven times in the death of my children.*
1075. **arcu**: probably of Diana, who had gone to Thebes with her brother to assist in avenging their mother's insult.
1077. **cum vestibus atris . . . demisso crine**: these were the usual signs of mourning among the ancients. Cf. the mourning of the nymphs in ll. 718–719. And again of the dryads in *Metamorphoses*, VIII, 778–779: —

    Omnes germanae Cererem cum vestibus atris
    maerentes adsunt.

1080. **imposito**: take with **ore**, *pressing her lips* upon her brother, *to kiss him.*
1084. **videres**: potential subjunctive
1086. **ultima restabat**: see the illustration.
1089. **pro qua**: the antecedent of **qua** is the omitted subject of **occidit**.
1093. **genis**: in genis.
1094. **ipsa . . . congelat**: cf. the similar transformation in l. 730.
1095. **posse moveri**: cf. l. 845.
1099. **patriam**: Phrygia.
   montis: Mt. Sipulus in Lydia, where, according to Pausanias, the mountain side resembled the colossal figure of a weeping woman. There was also a fountain on the mountain, which had the property of turning objects to stone.

TABLE V. — THE DESCENT OF AMPHION AND NIOBE

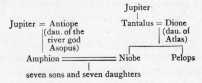

BOOKS OF REFERENCE. — Niobe: *Age of Fable*, pp. 136–139; Guerber, pp. 93–96. Latona: Cox; Guerber, pp. 61–62; Seeman, pp. 203–206.

IX. THE FLOOD

After the iron age the people of the earth became so depraved that the gods decided to purge it thoroughly by means of a flood. When this was done, only two living beings were left, — Deucalion and Pyrrha. Like Philemon and Baucis, they were saved by their goodness, and through the aid of the oracle of Themis repeopled the earth by means of stones, which, when thrown over their heads, became human beings.

1101. **placet**: sc. **ei (Iovi)**.
   sub undis: read in connection with this the account of the flood in Genesis.
1103. **Aeoliis in antris**: cf. *Aeneid*, I, 52–54: —

   Hic vasto rex Aeolus antro
   luctantis ventos tempestatesque sonoras
   imperio premit ac vinclis et carcere frenat.

1103. aquilonem: which brought cold and dry weather, while the south wind was supposed (in Italy) to cause rain.

1104. inductas: sc. caelo.

1106. vultum: for the case, cf. pectora, l. 674. So also colores, l. 1111.

1107. capillis: ex capillis. So fronte for in fronte. Find as many other instances of this as you can, in what you have read.

1112. concipit Iris: according to the ancients, the rainbow itself drew water and then gave it back to the earth in rain.

1114. vota: the "hopes" of the farmers, the abstract being used for the concrete, as in l. 921.

1115. Iovis ira: Iuppiter iratus.

1116. caeruleus frater: Neptune. For the epithet, see also l. 356.

1118. hortamine: abl. with utendum; sc. mihi.

1120. domos: the fountains, the homes of the river gods.

1121. immittite habenas, ora relaxant, defrenato: all strictly applicable to horses. Find the lines in Phaëthon where the same words are used.

1122. fontibus: dat. of reference.

1127. satīs: distinguish carefully from satĭs, *enough*.

1128. suis: refers to penetralia, not to the subject of rapiunt.

penetralia: really the inner part of the house, where the images of the gods (sacris) were kept, but here used in general for *temples*.

1130. Prose order: altior tamen unda huius culmen tegit. Huius refers to domus.

1134. cymba: like fronte, l. 1108. It is thought that Ovid, in his desire to bring the scene vividly before his readers, goes too much into detail in the lines that follow.

1138. si fors tulit: forte, *if it happened so.*

1140. graciles gramen: note the double alliteration in this line.

1143. Nereides: see above, ll. 359 and 580.

1144. incursant: the same word that was used in the case of Phaëthon when he, too, was out of his element.

agitata: another case of "anticipation," like abdita, l. 955.

1145. nat lupus inter oves: a similar proceeding has been observed more than once in the West in case of prairie fires, when different animals have forgotten their natural enmities in seeking a common safety.

1146. vires fulminis: a reference to the force and lightning speed with which the boar strikes with its tusks; the metaphor is common in Roman poetry.

1147. ablato: *i.e.* by the waters.

1151. novi: *new, strange* to them, with the idea also, perhaps, of *horrible*.

1152. maxima pars: of men, as well as of beasts.

1153. inopi victu: inopia victus.

1157. verticibus duobus : in *Metamorphoses*, II, 221, this mountain is called **Parnasus biceps,** although there was in reality but one prominent peak. There are, however, twin peaks famous in antiquity in connection with the worship of Dionysus.

1159. hic : take with **adhaesit,** *while he clung here* (to the peak).

1160. consorte tori : Pyrrha, daughter of Epimetheus and Pandora.

1161. Corycidas : so-called from a cave on Mt. Parnassus sacred to the nymphs.

numina montis : *i.e.* the other divinities, especially the Muses.

1162. Themin : the daughter of Uranus and Gaea or Terra, from whom she had received the Delphic oracle. It did not fall to Apollo until much later. Observe the Greek acc. case-ending of **Themin.**

1163. amantior : note that participles may be compared when used as adjectives. So Cicero's **amantissimos reipublicae,** *most devoted to the republic.*

aequi : H. 451, 3 (399, II); M. 574; A. 349, c; G. 375; B. 204, a.

1169. aquilone : see l. 1103, where this wind was confined in the caves of Aeolus.

1171. posito tricuspide telo : deposito tridente, l. 1124.

1173. umeros : Greek acc.

1174. caeruleum : used several times before as an epithet of sea divinities. Triton was not only the color of the sea, but covered, like the hulk of an old vessel, with barnacles and seaweed.

conchae : dat. with **inspirare.**

1177. undis : dat. like **saxis,** l. 712. So also **quibus undis** in l. 1178. The waves here are personified.

telluris : *i.e.* those from the rivers, etc., which had covered the land.

1182. diem longam : *long time.* Observe the gender of **diem** here.

nudata : *i.e.* **aquis,** not **foliis.**

1187. soror : Pyrrha's father, Epimetheus (see Table VI), was brother to Prometheus, the father of Deucalion; so that she was in reality his cousin. Compare with this line Andromache's words to Hector (*Il.* VI, 429) : —

> " Hector, thou
> Art father and dear mother now to me,
> And brother and my youthful spouse besides." (Bryant.)

1189. turba : cf. the use of this word in l. 989, where the number of the **turba** is the same.

1190. haec . . . : *this confidence* (which we have now) *in our own lives is not yet sufficiently assured.*

1194. modo : with long o, so the abl. of the noun **modus.** The adv. **modo** has by exception o short.

1194. **quo consolante**: abl. absol.: *who consoling would you grieve*, i.e. *who would console you in your grief?*

1197. **paternis artibus**: read the story of Prometheus, who had made men of clay.

1199. **genus in nobis restat mortale**: nos duo turba sumus, l. 1189.

1201. **placuit**: sc. eis, *they resolved.*

1202. **per sacras sortes**: a general expression for consulting the oracle. It does not here mean necessarily casting lots.

1203. **Cephisidas**: see on a map that the Cephisus flows very near to the base of Mt. Parnassus.

1204. **ut, sic**: see in the vocabulary the peculiar meaning of these words.

1205. **inde**: ex Cephiso.

libatos: *consecrated* by pouring out a little in honor of a god, or perhaps here used in the rare sense of *drawn, taken up.* The act was one of purification, before entering the sacred presence of the oracle.

1212. **victa**: *moved, won over.*

1213. **Themi**: dic and the punctuation indicate the case of this word, a Greek form.

1214. **mersis rebus**: *the flood-swept world.*

1220. **det**: indirect discourse after **rogat** for the imperative of the direct discourse. She asked pardon because **parere recusat.**

1221. **iactatis ossibus**: abl. absol.; but render "*by throwing her bones.*" No worse act of impiety than this could be thought of by the ancients.

1222. **caecis obscura latebris**: *shrouded in dark mystery.*

1225. **fallax est sollertia nobis**: *my skill is at fault.*

1226. **oracula**: the subject of both verbs.

1227. **lapides . . . ossa reor dici**: *I think that stones are called bones*, i.e. *that stones are meant by bones.*

1229. **Titania**: both Pyrrha and Deucalion were the grandchildren of Iapetus, who was a Titan. See Table VI.

1233. **sua post vestigia**: post terga sua.

1234. **credat, sit**: present subjunctive where an imperfect would be looked for, as in l. 518.

nisi sit: *i.e.* if it had not been believed for ages.

1236. **mora**: *by delay*, i.e. *after a time.*

1238. **ut . . . sic**: cf. l. 1204: *though some form of a man, yet not clearly outlined, can be made out.*

1239. **de**: *in the case of.*

1241. Prose order: quae pars ex illis aliquo suco fuit umida et terrena, ea (pars) versa est.

1242. **in corporis usum**: *i.e.* to be used as flesh.

TABLE VI.—THE DESCENT OF DEUCALION AND PYRRHA

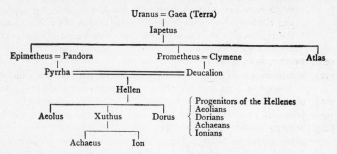

Uranus = Gaea (Terra)

Iapetus

Epimetheus = Pandora   Prometheus = Clymene   Atlas

Pyrrha ========================= Deucalion

Hellen

Aeolus   Xuthus   Dorus   { Progenitors of the Hellenes
                                 { Aeolians
                                 { Dorians
                                 { Achaeans
                                 { Ionians

Achaeus   Ion

BOOKS OF REFERENCE. — Deucalion and Pyrrha: *Age of Fable*, pp. 24–26; Cox; Guerber, pp. 36–38; Seeman, p. 190.

───◆───

X. PERSEUS AND ANDROMEDA

Perseus, the son of Danaë and Jupiter, was a hero of the type of Hercules. Among other wonderful exploits he slew the Gorgon Medusa, whose head had the power of turning to stone all who looked upon it. While on his way home with this head as a trophy, he asked shelter of the Titan Atlas, who refused, and was turned to stone for his inhospitality. Continuing his journey, Perseus came upon Andromeda, the daughter of Cepheus of Ethiopia, exposed on a cliff as prey to a sea monster. He stayed his flight to kill the creature, and received the hand of Andromeda as his reward. At the wedding feast he related to the guests the story of the capture of the Gorgon.

1248. **viperei spolium monstri**: the Gorgon Medusa, with its head of snaky hair.

1249. **aëra carpebat**: like **carpe viam** in l. 809 the air being for the time his **viam**.

tenerum: tenuem.

alis: which Mercury had loaned him for the flight.

1253. **colubris**: take with both adjectives.

1254. **per immensum**: cf. profundum, l. 1172.

1258. **Arctos, Cancri bracchia**: *i.e.* the extreme North and the extreme South

GORGO
(From an Ancient Terracotta)

1261. **Hesperio**: used of any place in the unknown West, here Mauretania
in Africa, where Atlas was king. He was son of the Titan Iapetus
and brother of Prometheus and Epimetheus (see Table VI). Since
the rebellion of the Titans he had been condemned to support the
heavens on his shoulders.

1262. **Lucifer, Aurora**: cf. ll. 461–463, 767–768.

1264. **hominum cunctos**: by a Greek construction for **homines cunctos**.
The acc. is usual even in prose with **praestans** in the sense of *excel*.

1265. **ultima**: *i.e.* the farthest to the West.

1266. **pontus**: of course the ocean called after Atlas himself, the Atlantic.

1267. **aequora subdit . . .** : see ll. 416, 417.
axes: currus, as before. The epithet is transferred as frequently in
Ovid. So, too, in Vergil, as the familiar line (*Aen.* I, 168), hic fes-
sas non vincula navis ulla tenent.

1268. **illi**: *of his*, dat. of reference.

1269. **premebant**: plural, as the subject **vicinia** is plural in sense: *no neighbors limited his land.*

1270. **arboreae frondes**: again, as in ll. 88–89, Ovid describes a tree of
golden branches and leaves, as well as fruit, though usually it is represented as bearing merely golden apples. These apples are generally given as belonging to the Hesperides.

1274. **rerum**: rerum gestarum.

1276. **Themis Parnasia**: cf. l. 1162.

1278. **Iove natus**: the oracle referred to Hercules, who was to kill the
watch dragon and steal the golden fruit, but Atlas naturally understood it to be Perseus and acted accordingly.

1283. **quam mentiris**: *of which you falsely boast.*
longe absit: *be far from (helping) you, be of no avail*, hence the dat.
tibi, rather than the abl. of separation.

1285. **fortia**: sc. dicta.

1287. **gratia**: amicitia.

1289. **retroversus**: because the Gorgon's head had the unpleasant property
alluded to in the introductory note, Perseus had conducted opera-
tions against Medusa by the aid of a polished shield, in which he
beheld the reflection of the Gorgon and not herself. See ll. 1413–
1414.

1296. **aeterno carcere**: in the caves in the Lipari islands already mentioned
in l. 1103.

1297. **operum**: objective gen.

1298. **pennis ligat . . . pedes**: in prose **pennas pedibus adligat**, referring, of course, to the sandals which Mercury had loaned him.
ille: Perseus.

1299. **telo unco**: also a loan from Mercury, a short, sharp sword called *harpé*.
accingitur: like a Greek middle verb, *girds himself.*

1302. **Cephea**: *of Cepheus*, king of Ethiopia, according to Ovid's account, and brother of Egyptus and Danaus.

1303. **maternae linguae**: Cassiopeia, queen of Ethiopia, had boasted that she was more beautiful than the Nereids, whereupon Neptune had sent a deluge upon her kingdom. The oracle of Jupiter Ammon, in Libya, had declared that in order to avert this calamity Andromeda must be exposed to the attacks of a sea monster. The girl accordingly had been chained to a rock near the sea, and it is there that Perseus finds her in l. 1305.

1306. **Abantiades**: Perseus, whose grandfather Acrisius was son of Abas, king of Argos. See Table VII.

1309. **correptus**: *fascinated.*

1313. **requirenti**: sc. **mihi.**

1317. **quod potuit**: id quod potuit, *i.e. the only thing she could do.*

1318. **instanti**: sc. **ei**, as **mihi** with **requirenti** above. (*To him*) *as he urged her again and again.*

sua ne . . . videretur: depends upon **indicat**: *that she might not seem to wish to conceal* (literally, *to be unwilling to admit*) *any fault of her own.* **Sua** is emphatic in contrast with l. 1320.

1320. **quantaque fiducia**: *i.e.* how much her mother had presumed upon her beauty. Although Andromeda wished Perseus to know that she was being punished for no fault of her own, she did not wish to deal harshly with her mother.

1323. **possidet**: when taken in connection with **immensa**, this shows the vast size of the beast.

1325. **illa**: Cassiopeia. See l. 1303.

1326. **dignos**: *i.e. suited to.*

1328. **lacrimarum**: objective gen., corresponding to **ad opem**, *time for tears.*

1329. **vos**: acc. with **manere.**

1330. **peterem**: the imperfect subjunctive instead of the present, as, in l. 518, the present was used for the imperfect. The condition is not contrary to fact.

Perseus: in both this line and the next is in apposition with **ego.**

1333. **praeferrer**: the apodosis to **peterem.**
gener: *as son-in-law.*

1334. **et**: *also.*
faveant modo: dummodo faveant.
tempto: temptabo.

1335. **mea, meā**: the first is a pred. adj. after **sit**; the second, abl. with **virtute.**

1335. **servata**: conditional.

1337. **dotale**: an anachronism, as in early times the wife was purchased from her parents.

1341. Prose order: quantum medii caeli Balearica funda plumbo transmittere potest. Cf. l. 932.

   Balearica: the inhabitants of the Balearic islands were celebrated in history for their skill in slinging, and no army was considered complete without a body of Balearic slingers.

1346. **Iovis praepes**: the eagle, which was sacred to Jupiter.

1347. **praebentem Phoebo**: *i.e.* basking in the sunshine.

1348. **occupat aversum**: a common use of **aversus**.

1349. **cervicibus**: in cervice.

1352. **Inachides**: Perseus, since he was born at Argos, the first king and founder of which was Inachus, son of Oceanus.

1353. **sublimis**: pred. adj., agreeing with the subject of **attollit**, instead of the object. Supply **se** with **subdit** and **versat**.

1357. **obsita conchis**: cf. the description of Triton in l. 1173.

1361. **graves**: by anticipation; *so as to become heavy*. Find other adjectives or participles used in this way.

1362. **bibulis**: *i.e.* from the monster's blood.

1365. **eo**: scopulo.

1367. **cum plausu clamor**: plausus et clamor, hence a plural verb, **implevere**.

1373. **caput**: acc. Scan, to determine the case of **dura**, which agrees with **harena**.

1374. **mollit**: *i.e.* strews so as to be mollis, *carpets*.

1376. **recens**: *i.e.* just broken off.

1377. **rapuit**: a stronger word than **percepit** below, expressing the suddenness of the change.

1383. **capiant ut**: ut capiant, explaining the preceding line; *i.e.* according to Ovid's natural history, coral was a plant which, springing from the seeds thus sown and growing beneath the water, hardened instantly upon exposure to the air (**tacto ab aere**).

1385. **dis tribus**: the three who had aided him in his undertaking: Mercury had, as we have seen, loaned him his winged sandals and *harpē;* Minerva had given him a helmet, spear, and shield; while Jupiter was his father, and had been of great moral assistance.

1388. **Alipedi**: in what you have read, find several other allusions to this quality of Mercury.

1390. **rapit**: shows the promptness with which Perseus claims his reward, while **indotata** shows his love for her. Compare the use of **rapuit** in l. 1377, and see note.

1391. praecutiunt: at the head of the marriage precession. Here the gods of Marriage and Love act the part of servants.

1394. aurea: *decked with gold.*

1396. Cepheni proceres: *i.e.* the Ethiopians.

1397. munere: take with **functi**.

1400. qui: Cepheus.

1403. Agenorides: Perseus was not a direct descendant from Agenor. It is thought by many that this is an oversight of Ovid, due to the great haste with which the poem was written. Make a list of all the names by which Perseus is called in this chapter.

gelido: this seems rather early for Perseus to apply this word to Atlas,

PEGASUS

as it is only a few hours after the man was changed into a mountain. The description of the cave is inaccurate too, as the adventure happened before Atlas was transformed.

1405. sorores: the Graeae, two old women, Pephredo and Eryo, daughters of Phorcys and Ceto. They were said to have only one eye and one tooth, which they used by turns, as described.

1408. cepisse manu: and had refused to return, it is said, until the helpless old women had told him how to find his way to the home of the Gorgons.

1412. ex ipsis: cf. l. 7, teque ipsa carebis.

1413. Prose order: seque aere repercusso clipei, quod laeva gerebat, formam Medusae horrendae adspexisse.

1414. aere: the mirrors of the ancients were usually of polished brass.

1417. matris: *i.e.* Medusae; the winged horse Pegasus and the giant Chrysaor
sprang from the blood of Medusa. Pegasus was destined to play an important part in mythology. He was caught and tamed by Minerva, and
presented by her to the Muses. Afterward he became the property
of Bellerophon, and his companion in a number of exciting adventures.

TABLE VII. — THE DESCENT OF PERSEUS AND ANDROMEDA

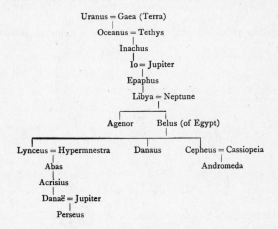

TABLE VIII. — THE GRAEAE AND GORGONS

(See also Table III)

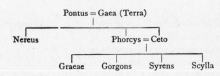

It will be seen, by Table III, that the more respectable members of the
family of Pontus and Gaea were descended from Nereus, while the children
of Phorcys and Ceto were, taken as a whole, a sorry lot.

BOOKS OF REFERENCE. — Perseus and Andromeda: *Age of Fable*, pp. 142–
150; Cox; Guerber, pp. 240–249; Kingsley's *Andromeda; Wonder Book.*
Medusa: *Age of Fable*, p. 141; Guerber, pp. 242–244.

TABLE IX. — THE DESCENTS OF THE PRINCIPAL GODS

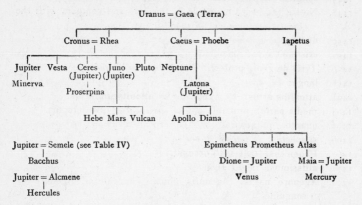

XI. THE SEARCH OF CADMUS

Cadmus, son of Agenor, king of Phoenicia, goes in search of his sister Europa, who has been carried off by Jupiter in the form of a white bull.

1422. **imagine tauri:** the disguise which Jupiter (**deus**) had assumed in order to carry off Europa.

1424. **ignarus:** i.e. ignorant of what had happened.
 perquirere: per orbem quaerere.
 raptam: sc. sororem.

1425. **poenam:** in apposition with **exsilium.**

1426. **sceleratus:** *cruel* toward his son, but *tender* (**pius**) toward his daughter.

1427. **possit:** for mood cf. **agat, 410.**

1432. **aratri:** like **flammae, 471.**

1434. **fac condas:** *see that you found.* H. 566 (498), A. 449 c.
 Boeotia: predicate adjective.
 vocato: the so-called future imperative.

1435. **Castalio antro:** the grotto in which the oracle of l. **1429** was situated.

1436. **ire:** in prose **euntem.**

1437. **servitii:** i.e. of the yoke.

1441. **cornibus altis:** abl. of cause with *speciosam.*

1443. **comites:** obj. of **respiciens.**

1448. Notice the order of words in this line and compare with the chiastic arrangement in 1440.

1450. **densus:** *overgrown.*

1453. **cristis et auro:** (hendiadys) *with crests of gold.*

1456. **Tyria de gente profecti:** *men of the Tyrian race.*

1458. **longo:** i.e. *deep.*

1461. **attonitos artus:** by hypallage for **attonitorum artus.**

1464. **media parte:** probably abl. of specification with **erectus.**

1465. **quanto—qui separat:** *as* (the serpent) *which lies between.*

1466. **si spectes:** *if you see, if one sees.*

1467. **Phoenicas:** take with **occupat.**

1471. **altissimus:** i.e. at noon.

1472. **Agenore natus:** Agenoris filius. For case of **Agenore** cf. **sanguine,** 438.

1477. **supra:** *i.e.* stretched out over the bodies of his victims.

spatiosi corporis: for case see note on **operum,** 251 and cf. **splendenti ferro,** 1474.

1483. **mota forent:** mota essent; cf. **coissent,** 127 and notice a similar apodosis.

1484. **loricae—defensus:** *protected by its scales as by a coat of mail*

1489. **dolore:** abl. of cause.

1492. **ferrum:** the iron head remained though the shaft of the spear had been broken off.

1494. **recens:** *fresh, additional.*

1497. **ore Stygio:** i.e. the depths of the earth.

1498. **orbem:** object of **facientibus.**

1509. **plagam sedere—arcebat:** *kept the stroke from sinking deep.*

1512. **usque sequens:** *following up.*

eunti: sc. **serpenti.**

1513. **fixa est:** *i.e.* by the spear point.

1515. **flagellari:** after **gemuit:** *groaned that its trunk was lashed* **ima parte caudae.**

1516. **spatium:** *the huge bulk.*

1519. Notice both the alliteration and the chiastic order of this line. In another place Ovid tells how Cadmus and his wife were in their old age changed into serpents (see the story of Cadmus in the *Age of Fable*). In *Paradise Lost* the Serpent is described:

> "Pleasing was his shape,
> And lovely; never since of serpent kind
> Lovelier; not those that in Illyria changed
> Hermione and Cadmus, nor the god
> In Epidaurus."

1523. **motaeque iubet supponere terrae:** *bade him plow the earth and plant in it.*

1524. **incrementa:** i.e. destined to become a nation.

1527. **fide maius:** *a thing incredible!* What literally?

1528. **acies:** here in its more literal meaning. Cf. **acer, acuo, acutus,** etc.

1531. **clipeata:** for agreement cf. **attonitos, 1461.**

1532. **festis:** i.e. on a holiday.

1533. Another alliterative line. **signa:** i.e. painted on the curtain. At the end of the play the curtain was raised from a roller at the bottom, not lowered from above as with us.

1537. **ne cape:** noli capere; cf. **ne dubita,** 449.

1541. **leto dederat:** sc. **eum,** referring to **ipse,** 1540.

1545. **brevis vitae spatium:** for **breve vitae spatium.**

1546. **matrem:** terram.

1547. **superstitibus:** abl. absolute with **quinque.**

1548. **humo:** dative of place to which, a common construction of poetry instead of the acc. with **ad** or **in.**

1550. **comites:** predicate acc. with **hos.**

1553. **exsilio:** *although an exile.* Translate also literally.

       soceri: for they were the parents of Harmonia or Hermione.

1554. **tanta:** *so noble.*

1555. **pignora** (sc. **amoris**): in apposition with **nepotes.**

XII. THE FLIGHT OF DAEDALUS

The mythical Daedalus, who had constructed the famous Labyrinth of Crete to contain the terrible Minotaur, lost the favor of King Minos and was imprisoned by him. He was released by Pasiphae, but could not escape from Crete, as Minos had seized all the ships on the island. Daedalus accordingly devised wings for himself and his son Icarus, and fled through the air. Icarus, however, did not obey his father's instructions, and on his first attempt came to grief.

1559. **Creten:** read in the *Age of Fable* or some other book of mythology the whole story of Daedalus and the Labyrinth.

1560. **loci natalis:** *i.e.* Athens, from which Daedalus had fled because in a fit of jealousy he had killed his nephew and pupil Perdix.

1562. **obstruat:** he (Minos) *may bar.* Cf. **placeat,** 407.

1563. **possideat:** a hortatory subjunctive expressing a concession.

1565. **naturamque novat:** *i.e. he changes the laws of nature.*

1566. **a minima:** abl. of source.

1567. **clivo:** i.e. like trees on a sloping hillside.
putes: like **putes** in 784.
rustica: cf. 822, where Pan's pipes are mentioned.

1569. **medias, imas:** sc. pennas.

1573. **renidenti:** *beaming* (with pleasure).

1575. **mollibat:** for **molliebat.** Notice the variation of tense in this sentence.

1576. **manus ultima:** cf. our term, *the finishing touch.*

1578. **mota:** i.e. by his wings.

1579. **medio limite:** compare with this the advice which that other adventurous youth received from his father: Medio tutissimus ibis, and later (488), inter utrumque tene. Compare also the result of disobedience in that instance.

1581. **ignis:** i.e. of the sun.

1582. **Booten:** *the Ox-driver,* a constellation near **Helice,** *the Great Bear.*

1583. **Orionis:** a famous huntsman accidentally killed by Diana and changed by her into a constellation.

1586. **maduere:** sc. lacrimis.
seniles: senis.

1588. **repetenda:** renovanda.

1589. **comiti:** how does this differ in meaning from **comitem** (timet)?

1591. **sequi:** what is the usual prose construction after **hortor?**

1595. **quique:** -que connects **obstipuit** and **credidit.**

1596. **Iunonia:** because Samos was especially sacred to Juno.

1597. **Samos, Delos, Paros, Lebinthos, Calymne:** islands in the Aegean Sea. The aviators had flown first North, then East.

1598. **dextra:** predicate adj. with **Lebinthos.**

1600. **caeli:** objective gen.

1604. **remigio:** the "oarage of his wings" mentioned by **Virgil.**

1606. **nomen:** the Icarian Sea, the waters about Samos.

1611. **tellus:** the island of Icaria (Icaros) west of Samos.

HELPS TO SCANSION

The Meter. — The *Metamorphoses* are written in **dactylic hexameter;** that is, each verse is composed of a succession of six groups of syllables called *feet*, the unit being a **dactyl**, — a foot made up of one long and two short syllables, as fōrsĭtăn [or in musical notation ♩ ♫]. For any foot, however, except the fifth, a **spondee** [as cūrsūs, = ♩ ♩] may be substituted, and the last must always be a spondee, or a **trochee** [as rūmŏr, = ♩ ♪]. So a complete line may be represented thus: —

Rarely, as in l. 763, a spondee is found instead of a dactyl in the fifth foot, when the verse is called a **spondaic** verse.

Scansion. — The separation of a verse into its component feet is called **scansion.** In scanning dactylic hexameter verse the stress of voice, or **ictus,** falls upon the first syllable in every foot. The syllable receiving the accent is called the **thesis** (*i.e.* the *putting down* of the foot in keeping time); the unaccented part is called the **arsis** (the *raising* of the foot). These terms correspond to the downward and upward beat in music.

Caesura. — The ending of a word within a foot is called a **caesura** (*cutting*). Most verses contain one or more prominent caesuras, coinciding with a pause in the sense. The most common place of the caesura is after the thesis or in the arsis of the third foot, dividing the verse into two nearly equal parts; though it is found frequently in the fourth foot, with an additional pause in the second foot. When the rhetorical pause comes, not within a foot, but at the end of one, the separation is called a **diaeresis.** Occasionally it happens that the caesura would naturally fall after an elided syllable, as in l. 198: —

utque lo|cum ‖ et vi|sa co|gnoscit in | arbore | formam.

The caesural pause came here probably after **locum,** though it is often written after **et,** giving the effect of a harsh shock.

Elision. — In scanning, a vowel or diphthong at the end of a word is partially suppressed before a word beginning with a vowel or **h**, as **tequ^e ipsa.** This is called **elision** (*bruising*). In the same way, words ending in **m** suppress the final syllable, as **faci^em et.** This, however, is called **ecthlipsis** (*squeezing*), instead of elision.

Hiatus. — The occasional omission of elision, as in l. 687, is called **hiatus** (*yawning*). The effect of the succession of vowel sounds is often corrected by a caesural pause before the following word.

Synaeresis or Synizesis. — Sometimes two syllables are contracted into one, as **nēscĭō.** This is known as **synaeresis or synizesis.**

Hints in Scansion. — After one or two trials a pupil who has any musical instinct will be able to scan most lines at sight. Some, however, will be compelled to scan in a more mechanical way, by separating a line into its feet according to the succession of long and short syllables. It will be a help to remember (1) that the ictus falls always on the first syllable of each foot; (2) that if the second syllable is long, the foot is a spondee, so that the third syllable also must be long, as it begins a new foot, as **vēlō₁cēs**; (3) if the second syllable is short, the foot must be a dactyl, hence the third also is short, and the fourth must receive the accent of the next foot, as **fŏrsĭtăn, āudieris.** If now the rest of the line does not at once become clear, a glance at the end will often remove any difficulties, for the last foot is always a trochee or a spondee, and the one before it usually a dactyl — in fact, the last two, and often three, feet are scanned in accordance with the regular prose accent of the words; so that the trouble, if any, will be found generally in the third and fourth feet. These will be seen, on examination, to be composed of four, five, or six syllables: if four or six, they will be, of course, two spondees or two dactyls, and the scansion of the verse is complete; if five, either a spondee and a dactyl or a dactyl and a spondee, the order in most cases easily determined by some familiar quantity.

The scansion of the *Metamorphoses* does not present very many difficulties; any irregularity which occurs will be pointed out in the following notes: —

1. **aúdĭĕrĭ́s**: made long by thesis.

9. The only rhetorical pause comes after **vivit** in the first foot, which is rather early in the line for a regular caesura. The other words are too closely connected for a marked pause.

19. There is also an important caesura in the elided syllable of the **second** foot. Cf. the following line. Do not make a pause after **et.**

30. **Aonio**: the first vowel is long, retaining the quantity of the Greek word, though preceding a vowel.

31. The chief caesura falls at the end of the second foot, and is therefore a diaeresis.

36. A strong diaeresis after the first foot, but no other important pause.

43. A caesura after the ictus of the second foot, to emphasize **facilem,** or in the more common place, in the third foot.

63. The pause after **optari** is rather artificial, unless we wish to emphasize the word. Notice the stronger pause in the first foot, which is a rather common thing with Ovid.

65. Observe the diaeresis after the first foot, of almost equal importance with the caesura noted.

71. As in ll. 9 and 63, an important break in the first foot.

73. Cf. l. 71.

77. Cf. l. 65.

83. This line has no marked pause in the sense. A caesura mark may be placed in the second, third, or fourth foot.

85. The strongest pause is at the diaeresis after the first foot. A slight pause may be made at the third foot, serving to emphasize **indigenae.**

86. The caesural pause at the end of the fourth foot (really a diaeresis) is called a *Bucolic* caesura, from its frequent occurrence in Greek pastoral poetry.

95. Cf. l. 83.

111. Like l. 65.

114. The pause in the third foot is an instance of *weak* or *feminine* caesura, as opposed to the *strong* or *masculine* caesura in the second and fourth feet. In the former case the caesura comes after the first syllable of the arsis. Find other similar lines.

118. The only important pause in the sense comes at the diaeresis after the first foot.

198. The real caesural pause is in the suppressed syllable of the second foot, though sometimes written after **et.**

199, 201. A Bucolic caesura. See l. 86.

208. Like l. 118.

209, 210, 211, 217. Like l. 65.

229. Like l. 9.

234. **Pēnēïă**: the second e is long, because it stands for the Greek ē.

239. Cf. l. 118.

242. A very unimportant caesura.

243. **nēscĭō**: a dissyllable by synizesis.

248. Cf. l. 63.

250, 266. Cf. l. 242.

267. The closely interlocked order of this line prevents any marked caesura.

283. Like l. 198.

313. Like l. 249.

314, 316. Cf. l. 118.

318. Cf. l. 63.

339. Like l. 249.

342. Like l. 118.

367. Clўmĕnēĭă: like Pēnēĭă l. 234.

381. A long line, but easy of scansion, as all the feet but the last are dactyls.

437. cavē has a long e here, like other verbs of the second conjugation; it is usually, however, short.

501. An apparently difficult line, owing to the succession of vowel syllables. Both the e and the o of Ēŏŭs are regularly long, standing for the corresponding Greek vowels, but here the e is short, while the final syllable of Pўrŏĭs is made long by the ictus and caesura:—

Íntere|á volu|crés Pyro|ĭs ‖ ĕt Ē|ŏŭs ĕt | Aéthon.

513. āĕră: has its first vowel long by nature from the Greek.

516. quădrĭĭŭgî: the second i is the consonant i of iugum.

537. Scorpiŏs: the final o is short, from the Greek declension ending -os.

575. Cycladăs: the final ăs in the Greek third declension is short.

577. delphinĕs: because of the Greek third declension.

582. āĕrĭs: cf. l. 513.

636. Nāĭdĕs: a word of the Greek third declension.

673. Orphēā: ē standing for Greek ē.

685. Persephonēn adiît: the ē long, standing for a Greek ē; the final syllable of adiit is lengthened by the ictus and caesura. Such a lengthening is called *diastole*.

688. rēcidimus: ē lengthened by the ictus. Cf. recidat, 1001.

709. mihī: the ī long before a strong pause.

714. Bēlĭdĕs: cf. delphinĕs, 577.

725. ăfŭĕrūnt: the ĕ is short by systole.

739. Ŏlĕnŏs: cf. Scorpiŏs, 537.

753. antēît: by synizesis.

763. A spondaic line: Órgia | trádide|rát cum | Cécropi|ó Eu|mól|po. Notice that the final o of Cecropio is not elided.

875. Note that the first e of rēfert is long, forming a spondee, Néc re|fért domi|nós, while rĕfert, from rĕfĕrō, would require another short vowel following.

956. Thīnēĭŭs: like Pēnēĭă, 234.

971. Plēĭădum: cf. Thīnēĭŭs, 956.

1001. rēcidat: cf. recidimus, l. 688.

1006. **Cadmēĭdă:** cf. **Plēĭădum,** l. 971.

1010. **Amphīŏnĕ:** a Greek name.

1036. A spondaic line.

1060. See line 1010.

1063. **Lātōīs:** retaining the quantities of the Greek word.

1133. **dēērant:** like **deinde,** often pronounced as a dissylable.

1143. **delphinĕs:** as in l. 577.

1197. **O uti|nam pos|sem: O** is not elided here before a vowel. This is generally so in the case of prepositions.

1203. **Cephisidăs:** cf. **Cycladăs,** l. 575.

1213. **Themī:** with final i short, from its declension in Greek.

1261. Notice that **a** in **Atlantis** is long here, while above, in l. 867, it is short. Cf. also ll. 1265 and 1277.

1302. **Cēphēăquĕ:** like **Cadmēĭdă,** l. 1006.

1375. **Phorcynidŏs:** with short **o,** according to the Greek declension.

1406. **Phorcidăs:** cf. **Cephisidăs,** l. 1203.

1411. The final **e** of -**que** suffers elision before the vowel which begins the following line. A line of this sort is called hypermetrical, and its joining with the succeeding line is termed *synapheia.*

1455. **vībrant:** i short here, but long in ll. 310 and 619. Cf. **rĕtrahebat,** l. 1508, **flăgellari,** l. 1515.

1481. **magnum magno:** read aloud and notice the effect of the juxtaposition.

1482. **illĭus,** as often in poetry.

1519. Notice the chiastic order.

1547. **Echīŏn:** like **Amphīone,** l. 1010. So also **Ōrīonis,** l. 1583.

1551. **Phoebēīs:** cf. **Cadmēĭdă,** l. 1006.

1563, 1590. *āĕra,* as in 513.

1598. **Lĕbinthŏs:** like **Scorpiŏs,** l. 537.

VOCABULARY

A

ā, interj., *ah, oh*, 73.

ab or **ā**, prep. w. abl., *away from, from*, of source or separation, 58, 159, 219, etc.; *from off*, 1018; of time, 655; of place, *on the right*, etc., 373, 1288, 1299; ab ortū, *in the east*, 460; ab oblīquō, *slant-wise, obliquely*, 116; *by*, of agent, 45, 63, 860, etc.; of means, 800, 1364; ā laevā, *in* or *with the left hand*, 836. *

Abantiadēs, ae, m., *descendant of Abas*, king of Argos; *Perseus*, the slayer of the Gorgon, 1306.

abdō, 3, didī, ditus, *put away; hide, conceal*, 955; *plunge, bury*, 1352; abdita, ōrum, as noun, *hidden ways*, 1408.

abeō, īre, iī, itus, *go away, go off*, 61, 776, 1344; *be changed, be converted*, 1291; *burst*, 277. *

ablātus, abstulī, see **auferō**.

abluō, 3, luī, lūtus, *wash off, bathe*, 635, 1372.

abrumpō, 3, rūpī, ruptus, *break off, break away*, 626.

absum, esse, fuī, futūrus, *be from* or *away, be absent*, 130, 760, 932; *go away*, 603; *be distant*, 725, 1341; *be far from helping*, 1283.*

absūmō, 3, sūmpsī, sūmptus, *take away; consume, exhaust*, 325. *

ac, see **atque**.

accēdō, 3, cessī, cessūrus, *come to, approach*, 389; *be added to*, 87, 915, 978, 1493. *

accēnsus, a, um, p. of accendō, *set fire to; in flames, ablaze*, 559. *

accingō, 3, cinxī, cinctus, *gird to* one; pass., *gird oneself, arm oneself*, 186, 1299. *

accipiō, 3, cēpī, ceptus (capiō), *take* (to one), *receive, accept*, 185, 720, 733, etc. *

acclīvis, e adj. (clīvus), *sloping, ascending*, 723.

acclīvus, a, um, adj. (clīvus), *sloping, inclined, ascending*, 367.

accommodō, 1, *fit to, adjust*, 1585.

accumbō, 3, cubuī, cubitum, *recline at dinner*, 897. *

ācer, ācris, ācre, adj., *sharp, keen, fierce*, 434; (too) *hot, glowing*, 904.

aciēs, ēī, f., *sharp point*, 1528. *

āctum, ī, n. (p. of agō), *thing done; act, deed*, 657.

acūmen, inis, n. (acuō, *sharpen*), *point, tip*, 1505.

acūtus, a, um, p. of acuō, *sharpen; sharp, pointed*, 252. *

ad, prep. w. acc., *toward, to,* 83, 144, 150, etc.; *for, to,* 142, 1329; *by,* 166; *near,* 681; *near, at,* 155; *at, at the sound of,* 212, 285; *at, in accordance with,* 15. *

addō, 3, didī, ditus (dō), *put to; put on,* 469; *add, give in addition,* 667, 1284, 1333, 1425; *consider also,* 418, 1554; *tell besides,* 1418. *

addūcō, 3, dūxī, ductus, *lead to; draw, tighten,* 237.

adēmptus, see **adimō.**

adeō, īre, iī, itus, *go to, approach,* 92, 1203; *visit,* 685, 868. *

adeō, adv., *to that point; to such an extent, so much,* 1230. *

adfectō, 1, freq. (adficiō), *strive after, seek, aspire to,* 406.

adferō, ferre, attulī, adlātus, *bear to, bring,* 675, 1112.

adficiō, 3, fēcī, fectus (faciō), *make (to); affect, injure, wound,* 1044.

adflō, 1, *breathe upon,* 324, 1470.*

adfor, 1, fātus, *speak to, address,* 1186. *

adgnōscō, 3, nōvī, nitus, *recognize, identify,* 764. *

adhaereō, 2, —, —, *stick to, cling (upon),* 1327.

adhaerēscō, 3, haesī, haesus, (adhaereō), *adhere; ground,* 1160.

adhūc, adv., *to this; still, yet, as yet, even yet,* 56, 230, 335, etc.

ādiciō, 3, iēcī, iectus (iaciō), *throw to; give in addition, give, add,* 97, 118, 654, etc.

adigō, 3, ēgī, āctus (agō), *drive to; drive, force,* 1060.

adimō, 3, ēmī, ēmptus (emō, *take*), *take away, remove,* 209, 552.

adiuvō, 1, iūvī, iūtus, *help, aid, assist,* 82, 322.

adlevō, 1, *raise; relieve, free, untwine,* 1038. *

adligō, 1, *bind* or *fasten to,* 1569.

admīror, 1, *marvel at, wonder,* 550.

admittō, 3, mīsī, missus, *let go to, quicken;* p. admissus, *swiftly moving, swift, rapid,* 314, 1026.

admoneō, 2, uī, itus, *warn,* 66.

admonitor, ōris, m. (admoneō), *reminder, prompter, summoner,* 1297.

admoveō, 2, mōvī, mōtus, *move to, bring near,* 276, 785, 794, 885.

adnuō, 3, uī, —, *nod to; make a sign, nod,* 348; *nod assent,* 774. *

adoleō, 2, oluī, —, *turn to vapor; kindle, burn, destroy by fire,* 274.*

adoperiō, 4, peruī, pertus, *cover over,* 939; *envelop, wrap, veil,* 161.

adōrō, 1, *call upon; reverence, honor, worship,* 1161, 1439. *

adripiō, 3, ripuī, reptus (rapiō), *snatch at, clasp,* 729.

adserō, 3, seruī, sertus, *lay claim to,* 244.

adsiduus, a, um, adj., *attending; unceasing, continual,* 418, 1008.

adspiciō, 3, spēxī, spectus, *look at, behold, observe, see,* 51, 380, 440, etc. *

adstō, 1, stitī, —, *stand near, stand by,* 495.

adsuētus, a, um, p. of adsuēscō, *accustom; accustomed, wonted, usual,* 513, 759.

adsum, esse, fuī, futūrus, *be with; be present, be at hand,* 341, 393,

830; *come, appear*, 674, 1325, 1523; *help, assist*, 82, 114. *

aduncus, a, um, adj., *bent to; curved*, 597, 1134.

adūrō, 3, ūssī, ūstus, *set fire to, burn*, 1581.

adventus, ūs, m., *coming, approach, arrival*, 765.

adversus, a, um, adj. (p. of advertō), *turned toward one; meeting, opposing, in one's face, exposed*, 310; *facing one, threatening*, 428; *in adversum, against, to meet*, 420. *

advertō, 3, vertī, versus, *turn (to), direct*, 977.

advolō, 1, *fly to; fly up, hasten to the rescue*, 1038.

Aegaeōn, ōnis, m., a sea giant with a hundred arms, 358.

aeger, gra, grum, adj., *sick; painful, sickening*, 640. *

aemulus, a, um, adj., *striving after, emulating*; as noun, f., *rival*, 258.

aēnus, a, um, adj. (aes, *copper*), *of copper or bronze*; as noun, n., *bronze vessel, kettle*, 885. *

Aeolius, a, um, adj. (Aeolus), *of Aeolus*, king of the winds, 1103.

aequālis, e, adj. (aequō, *level*), *equal, uniform, regular*, 374.

aequātus, a, um, adj. (p. of aequō, *level*), *leveled, made even*, 900. *

aequor, oris, n. (aequus), *level surface; sea, waters, waves*, 202, 354, 574, etc. *

aequoreus, a, um, adj. (aequor), *of the sea, from Neptune*, 58.

aequus, a, um, adj., *level; equal, the same, uniform*, 482; as noun,

n., *right, justice*, 1163; *ex aequō, equally*, 129. *

āēr, āeris, m., *air, sky*, 191, 248, 506, etc. *

aes, aeris, n., *copper, bronze*, 1414.*

aestās, ātis, f., *summer;* personified, 376. *

aestuō, 1 (aestus), of fire, *rage*, 131.

aestus, ūs, m., *agitation; heat*, 559 (pl.), 568. *

aetās, ātis, f. (aevum), *age, years*, 871; *old age*, 923; *youth*, 56. *

aeternus, a, um, adj. (aevum), *lasting, enduring, perpetual*, 1296.

aethēr, eris, m., *upper air, air, sky*, 483, 519, 545, etc. *

aetherius, a, um, adj. (aethēr), *of the upper air; of heaven, celestial*, 972, 1332.

Aethiops, opis, adj., *African;* as noun, m. pl., *the Ethiopians*, 567.

Aethōn, onis, m. *blazing;* one of the Sun's horses, 501.

aevum, ī, n., *eternity; time, the world*, 655; *age, old age*, 949.

Agēnor, oris, m., king of Phoenicia, 1472. *

Agēnoridēs, ae, m., *son of Agenor: Cadmus*, 1429; *Perseus*, 1403.

ager, agrī, m., *field, land*, 85, 755, 768, etc. *

agitō, 1, freq. (agō), *shake, move to and fro, toss*, 348, 1144.

agmen, inis, n. (agō), *troop, land*, 767; *agmina cōgō, bring up the rear*, 462. *

agna, ae, f., *ewe lamb*, 287.

agō, 3, ēgī, āctus, *drive, lead*, 410, 525, 544, etc.; *propel, row*, 1339; *bring, lead*, 66; *drive, shoot*, 1047;

give, render, 500, 1445; *open in*
(fissures), *receive*, 552; *pass,
spend*, 945; *celebrate*, 765; *be
buried in* (silence), 1185; *do*,
422, 532. *

agrestis, e, adj. (ager), *of the fields;
rustic, sylvan,* 829.

agricola, ae, m. (ager), *husbandman; farmer, planter,* 860.

āiō, defective verb [for agiō],
affirm, say, 44, 82, 246, etc. *

āla, ae, f., dim. [for axla] (axis),
wing, 867, 1105, 1149, etc. *

albēns, entis, adj. (p. of albeō, *be
white*), *white, whitish,* 844.

albidus, a, um, adj. (albus, *white*),
white, 1495.

āles, itis, adj., *winged,* 28; as noun,
bird, 1589. *

alimentum, ī, n. (alō, *nourish*),
nourishment, food, 599, 745,
1112.

ālipēs, edis, adj. (āla; pēs), *wing-
footed,* 396; as noun, *Mercury,*
1388.

aliquandō, adv., *at some time, for
once,* 661.

aliquis, qua, quod, pron. adj.
(quī), *some,* 643, 1241, 1593; as
noun, f., *some one, a girl,* 1; n.,
aliquid, *something,* 445, 987. *

aliter, adv. (alis = alius, *other*), *in
another manner, otherwise,* w.
neg. *just as,* 36, 189, 734; *in
another,* i.e. *the opposite, direction,* 431. *

almus, a, um, adj., *nourishing;
fostering, kindly,* 583. *

Alphēnor, oris, m., one of the sons
of Niobe, 1037.

altē, adv. (altus), *high, on high,*

188, 514, 1055, 1601; comp., *too
high,* 484. *

alter, tera, terum, gen. ius (alius,
other), *one, the other,* 122, 123,
256, 317, 319; *another, a second*,
1047, 1081, 1134; *other* (of two),
836, 973; quīlibet alter, *anybody
else,* 658. *

altor, ōris, m. (alō, *nourish*), *nour-
isher; foster father,* 771.

altus, a, um, adj. (p. of alō, *nourish*), *nourished; high, tall, lofty*,
412, 468, 545, etc.; *stately, lofty*,
124, 349; *at full height,* 966; in
altum, *high,* 1048; ab altō, *from
on high,* 1419; *deep,* 574; *thick*,
172; *profound,* 1185. *

alumnus, ī, m. (alō, *nourish*),
foster son, ward, 769.

alveus, ī, m. (alvus, *belly*), *hollow;
bed, channel,* 1180.

amāns, antis, adj. (p. of amō),
loving, regardful, 1163; as noun,
m. and f., *lover,* 135, 140, 175,
etc. *

ambāgēs, um, f. pl. (ambi-,
around; agō), *going around; digression, evasion,* 689. *

ambiguus, a, um, adj. (ambi-,
around), *ever-changing, many-
formed,* 357; in ambiguō, *in
doubt, uncertain,* 319. *

ambō, ae, ō, adj., *both,* 129, 221,
752, etc. *

ambrosia, ae, f., *ambrosia,* said to
be the food of the gods, 468.

ambūrō, 3, ūssī, ūstus, *burn round;
singe, scorch,* 550.

āmēns, entis, adj. (mēns), *out of
one's senses; frantic, frenzied,
wild,* 645, 668.

amictus, ūs, m. (amiciō, *wrap*), *mantle,* 171, 671. *

amīcus, a, um, adj., *friendly, loving,* 144. *

Ammōn, ōnis, m., epithet of Jupiter, worshiped in Africa in the form of a ram, 1304.

amnis, is, m., *river, stream,* 807, 813, 1117, etc.

amō, 1, *love,* 59, 78, 256, etc.; amātus, *beloved,* 206.

amor, ōris, m., *love, affection,* 68, 78, 127, etc.; *object of affection, love, "flame,"* 234; pl., *wooing,* 18; *love affairs,* 243; *lover,* 204; *Love, Cupid,* 262, 314, 696. *

Amphīōn, onis, m., husband of Niobe, king and founder of Thebes, 1010.

amplector, 3, plexus, *twine around; embrace,* 206, 751.

amplexus, ūs, m. (amplector), *embrace, caress,* 390, 1469. *

an, conj., *whether,* 319, 997; (whether) *or,* 51, 101, 117, 199, 697. *

ancora, ae, f., *anchor,* 1138. *

Andromeda, ae, f., daughter of Cepheus, king of Ethiopia, 1304.

anguicomus, a, um, adj. (anguis; coma), *with snaky hair,* 1331.

anguifer, era, erum, adj. (anguis), *covered with serpents,* 1373.

anguis, is, m., *serpent,* 1252, 1453; the constellation *Serpent,* 486.

anhēlitus, ūs, m. (anhēlō, *gasp*), *panting, panting breath,* 104, 139.

anhēlus, a, um, adj., *out of breath; panting,* 1266.

anīlis, e, adj. (anus), *of an old woman, feeble,* 883.

anima, ae, f., *air; breath,* 883; *life,* 623, 1036, 1042; *soul, spirit,* 177, 711, 748, 1198. *

animal, ālis, n. (anima), *living being; animal, creature,* 246.

animō, 1 (anima), *make alive, quicken,* 1252.

animōsus, a, um, adj. (animus), *animated, spirited,* 432; *proud,* 995.

animus, ī, m., *soul, mind, faculties, heart,* 196, 425, 529, etc.; *feeling,* 1193; *disposition, character,* 1399; pl., *mind,* 387; *courage,* 97; *spirits,* 435. *

annus, ī, m., *year,* 598, 694, 872, etc.; personified, 373; pl., *years, age,* 403, 760, 949. *

ānser, eris, m., *goose,* 921.

ante, adv., *before,* 64, 269, 736, 816; *formerly, previously,* 749, 1292; *ahead,* 1589; prep. w. acc., *before, in front of,* 344, 529, 950, etc. *

ante-eō, īre, īvī or iī, —, *go before, precede,* 753.

antīquus, a, um, adj. (ante), *former, ancient, of old times,* 610. *

antrum, ī, n., *cave, cavern, grotto,* 167, 580, 614, etc. *

anus, ūs, f., *old woman,* 871, 898.

Āonius, a, um, adj., *Aonian, Boeotian,* 30.

aper, aprī, m., *wild boar,* 1146, 1355. *

aperiō, 4, aperuī, apertus, *disclose,* 943; *open, unclose,* 1120. *

apertus, a, um, p. of aperiō, *uncovered; open, broad,* 1126; *exposed, bared, naked,* 650. *

Apollineus, a, um, adj. (Apollō), *of Apollo, Apollo's*, 255.

appāreō, 2, uī, itūrus, *come in sight, appear*, 1528.

appellō, 1, *speak to, address*, 1315.

aptō, 1 (aptus), *fit, adjust, place carefully*, 229. *

aptus, a, um, adj., *fastened; fitted, suitable, appropriate*, 227.

aqua, ae, f., *water*, (pl.) *waters*, 47, 159, 191, etc. *

aquila, ae, f., *eagle*, 288.

Aquilō, ōnis, m, the *north wind*, 1103, 1169; pl., *winds*, 480, 747.*

aquōsus, a, um, adj. (aqua), *abounding in water; watery, rain-*, 1255.

āra, ae, f., *altar*, 968, 998, 1063, etc.; the constellation, *Altar*, 487.

arātor, ōris, m. (arō), *plowman*, 1594.

arātrum, ī, n. (arō), *plow, plow-share*, 597, 1432, 1525.

arbitrium, ī, n. (arbiter, *spectator*), *judgment; will, choice, pleasure*, 565; *choice, power to choose*, 771.

arbor or **arbōs**, oris, f., *tree*, 88, 156, 162, etc. *

arboreus, a, um, adj. (arbor), *of a tree, tree-*, 106, 192, 1270. *

arbustum, ī, n. (arbor), *place where trees are planted; vine-yard*, 1127.

arceō, 2, arcuī, —, *shut up; keep away or out, restrain, drive away*, 743, 998, 1281, 1510. *

Arcitenēns, entis, adj. (arcus; tenēns, teneō), *bow-bearing;* as noun, m., Apollo, 1054.

Arctos, ī, f., the *Great Bear*, 480; pl., the *two Bears*, 1258.

arcus, ūs, m., *bow*, 246, (pl.) 429, 1075; *curve, arc*, 536, 1463; *zone*, 477; *arch*, 1451. *

ārdeō, 2, ārsī, ārsus, *be on fire; blaze, burn*, 129, 275, 557.

arduus, a, um, adj., *steep, lofty, high*, 157, 411, 724, etc.; *on high, towering*, 617, 1157, 1344; as noun, n. pl., *heights*, 929.

āreō, 2, uī, —, *be parched*, 552; p. ārēns, as adj., *parched, dry*, 782.

argenteus, a, um, adj. (argentum), *of silver, silver*, 456.

argentum, ī, n., *silver*, 352; (silver) *plate*, 906. *

argumentum, ī, n. (arguō), *evidence, proof, indication*, 1394.

arguō, 3, uī, ūtus, *complain of, find fault with, blame*, 841.

āridus, a, um, adj., *dry, parched*, 104, 554, 569, 586, 884; *burning*, 799. *

arista, ae, f., *top of an ear of grain; ear, head*, 96, 274, 782.

arma, ōrum, n., *implements; weapons*, 238, 1536, 1548. *

armentum, ī, n. (arō), *cattle for plowing; cattle, oxen*, 295, 1268. *

armus, ī, m., *shoulder*, 1018, 1351.

arō, 1, *plow, till*, 1135.

ars, artis, f., *art, skill, science, means*, 306, 1198, 1214, etc. *

artifex, icis, m. and f. (ars), *master of an art; artist, professional*, 837. *

artus, a, um, adj., *close, tight*, 1031. *

artūs, uum, m., *joints, limbs*, 329, 647, 1038, 1461. *

arvum, ī, n. (arvus, *plowed*), *plowed land; field,* pl., *lands, country,* 88, 154, 315, etc. *

arx, arcis, f., *castle, citadel,* 381, 1006; *summit, height,* 249, 617. *

ascēnsus, ūs, m. (ascendō, *climb*), *climbing; ascent, approach,* 819.

asellus, ī, m., dim (asinus, *ass*), *little ass, ass's colt,* 847.

asper, era, erum, adj. (ab; spēs), *without hope; rough, prickly,* 292. *

aspergō, inis, f. (aspergō, *scatter*), *sprinkling, drops,* 192, 1361, 1507.

astrum, ī, n., *constellation, star,* 1157.

astus, ūs, m., *adroitness, cunning, craft,* 1407.

at, conj., *but, at least, but on the other hand,* 72, 225, 254, etc. *

Atalanta, ae, f., daughter of Schoeneus, of Boeotia, 6.

āter, tra, trum, adj., *dark, black,* 192, 232, 1077, 1484. *

Atlantiadēs, ae, m., *Mercury,* grandson of Atlas, 867.

Atlās, antis, m., son of Iapetus, a Titan, 607. *

atque or **ac,** conj., *and in addition; and,* 18, 52, 111, etc.; simul ac, *as soon as,* 515. *

ātrium, ī, n., *forecourt; hall,* 36, 462, 607, 1395.

attollō, 3, —, —, *lift up, raise,* 211, 1354.

attonitus, a, um, adj., *thunderstruck, astounded, spellbound,* 797, 918, 1461.

auctor, ōris, m. (augeō), *increaser; author, giver,* 114, 436, 592, 795, 1439; *founder, originator,* 1273; *father, sire,* 969.

audāx, ācis, adj., *bold, daring, fearless,* 163, 1077, 1599.

audeō, 2, ausus sum, *dare, venture,* 577, 582, 683, etc.; audentēs, as noun, *those who dare,* 27. *

audiō, 4, *hear,* 1, 1019, 1177, etc.; *hear of,* 967.

auferō, ferre, abstulī, ablātus, *bear* or *take away, remove, carry off,* 423, 694, 946, 1259, 1402; *sweep away,* 1147; *bear back, uplift, raise,* 32.

augeō, 2, auxī, auctus, *increase, enlarge,* 1293; *heighten, enhance,* 312; *swell, increase the number of,* 575.

augurium, ī, n. (augur, *diviner*), *divination; interpretation,* 1229. *

auguror, 1 (augur, *diviner*), *imagine, suppose, surmise,* 697.

Augustus, ī, m. (augeō), *consecrated one;* epithet of Octavius Caesar: as adj., *of Augustus,* 343.

aulaeum, ī, n., *tapestry; curtain,* 1532. *

aura, ae, f., *air* in motion; *air, wind, breeze,* 32, 83, 203, etc.; *air of heaven,* 1042; efferre sub aurās, *bring to light, make known,* 852. *

aurātus, a, um, adj. (aurum), *covered with gold, gilded,* 938. *

aureus, a, um, a' (aurum), *of gold, golden,* 91, 455, 757, etc.; *glittering, splendid,* 1394. *

aurīga, ae, m. and f., *charioteer, driver,* 623, 638.

auris, is, f., *ear,* 144, 732, 825, etc. *

aurōra, ae, f., *morning, dawn, day-*

break, 148, 461, 492; personified, *Aurora*, 1263.

aurum, ī, n., *gold*, 89, 350, 773, etc.; *golden apple*, 108, 116.   *

auspicium, ī, n. (auspex, *interpreter of bird omens*), *omen, sign, portent*, 678.

auster, trī, m., *the south wind*, 860.*

austrālis, e, adj. (auster), *of the south wind; southern*, 480.

ausum, ī, n. (audeō), *bold deed, undertaking, daring*, 81, 639.

ausus, see **audeō.**

aut, conj., *or, or else*, 71, 142, 564, etc.; aut . . . aut, *either . . . or*, 1225, 1226, 1479, 1480.   *

autem, conj., introducing antithesis, following emphatic word, *but, on the contrary*, 1073.

autumnālis, e, adj. (autumnus), *of autumn, autumnal*, 902.

autumnus, ī, m., *autumn*, personified, 377.

auxiliāris, e, adj. (auxilium), *aiding, helping, auxiliary*, 1116.

auxilium, ī, n., *aid, help, assistance, support*, 1202, 1326, 1369.   *

avēna, ae, f., *oats; straw*, 1568.

Avernus, a, um, adj., *of Avernus*, a lake near Cumae, the fabled entrance to the lower world, 721.

āversor, 1 (āvertō, *turn away*), *turn away, shrink from*, 260.

āversus, a, um (p. of āvertō, *turn away*), *turned away; from behind, in the rear*, 1348.

avidus, a, um, adj., *eagerly longing, greedy, eager*, 726, 793, 1349, 1356.   *

avis, is, f., *bird*, 1571.

avītus, a, um, adj. (avus), *of a grandfather, ancestral*, 1028.

āvius, a, um, adj. (via), *out of the way*; n. pl. as noun, *unfrequented places, pathless regions, solitudes*, 261, 546.

avus, ī, m., *grandfather*, 47, 972, 973.

axis, is, m., *axle, axle tree*, 455, 628; *chariot, car*, 407, (pl.) 496, 1267; *axis of the heavens*, 423; *axis of the world, globe*, 608, 972.

B

Babylōnius, a, um, adj. *of Babylon, Babylonian*, 166.

bāca, ae, f., *berry; fruit, olive*, 901.

baccha, ae, f., *female Bacchanal, Bacchante*, 759.

Bacchus, ī, m., son of Jupiter and Semele, god of wine and of inspiration, 755.   *

baculum, ī, n., *stick, staff*, 930, 1594.

bālaena, ae, f., *whale*, 357.

Baleāricus, a, um, adj., *of the Balearic Islands* in the Mediterranean; *Balearic*, 1341.

barba, ae, f., *beard*, 1107, 1290.

barbaricus, a, um, adj., *foreign, barbaric, rude*, 830.

Baucis, idis, f., wife of *Philemon*, 871.

beātus, a, um, adj. (p. of beō, *bless*), *happy, fortunate*, 1557. *

Bēlides, um, f., *the Danaides*, grand-daughters of Belus, King of Egypt, 714.

bellicus, a, um, adj. (bellum), *warlike, fierce in war*, 1386.

bellum, ī, n., *war*, 1538.   *

bēlua, ae, f., *beast, monster,* 1322, 1360.

bene, adv. (bonus), *well, fairly,* 395, 696, 1435; *skillfully,* 663.

Berecyntius, a, um, adj., *Berecyntian, Phrygian,* 776.

bibulus, a, um, adj. (bibō, *drink*), *soaked, wet,* 1362; *porous,* 1376.

bicolor, ōris, adj., *two-colored,* 901.

bicornis, e, adj. (cornū), *with two horns; two-pronged,* 887.

biforis, e, adj. (foris, *door*), *with two doors; double, folding,* 352.

bis, num. adv., *twice,* 766.   *

blanditia, ae, f. (blandus), *caressing;* pl., *loving words, endearments,* 137, 313.

blandus, a, um, adj., *caressing, coaxing, soft,* 83, 267, 448.   *

Boeōtius, a, um, adj., *Boeotian, Theban,* 1434.

bonus, a, um, adj., *good, excellent; kindly,* 915; as noun, n., *excellence,* 4; pl., *blessings,* 445, 986. *

Boōtēs, ae, m., *the Ox-driver,* a constellation near the Great Bear, 1582.

boreās, ae, m., *the north wind,* 526.

bōs, bovis, m. and f., *bull, ox, cow,* 164, 1431, 1441.

bracchium, ī, n., *forearm, arm,* 283, 331, 581, etc.; *claw,* 430, 431, 536.

brevis, e, adj., *short,* 1245, 1329, 1545, 1566.   *

būstum, ī, n., *tomb, grave,* 155, 947.

buxum, ī, n., *boxwood,* 201.

C

cacūmen, inis, n., *extremity; peak, point, top,* 333, 348, 953, etc.

Cadmēis, idis, f. adj., *of Cadmus, Theban,* 1006.

Cadmus, ī, m., son of Agenor, king of Phoenicia, 974.

cadō, 3, cecidī, cāsūrus, *fall,* 290, 633, 1251; *fall dead,* 1039, 1540, 1544; *set,* 1260.   *

cādūcifer, ī, m. adj. (cādūceus, *herald's staff*), *bearing a herald's staff,* 867.

caecus, a, um, adj., *blind; dark, hidden,* 1082, 1222.   *

caedēs, is, f., *cutting; killing, slaughter,* 65, 164, 227; *blood,* 192; *wound,* 230.   *

caedō, 3, cecīdī, caesus, *cut; strike, lash,* 669.

caelestis, e, adj. (caelum), *of heaven, heavenly, celestial,* 484, 1201, 1230; m. pl., *gods, divinities,* 968.   *

caelicola, ae, m. (caelum), *god, deity,* 877.

caelō, 1 (caelum, *chisel*), *carve, emboss,* 354, 905, 939.   *

caelum, ī, n., *sky, heavens, heaven,* 355, 365, 412, etc.; *the air, space,* 1342.   *

caeruleus, a, um, adj. (caelum), *like the sky; dark blue* or *green, dark,* 356, 1116, 1174, 1459, 1605.

caerulus, a, um, adj. (caelum), *like the sky; blue, dark blue,* 826.

caespes, itis, f. (caedō), *cut sod; turf,* 1385.

calamus, ī, m., *reed, cane,* 829.

calcō, 1 (calx, *heel*), *tread, trample,* 377, 693.

calēns, entis, adj. (p. of caleō, *be warm*), *hot,* 908.   *

calidus, a, um, adj., *warm, hot,* 563, 1027.

cālīgō, inis, f., *thick air; darkness, gloom,* 564, 724, 1106.

callidus, a, um, adj. (calleō, *be experienced*), *practiced;* with force of adv., *slyly, stealthily,* 160.

calor, ōris, m., *warmth, heat,* (pl.) 482.

Calymnē, ēs, f, one of the Sporades, 1598.

campus, ī, m., *plain, field, grounds,* 115, 1007, 1126; *expanse, stretch,* 573, 1156. *

Cancer, crī, m., *Crab,* 431.

candēns, entis, p. of candeō, *shine; shining, glowing,* 608.

candēscō, 3, —, — (candeō, *shine*), *begin to glow, grow hot,* 561.

candidus, a, um, adj. (candeō, *shine*), *shining white; white, snow-white,* 914; *white (marble),* 37.

candor, ōris, m., *dazzling whiteness,* 35.

cānēscō, 3, —, — (cāneō, *be white*), *grow white, whiten,* 553.

canis, is, m. and f., *dog, hound,* 315, 736, 1355.

canistrum, ī, n., *plaited basket,* 912. *

canna, ae, f., *reed, cane,* 870; pl., *reed pipes,* 839.

canō, 3, cecinī, —, *make music, sing, play,* 342, 830. *

canōrus, a, um, adj. (canor, *melody*), *melodious, tuneful,* 356.

cantus, ūs, m., *singing, song, notes,* 823, 1393. *

cānus, a, um, adj., *white, hoary,* 378, 1107; *yellow, ripened,* 96. *

capella, ae, f., *she goat,* 1140.

capillus, ī, m. (caput), *hair;* pl., *hair, tresses,* 259, 279, 311, etc.

capiō, 3, cēpī, captus, *take; take, catch, seize,* 761, 1408, 1536, 1537; *take in, comprehend,* 788; *take on, receive,* 1383; *receive, embrace,* 1180; *charm,* 838; *enslave,* 129. *

Capitōlium, ī, n. (caput), *Capitol* at Rome (pl.), 342.

captīvus, a, um, adj., *taken prisoner; captured, captive,* 257.

captō, 1, freq. (capiō), *strive to seize,* 712, 1574, 1593; *watch* or *listen for,* 139.

caput, capitis, n., *head,* 345, 348, 388, etc. *

carbasus, ī, f., *fine linen; sails,* 1022.

carcer, eris, m., *prison, jail,* 1296; *barrier, starting place* in a race course, 93. *

cardō, inis, m., *hinge,* 160. *

careō, 2, uī, itūrus, *be without,* 7; *be deprived of, lack,* 510, 1604.

cārica, ae, f., *dried fig* (from Caria), 911.

carīna, ae, f., *keel* of a ship, 1139.

carmen, inis, n., *song, verse,* 300, 637, 686, etc.

carpō, 3, carpsī, carptus, *pick, pluck,* 713; *crop, graze,* 1140; *make, pass over, tread,* 723, 809, 1433, 1584; *pass through, cleave,* 1249, 1595. *

cārus, a, um, adj., *dear, darling, precious,* 53, 210, 268, 758, 1555.*

casa, ae, f., *cottage, hut,* 873, 936.

Cassiopē, ēs, f., *wife of Cepheus and mother of Andromeda,* 1370.

Castalius, a, um, adj., *of Castalia, at Delphi*, 1435.

cāsus, ūs, m., *falling; fate, ill chance, misfortune*, 209, 951. *

catēna, ae, f., *chain, fetter*, 735, 1311, 1370.

cauda, ae, f., *tail*, 537, 1358, 1515.

causa, ae, f., *cause, reason, motive*, 219, 289, 291, etc. *

cautēs, is, f., *pointed rock, crag*, 1305.

caveō, 2, cāvī, cautus, *be on one's guard, take heed, beware*, 437.

cavus, a, um, adj., *hollow, excavated, concave*, 827, 907, 1357. *

cecidī, see **cadō**.

Cecropius, a, um, adj. (Cecrops, the most ancient king of Attica), *of Cecrops, Attic, Athenian*, 763.

cēdō, 3, cessī, cessūrus, *give way*, 1502; *go away, depart*, 813; *yield*, 729, 996, 1510; *yield in rank, be inferior*, 246.

celeber, bris, bre, adj., *frequented, abounding*, 865; *surrounded, numerously attended*, 962.

celer, eris, ere, adj., *swift, quick, speedy, fleet*, 94, 110, 321, etc.; *quickly*, 467, 1350.

cēlō, 1, *hide from; hide, conceal*, 385, 848, 1316. *

celsus, a, um, adj., *high, lofty*, 1482, 1581. *

Cēphēnī, ōrum, m., *people of Cepheus*, 1396.

Cēpheus, ī, m., *a king of the Ethiopians*, 1370.

Cēphēus, a, um, adj., *of or belonging to Cepheus*, 1302.

Cēphīsis, idis, adj., *of the Cephisus*, 1203.

Cēphīsus, ī, m., *a river in Phosis and Boeotia*, 1440.

cēra, ae, f., *wax*, 907, 1569, 1574, etc.

cērātus, a, um, adj. (cēra), *covered with wax, waxed*, 822.

Cereālis, e, adj. (Cerēs), *belonging to Ceres, of Ceres*, 791, 792. *

Cerēs, eris, f., *daughter of Saturn, goddess of agriculture; grain*, 782. *

cernō, 3, crēvī, certus; *distinguish, make out, perceive*, 481. *

certāmen, inis, n. (certō, *contend*), *contest, struggle, competition*, 1, 13, 25, 824.

certē, adv. (certus), *really; without doubt, surely, unmistakably*, 339, 1333, 1562. *

certō, 1 (cernō), *match; strive*, 728.*

certus, a, um, adj. (p. of cernō), *determined*, 708; *unmistakable*, 173, 240, 439; *assured, proved, true*, 223, 1191; *sure, steady*, 415; *sure* (of aim), *unerring, deadly*, 301, 302; *perfect, regular*, 1014; certum faciō, *inform*, 1057. *

cerva, ae, f. (cervus), *hind, deer*, 287.

cervīx, īcis, f., *head joint, neck, shoulder*, 267, 324, 435, etc. *

cervus, ī, m., *stag, deer*, 1147. *

cessō, 1, freq. (cēdō), *be remiss; be inactive, idle* or *unoccupied*, 590; tempora cessāta, *lost time*, 110. *

(cēterus), a, um., adj., *the other, remaining, rest*, 364, 420; n. pl., *all else, the rest*, 488, 846, 934, etc.*

ceu, adv. (for ce-ve), *as, like as, just as*, 1500.

(chaos), —, n., *the unformed world, void, empty space*, 610, 700.

chorus, ī, m., *dance in a ring; band* of singers or dancers, *train, troop*, 756. *

chrȳsolithos, ī, m., *goldstone; chrysolite, topaz*, 457.

Cicones, um, m., *a Thracian tribe, on the Hebrus River*, 672.

cingō, 3, cīnxī, cīnctus, *go around; surround, encircle*, 125, 330, 354; *crown, wreathe*, 375, 827; *gird up*, 1216; *coil, knot*, 1499. *

cinis, eris, m., *ashes, embers*, 557, 562, (pl.) 881.

circuitus, ūs, m. (eō), *going round; arc*, 430.

circum, prep. w. acc., *around, about*, 388, 827; as adv., 1301. *

circumdō, dare, dedī, datus, *surround, encircle, enwrap*, 583, 863, 1098. *

circumferō, ferre, tulī, lātus, *bear around; cast* or *sweep about*, 966.

circumfluō, 3, flūxī, —, *flow about*, 1495.

circumlitus, a, um, adj., *spread over, covered, plated*, 806.

circumsonus, a, um, adj., *sounding around; barking around*, 1355.

circumspiciō, 3, spēxī, spectus, *look about, cast a glance around*, 443, 605.

circumstō, 1, stetī, —, *stand around; surround, beset*, 664.

cithara, ae, f., *lyre*, 340, 839. *

citius, adv. (citō, *quickly*), *sooner*, 703.

citrā, adv., *on this side; less than*, 48.

citus, a, um, adj. (p. of cieō, *set in motion*), *quick, swift, rapid, flying*, 32, 325, 423. *

cīvīlis, e, adj. (cīvis, *citizen*), *of citizens, civil*, 1538.

clādēs, is, f., *destruction; misfortune, calamity, disaster*, 592.

clāmō, 1, *call, cry out, shout aloud*, 209, 1088, 1605.

clāmor, ōris, m., *loud call, shout, shouting*, 97, 1367. *

Claros, ī, f., *a town in Ionia, containing a famous temple of Apollo*, 298.

clārus, a, um, adj., *clear, bright, shining, gleaming, sparkling*, 350, 372, 458, 1297; *loud, piercing*, 205. *

claudō, 3, clausī, clausus, *shut up, imprison*, 1296; *inclose, shut in*, 1103, 1279, 1561; *close, bolt, bar*, 869. *

clipeātus, a, um, adj. (clipeum), *shieldbearing*, 1531.

clipeum, ī, n., *round, metal shield*, 1413.

clīvus, ī, m., *slope, hillside*, 819, 931, 1567; *sloping surface*, 899.

Clymenē, ēs, f., *daughter of Tethys, wife of Merops, mother of Phaëthon*, 385.

Clymenēius, a, um, adj., *of Clymene*, 367.

coāctus, see cōgō.

coarguō, 3, uī, —, *expose, prove, make known*, 861.

coctilis, e, adj. (coquō, *burn*), *burnt; of burnt bricks*, 125.

coeō, īre, īvī or iī, itus, *come together, be united*, 127; *meet*, 150.

(coepiō), 3, coepī, coeptus, *begin, commence*, 859, 1235, 1507, etc.;

coeptus, *begun* (to be fashioned), 1239; as noun, n., *undertaking, work,* 1576. *

coerceō, 2, uī, itus (arceō), *enclose, confine,* 259; *check, curb, restrain,* 1015, 1178.

cognōscō, 3, gnōvī, gnitus; *perceive, see, know, recognize,* 198, 204, 214, 1517; *feel,* 509; *learn, find out,* 524. *

cōgō, 3, coēgī, coāctus (con-agō), *drive together; marshal* (agmen), *bring up the rear,* 462, 767; *force, compel,* 117; *coagulate, curdle,* 903. *

cohors, hortis, f., *court; band, company, bodyguard,* 759.

collis, is, m., *elevation, hill,* 863, 1134, 1179. *

collum, ī, n., *neck,* 279, 448, (pl.) 586, etc. *

colō, 3, coluī, cultus, *till; cherish, worship,* 961, 968, 997; *take up, cultivate, inhabit,* 814. *

colōnus, ī, m., *farmer, peasant,* 1113. *

color, ōris, m., *color, hue, complexion,* 194, 199, 232, etc.

colubra, ae, f., *serpent, snake,* 691, 1253, 1415.

columba, ae, f., *dove,* 288.

columna, ae, f., *pillar, column,* 349, 937. *

coma, ae, f., *hair* of the head, 89, 206, 340, etc.; *head,* 472, 826. *

comes, itis, m. and f., *attendant, companion,* 219, 764, 962, etc.

comitō, 1 (comes), *accompany, attend, follow,* 679, 929. *

comminus, adv. (manus), *hand to hand, at close quarters,* 1540.

committō, 3, mīsī, missus, *bring together, build,* 975; *intrust, commend, commit,* 517. *

commūnis, e, adj., *common, held in common,* 133, 943.

commūniter, adv. (commūnis), *together, in common,* 1051.

cōmō, 3, cōmpsī, cōmptus (emō, take), *gather; arrange, adorn,* 280.

compāgēs, um, f., *joining together, joints,* 1451. *

compescō, 3, uī, —, *check, quench, subdue,* 624; *allay, assuage,* 169.

complector, 3, plexus, *clasp, embrace,* 336. *

complexus, ūs, m., *embrace, clasp,* 1038.

compōnō, 3, posuī, positus, *bring together, arrange,* 1570; *lay to rest, bury,* 224.

comprecor, 1, *pray to; supplicate, entreat, beg,* 81. *

comprēndō, 3, prēndī, prēnsus, *bind together; catch, seize,* 319.

cōnāmen, inis, n. (cōnor), *effort,* 1481.

concavō, 1, —, ātus, *hollow out, curve,* 536.

concha, ae, f., *conch shell, shell,* 1174, 1357.

conciō, 4 (concieō, 2), cīvī, citus, *set in motion, urge on, shoot, impel,* 1032; p. concitus, *swift,* 1338; *swollen,* 1500.

concipiō, 3, cēpī, ceptus (capiō), *take hold of; catch, gather, draw up,* 1112; *catch, take* (fire), 23; w. animō, *grasp, form, conceive,* 425; w. precēs, *utter prayers, pray,* 919.

concitus, see **conciō.**

conclāmō, 1, *cry aloud, cry out,* 1016, 1324.

concordō, 1 (concors), *agree; harmonize, sound in harmony,* 300.

concors, cordis, adj. (cor), *in accord, in harmony,* 945.

concutiō, 3, cussī, cussus (quatiō), *strike together; shake up,* 892; *shake,* 398, 588.

condiciō, ōnis, f., *agreement, stipulation, terms,* 10.

condō, 3, didī, ditus, *put together, found,* 1434; *hide, bury,* 585, 641, 648, 1452, 1611; *preserve,* 902. *

cōnferō, ferre, tulī, lātus, *bring together; match, join,* 1031; *contend, contest,* 44.

cōnfīdō, 3, fīsus sum, *have confidence in; be proud, boast,* 739. *

cōnfiteor, 2, fessus (fateor), *acknowledge, admit, confess,* 400, 1423.

cōnfugiō, 3, fūgī, —, *flee, take refuge, run to save oneself,* 925. *

cōnfundō, 3, fūdī, fūsus, *blend, mix, confuse,* 610.

congelō, 1, *freeze together; petrify, harden,* 1095.

cōniciō, 3, iēcī, iectus (iaciō), *throw together; plant, fix,* 1511.

coniugium, ī, n., *union; marriage, wedlock,* 54, 62, 75.

coniungō, 3, iūnxī, iūnctus, *join; passus, walk together,* 752. *

coniūnx, iugis, m. and f., *husband, wife,* 5, 6, 12, etc. *

conlābor, 3, lāpsus, *fall together; fall, sink down,* 1083.

conligō, 3, lēgī, lēctus (legō), *gather, collect,* 668, 886, 913. *

cōnor, 1, *undertake, attempt, try,* 1081.

cōnscendō, 3, scendī, scēnsus (scandō, *climb*), *mount,* 1011. *

cōnscius, a, um, adj. (sciō), *knowing in common;* as noun, m., *witness, confidant,* 130. *

cōnsenēscō, 3, senuī, —, inch., *grow old together, grow old,* 873. *

cōnsequor, 3, secūtus, *follow up; overtake, come up with,* 113, 1024.

cōnsīderō, 1, *examine, survey,* 1516.

cōnsīdō, 3, sēdī, —, *take one's seat, sit,* 825. *

cōnsilium, ī, n., *council; counsel, advice,* 494. *

cōnsistō, 3, stitī, stitus, *stand, stop,* 966; *remain standing, keep one's foothold,* 407; *alight,* 249, 1261; *take one's stand, post oneself,* 42, 138, 370; *remain,* 1488. *

cōnsōlor, 1, *encourage; comfort, console,* 1194.

cōnsors, sortis, m. and f., *sharer, partner,* 1160.

cōnspiciō, 3, spēxī, spectus, *look at attentively; get sight of, perceive, espy,* 952, 1302, 1363. *

cōnsternō, 1, *terrify, alarm, affright, strike with terror,* 625.

cōnsuēscō, 3, suēvī, suētus, *accustom, habituate, inure,* 577, 895.

cōnsulō, 3, suluī, sultum, *meet and consider; take thought or have regard (for), consult (for),* 489, 611, 1430.

cōnsūmō, 3, sūmpsī, sūmptus, *use up; devour, consume,* 180.

contāctus, ūs, m., *touching; contact, touch,* 781.

contemnō, 3, tempsī, temptus, *value little; despise, disdain, scorn,* 823.

contendō, 3, tendī, tentus, *stretch; vie, contend, measure strength,* 11.*

contentus, a, um, adj. (p. of contendō), *stretched; tight, taut,* 1075.

contentus, a, um, adj. (p. of contineō), *content, satisfied, pleased,* 243, 1115.

conterminus, a, um, adj., *adjoining, neighboring,* 157, 862.

conterreō, 2, terruī, territus, *frighten, terrify,* 1076.

conticēscō, 2, ticuī, — (taceō), *become still, cease speaking,* 1082.

contiguus, a, um, adj., *bordering, neighboring, adjoining,* 124.

contineō, 2, tinuī, tentus (teneō), *hold together; bound, hem in,* 479.

contingō, 3, tigī, tāctus (tangō), *touch, reach,* 471, 499, 530, etc.; *attain, attain to,* 405, 1380; *come to, be given to,* 1238, 1554. *

contrā, adv., *opposite; to the other side,* 147. *

contrahō, 3, trāxī, trāctus, *draw together, contract, shrink,* 573, 584.

contrārius, a, um, adj. (contrā), *lying over against; in the opposite direction,* 421; in contrāria, *in the opposite direction, backward,* 625. *

cōnūbium, ī, n. (nūbō), *marriage, wedlock,* 59, (pl.) 262, 272. *

cōnus, ī, m., *apex; crest, plume,* 1529.

convellō, 3, vellī, volsus, *tear away, separate,* 793. *

conveniō, 4, vēnī, ventus, *come together; meet,* 155; *be fitted* or *suited to, befit,* 403.

convertō, 3, vertī, versus, *turn round; turn, change,* 1412. *

convīcium, ī, n., *loud noise; abusive words, abuse, injury,* 999.

convīvium, ī, n., *meal in company;* pl., *feast, banquet,* 1896. *

convocō, 1, *call together, assemble, summon,* 1117.

cōpia, ae, f., *abundance, plenty,* 799, 983; *access,* 505. *

cor, cordis, n., *heart,* 1055, 1071. *

cornū, ūs, n., *horn,* 428, 1441; *of the moon, tip, extremity,* 465; pl., *bow,* 237. *

cornum, ī, n. (cornus, *cornel cherry tree*), *cornel berry,* 902.

corōna, ae, f., *crown, garland, wreath,* 39, 375, 761. *

corpus, oris, n., *body, form,* 179, 206, 225, etc.; *person,* 773; *bodily presence,* 141; *flesh,* 1242; *skin,* 35; *beauty,* 19; pl., *limbs,* 309. *

corrigō, 3, rēxī, rēctus (regō), *make straight; improve, better, amend, change* (for the better), 111, 437.

corripiō, 3, ripuī, reptus (rapiō), *seize, snatch up, grasp,* 493; *attack, sweep away,* 551; *captivate, fascinate, charm,* 1309; *take up, begin,* 506. *

cortex, icis, m., *bark,* 335, 882.

Cōrycides, um, f. adj., *of Corycium,* a cave in Mt. Parnassus, *Corycian,* 1161.

costa, ae, f., *rib,* 1358. *

crātēr, ēris, m., *mixing-bowl, bowl,*
906, 916. *

crēber, bra, brum, adj., *thick,*
abundant, 858. *

crēdō, 3, didī, ditus; *give credence,*
believe, trust, 387, 438, 566, etc. *

cremō, 1, *burn, consume,* 484.

creō, 1, *produce, bear,* 688, 1537;
creātī, *children,* 995.

crepitō, 1, —, —, freq. (crepō,
rattle), rustle, murmur, 89.

crēscō, 3, crēvī, crētus, *grow, in-*
crease, be enlarged or *strengthened,*
127, 331, 694, etc.

Crētē, ēs, f., the island of *Crete,*
1559.

crīmen, inis, n., *judgment, fault,*
offense, guilt, sin, 265, 738, 811.

crīnis, is, m., *hair;* pl., *locks, tresses,*
33, 324, 331, etc. *

crīnītus, a, um, adj. (crīnis), *hairy,*
draconibus, *with dragon locks,*
1402. *

crista, ae, f., *crest,* 1453.

croceus, a, um, adj. (crocus),
saffron colored, yellow, 671. *

crūdēlis, e, adj. (crūdus, *bloody*),
rude, unfeeling, merciless, cruel,
62, 746, 1069. *

cruentātus, a, um, adj. (p. of cru-
entō, *make bloody), blood-*
stained, bloody, 171.

cruentus, a, um, adj., *blood-*
stained, bloody, 61, 200, 1251. *

cruor, ōris, m., *blood, gore,* 188,
207, 1042; *bloodshed, killing,* 228.

crūs, crūris, n., *leg, limb,* 291, 1044,
1147; pl., *heels,* 1026.

cubīle, is, n., *resting place; couch,*
bed (pl.), 76. See **sociō.**

culmen, inis, n. (for columen),

summit; roof, gable, 1130, (pl.)
1136.

culpa, ae, f., *fault, blame, guilt,* 70,
385.

culpō, 1 (culpa), *blame, criticise,*
condemn, 22.

cultor, ōris, m., *tiller; worshiper,*
1168.

cultus, ūs, m., *labor;* pl., *manner of*
life, 1398.

cultus, see **colō.**

cum, prep. with abl., *with, together*
with, in the company of, 11, 27,
44, etc. *

cum, conj., *when, while, after,*
since, 36, 80, 93, etc. *

cunctor, 1, *delay, linger, hesitate,*
453; *object, resist,* 1285.

cūnctus, a, um, adj. (for coniūnc-
tus), *all in a body, all together,*
all, 247, 558, 750, 1264; as noun,
m. pl., *everybody,* 1333. *

cupīdō, inis, f., *desire, longing,*
eagerness, 107, 452, 1600; *love,*
passion, 77; personified, *Love,*
Cupid, 235. *

cupidus, a, um, adj., *longing, eager,*
desirous, 751, 1312.

cupiō, 3, īvī, ītus, *long for, desire,*
wish, 272, 273, 525, etc.

cūr, interrog. adv., *why? where-*
fore? 25, 64, 602, etc. *

cūra, ae, f., *trouble; care, regard,*
anxiety, 64, 442, 745, 961. *

cūralium, ī, n., *coral,* (pl.) 1382.

cūrō, 1 (cūra), *care for; care, care*
to know, 262.

currō, 3, cucŭrrī, cursus, *run, has-*
ten, 24, 293, 516, 549; *fly,* 1579. *

currus, ūs, m., *chariot, car,* often
pl. for sing., 395, 410, 422, etc. *

cursus, ūs, m., *running, race, course*, 1, 11, 16, etc.; *pace, step*, 307; *journey*, 1418; pl., *course*, 108, 1015, 1123.   *

(curvāmen, inis), n. (curvō), *curving, curve, bend, sweep*, 478, 1487, 1570.

curvātūra, ae, f. (curvō), *curve*, 456.

curvō, 1 (curvus), *curve, round*, 430, 431, 540, 1514.

curvus, a, um, adj., *crooked; curved, rounding*, 511, 576, 1139, 1432; *bent*, 1352.

cuspis, idis, f., *point, head, tip*, 252, 1504; *sting*, 540.   *

custōdia, ae, f. (custōs), *guard, guardian*, 921.

custōs, ōdis, m. and f., *guard, guardian*, 343; pl., *parents*, 152.

cutis, is, f., *skin*, 1485.

Cyclades, um, f., a group of islands in the Aegean, 575.

cymba, ae, f., *boat, skiff*, 1134.

Cynthus, ī, m., a mountain in Delos, the birthplace of Apollo, 993.   *

Cyprius, a, um, adj., *of Cyprus*, an island in the Mediterranean, *Cyprian*, 86.

Cytherēa, ae, f., *Venus*, from Cythera, an island sacred to her off the coast of Lacedaemon, 81.*

D

Daedalus, ī, m., the mythical builder of the Labyrinth, 1559.

Damasichthōn, onis, m., a son of Niobe, 1043.

damnō, 1 (damnum), *condemn*, 18; *curse*, 846.

damnōsus, a, um, adj. (damnum), *hurtful, fatal*, 1591.

damnum, ī, n., *hurt, harm, curse*, 803; *destruction, loss*, 554, 1213.

Danaē, ēs, f., daughter of Acrisius, king of Argos, 787.

Daphnē, ēs, f., a nymph, 234.

(daps, dapis, f., *feast;* pl., *feast, viands*, 790, 793, 794, 920.   *

dē, prep. w. abl., *down from, from*, 813, 889, 913, etc.; *from, out of, of*, 105, 1010, 1088, etc.; *from, made of*, 892, 957, 1385; *in*, 508, 632; *by*, 1247; *about, concerning*, 5, 730.   *

dea, ae, f. (deus), *goddess*, 114, 647, 979, etc.   *

dēbeō, 2, uī, itus [for dehibeō (habeō)], *withhold; owe, ought*, 143, 263, 264, 702, 1558.

decēns, entis, adj. (p. of decet), *becoming; comely, fair, charming*, 309.

dēcerpō, 3, psī, ptus (carpō), *pluck off, gather*, 90, 782.

decet, 2, decuit, impers., *it is proper, beseems, befits*, 239, 362.

dēcidō, 3, cidī, — (cadō), *fall off, fall down, fall*, 1149.

dēclīnō, 1, *bend aside; turn aside, alter*, 108, 486.

dēclīvis, e, adj. (clīvus), *inclining;* as noun, n., *slope, descent*, 547.

decor, ōris, m., *comeliness, beauty, charm*, 30, 31, 270.

decōrus, a, um, adj. (decor), *beautiful, charming, lovely*, 964. *

dēcrēscō, 3, crēvī, crētus, *grow less, shrink, diminish, recede*, 603, 1181.

dēcurrō, 3, cucurrī or currī, cursus, *run down; run off, run*, 38.

decus, oris, n., *grace; glory, splendor, beauty*, 652. *

dēdecus, oris, n., *disgrace, shame*, 852.

dēdūcō, 3, dūxī, ductus, *lead off, conduct*, 454; *unfurl*, 1022.

dēfendō, 3, fendī, fēnsus, *ward off; protect, defend*, 1484.

dēferō, ferre, tulī, lātus, *bring down*, 885; *waft*, 83.

dēficiō, 3, fēcī, fectus (faciō), *withdraw; unmake,* (orbem) *be eclipsed*, 652; intr. *fail*, 726.

dēfleō, 2, flēvī, flētus, *weep at, bemourn, bewail*, 570, 682, 935.

dēfluō, 3, flūxī, fluxus, *flow down; sink down, fall*, 1018. *

dēfōrmis, e, adj. (fōrma), *unsightly, unshapely*, 1141.

dēfrēnātus, a, um, adj., *unbridled; unrestrained*, 1123.

dēlābor, 3, lapsus, *glide down, descend*, 1522.

dēlēniō, 4, *soothe, charm*, 831.

dēlīctum, ī, n., *fault, wrongdoing*, 1318.

Dēlius, a, um, adj., *of Delos, Delian;* as noun, *Apollo*, 236.

Dēlos, ī, f., one of the Cyclades, birthplace of Apollo and Diana, 1597.

Delphicus, a, um, adj., *of Delphi,* a famous oracle of Apollo in Phocis, *Delphic*, 297.

delphīn, īnis, m., *dolphin*, 577, 1143.

dēlūbrum, ī, n., *place of cleansing; temple, shrine*, 425, 944, 1207.

dēmēns, mentis, adj. (mēns), *insane, mad, foolish*, 71.

dēmittō, 3, mīsī, missus, *send down*, 1102; *plunge, thrust*, 186, 1457; *let down*, p. dēmissus, *hanging down, disheveled*, 1078; comp. *too low*, 1580. *

dēmō, 3, dēmpsī, dēmptus (emō, take), *take away, remove, take*, 274, 783, 986.

dēnique, adv., *and thenceforward: at length, at last, finally*, 105; *in short, in fact*, 443.

dēns, dentis, m., *tooth*, 680, 793, 794, etc.; Indus, *ivory*, 835.

dēnsus, a, um, adj., *dense, thickset*, 1450; *clouded*, 724.

dēpendeō, 2, —, —, *hang from; hang down, be suspended*, 1392. *

dēplōrō, 1, *weep bitterly; mourn, lament, bewail*, 1113.

dēpōnō, 3, posuī, positus, *lay* or *put aside*, 389, 991; *quench, slake*, 165.

dēprecor, 1, *avert by prayer; plead against*, 446.

dēprēndō, 3, prēndī, prēnsus, *take away; seize, catch*, 1137; *discern, detect*, 442, 1427.

dērigēscō, 2, riguī, —, inch., *become stiff, grow rigid*, 1091.

dēscendō, 3, scendī, scēnsus (scandō, *climb*), *climb down; go down, descend*, 683, 691, 1232, etc.

dēserō, 3, seruī, sertus, *leave, forsake, abandon*, 755, 1600. *

dēsieram, see dēsinō.

dēsinō, 3, siī, situs, *leave off, cease, finish*, 395, 1004; *end* (in), *go off* (into), 1359.

dēsistō, 3, stitī, stitus, *leave off,
cease, stop,* 70, 1095. *

dēsōlātus, a, um, adj. (p. of
dēsōlō, *leave alone*), *left alone;
abandoned, deserted,* 1185.

dēspectō, 1, —, —, intens. (dēspiciō), *look down on,* 1257. *

dēspiciō, 3, spēxī, spectus, *look
down (upon),* 519, 1465. *

dēsum, esse, fuī, futūrus, *be want-
ing, be lacking, fail,* 1133. *

dēterreō, 2, uī, itus, *frighten off;
deter, discourage,* 41.

dētrahō, 3, trāxī, trāctus, *draw off;
take away, remove,* 387; *pull off,
pluck,* 779.

Deucaliōn, ōnis, m., son of Prometheus, king of Thessaly; father
of Hellen, from whom the
Hellenes took their name, 1159.

deus, ī, m., *god,* 5, 8, 27, etc. *

dēvius, a, um, adj. (via), *out of the
way;* n. pl., *byways,* 1409.

dēvoveō, 2, vōvī, vōtus, *devote;
curse,* 1610. *

dexter, tera, terum, and tra, trum,
adj., *on the right side, right, right
hand,* 366, 1018, 1351, 1386,
1598; comp. dexterior, *right,*
486. *

dextra, ae, f. (dexter, sc. manus),
right hand, hand, 334, 409, 791,
etc.; ā dextrā, *on the right,* 373. *

Diāna, ae, f., sister of Apollo, goddess of light and of the moon,
269. *

dīcō, 3, dīxī, dictus, *say, tell,
speak,* 3, 5, 18, etc.; *call, name,*
85, 218, 304, etc.; *appoint,* 162;
shout, cry, 98. *

Dictaeus, a, um, adj. *of Dicte,* a

mountain in Crete, *Dictaean,*
1423.

dictum, ī, n. (p. of dīcō), *that said;
speech, word,* 101, 451, 954, etc. *

diēs, ēī, m. and f., *day, daylight,*
396, 642, 653, etc.; *time,* 1182;
personified, 373. *

diffīdō, 3, fīsus sum, *distrust,* 1231.

diffugiō, 3, fūgī, —, *flee in all directions, scatter, disperse,* 462.

diffundō, 3, fūdī, fūsus, *spread by
pouring,* 694; *relax, cheer, glad-
den,* 1398. *

digitus, ī, m., *finger,* 282, 785.

dīgnus, a, um, adj., *worthy, de-
serving, befitting, becoming,* 74,
176, 942, etc.; est, *deserve,* 391. *

dīgredior, 3, gressus, *go away,
depart,* 672.

dīmittō, 3, mīsī, missus, *send
down, send forth,* 621; *set at
work,* 1564. *

dīmoveō, 2, mōvī, mōtus; *remove,
take away,* 881; *separate, part,*
1340.

dīrēctus, a, um, adj. (p. of dīrigō,
lay straight), *straight,* 477. *

dīripiō, 3, ripuī, reptus (rapiō),
snatch apart; tear off, tear, 1473.

dīrus, a, um, adj., *ill-omened;
dreadful, awful, impious,* 999. *

dīs, dītis, adj., *rich, wealthy,* 425. *

discēdō, 3, cessī, cessus; *depart,
withdraw,* 158, 857, 1215.

discors, cordis, adj. (cor), *at vari-
ance; contradictory, different,*
1254.

discrīmen, inis, n., *that which
parts; difference, distinction,*
1132; *risk, peril, hazard, danger,*
53. *

dīsiciō, 3, iēcī, iectus (iaciō), *throw asunder; part, disperse, scatter*, 1169. *

dispār, paris, adj. (pār), *unequal, unlike*, 1568.

dispēnsō, 1, *distribute, dispense*, 1067.

dissiliō, 4, uī, — (saliō, *leap*), *leap apart; gape open, yawn, crack*, 571.

dissuādeō, 2, suāsī, suāsus, *advise against; dissuade*, 401.

dīstō, 1, —, —, *stand apart; be far removed, be different*, 989, 1062.

diū, adv., *by day, all day; long, a long while*, 103, 889, 924, etc. *

diurnus, a, um, adj., *of the day*, i.e., *of the sun*, 1263.

dīvellō, 3, vellī, volsus, *tear apart, rend in pieces*, 179.

dīversus, a, um, adj. (p. of dīvertō, *turn aside*); *different, various, different kinds of*, 251, 362, 1085, 1101; *apart, distant, remote*, 634; *separate, opposite*, 145. *

dīves, itis, adj., *rich, wealthy*, 443, 797. *

dō, dare, dedī, datus, *give, grant, bestow, vouchsafe, commit, consign*, 12, 84, 93, etc.; *exchange*, 142; *make*, 910; *cause*, 235; *utter*, 40, 1215, 1223, 1276; *render, offer*, 499; *fulfill*, 400; *give up*, 654; *bestow, inspire*, 82; *inflict*, 240; *blow*, 311; *draw*, 1509. *

doceō, 2, uī, doctus, *cause to know; teach, show*, 92. *

doctus, a, um, adj. (p. of doceō), *taught; skillful, skilled*, 837.

doleō, 2, uī, itūrus, *feel pain; grieve, lament*, 1194. *

dolor, ōris, m., *pain, hurt, suffering, grief, sorrow*, 291, 1034, 1056, etc.; *grievance*, 999. *

domina, ae, f. (dominus), *mistress*, 975.

dominus, ī, m., *master, owner, lord*, 306, 686, 817, etc. *

domō, 1, domuī, domitus, *overcome, subdue, master*, 669, 1153; *soften, boil soft*, 890.

domus, ūs, f., *house, dwelling house, home*, 124, 133, 153, etc.; *household, family*, 876, 1369. *

dōnec, conj. (dōnicum, *until*), *as long as, while*, 949; *until, till at length*, 721, 809, 1511. *

dōnō, 1 (dōnum), *give as a present; give, present*, 784.

dōnum, ī, n., *gift, present*, 425, 722, 772, 792. *

Dōris, idis, f., daughter of Oceanus and wife of Nereus, 359.

dōs, dōtis, f., *marriage portion, dowry*, 87; *endowment*, 1334.

dōtālis, e, adj. (dōs), *of a dowry; (given) as a bridal gift*, 1337.

dracō, ōnis, m., *serpent, dragon*, 1280, 1347, 1402.

dubitō, 1 (dubius), *be uncertain, doubt, hesitate, not know*, 51, 117, 200, etc.; pass., *be questioned, doubted*, or *suspected*, 368, 997.

dubius, a, um, adj., *doubtful*, 100; as noun, n., *doubt, uncertainty*, 1230. *

dūcō, 3, dūxī, ductus, *lead, conduct, guide*, 487, 762; *lead off, lead away*, 121; *lead out*, 469; **take** *on, receive,* **132,** 1236; *ply, row,* 1135. *

dulcēdō, inis, f. (dulcis, *sweet*), *sweetness, charm,* 838.

dum, conj., *so long as, while,* 27, 38, 61, etc.; *until,* 1262, 1512. *

duo, ae, o, num. adj., *two,* 175, 226, 250, etc.

duplicō, 1 (duplex), *double; double up, bend double,* 1082.

dūritia, ae, f. (dūrus), *hardness,* 1383, 1485, 1486.

(dūritiēs, ēī), dūritiem, f. (dūrus), *hardness,* 1235.

dūrus, a, um, adj., *hard* (to the touch), *rough, tough, unyielding,* 1009, 1094, 1305, 1373, 1504; *hard, cruel, harsh,* 60. *

dux, ducis, m. and f., *leader, commander, general,* 341; *guide,* 1433, 1584, 1600. *

E

ebur, oris, n., *ivory,* 351; (ivory) *scabbard,* 215. *

eburneus, a, um, adj. (ebur), *of ivory; ivory-, white as ivory,* 33.

ecce, interj., *lo! see! behold! here!* 163, 195, 441, etc.

Echīōn, ōnis, m., one of the race that sprang from the dragon's teeth, 1547.

ēdō, 3, didī, ditus, *give out; publish, tell, declare,* 391; *utter,* 940.

ēdoceō, 2, uī, ctus, *teach thoroughly; show forth, explain,* 1400.

ēdūcō, 3, dūxī, ductus, *lead forth; draw out,* 1041; *draw up,* 1534. *

efferō, ferre, tulī, lātus, *bring out,*

extend, 1458; *proclaim, publish,* 852; pass., *be buried,* 1072. *

efficiō, 3, fēcī, fectus (faciō), *make out; bring about that, make, cause, render,* 772, 874, 1451. *

efflō, 1, *breathe out, exhale,* 433.

effluō, 3, flūxī,—, *flow out; slip out, escape, be lost,* 1022, 1460.

effodiō, 3, fōdī, fossus, *dig out; dig up, excavate,* 854. *

effugiō, 3, fūgī,—, *escape, avoid,* 7, 480, 1356; *be free from,* 798. *

effulgeō, 2, fulsī, fulsus, *shine forth,* 492.

effundō, 3, fūdī, fūsus, *pour out, waste, shed,* 1042, 1119. *

egeō, 2, eguī, —, *be in want; lack, need, want,* 415; *egēns* as adj., *lacking, without,* 790. *

ego, meī, mihi, mē, pers. pron., *I,* 11, 22, 26, etc. *

ēgredior, 3, ēgressus (gradior), *go forth; go up* or *out, proceed, go,* 161, 172, 484. *

ei, interj., *Oh! alas!* 305, 1016.

ēiaculor, 1, *shoot out, throw out, spurt out,* 191, 1048.

ēiectō, 1, intens. (ēiciō, *throw out*), *cast forth, throw out,* 562.

ēlīdō, 3, ēlīsī, ēlīsus (laedō), *strike out; dash, cleave,* 248.

ēlūdō, 3, lūsī, lūsus, *avoid, evade, escape,* 924; *deceive, cheat,* 787.

ēluō, 3, uī, ūtus, *wash off, wash away,* 811.

ēmicō, 1, cuī, cātus, *spring out; break forth, shoot (forth),* 94, 1049; *dart forward, spurt,* 188.

ēminus, adv. (manus), *beyond the reach of hand; from afar,* 1540.

ēmittō, 3, mīsī, missus, *send out, send forth,* 1105.   *

ēn, interj., calling attention, *lo! behold! see!* 594, 607, 995.   *

enim, conj., postpositive, *for, in fact,* 3, 670, 982, etc.; sed enim, *but in fact, but,* 312; neque enim, *for . . . not,* 370, 612.   *

ēnītor, 3, nīxus or nīsus, *make one's way, struggle up,* 412.

ēnsis, is, m., *two-edged sword, blade,* 214, 1359, 1540, 1583.

eō, īre, īvī or iī, itūrus, *go, walk, run, fly,* etc., 29, 423, 544, etc.; *move,* 1097; *pass,* 642.   *

eōdem, adv. (īdem), *to the same place,* 733; *to the same (thing), to this,* 978.   *

Ēōus, a, um, adj., *of the morning;* as noun, m., *Dawn,* 501.

Epimēthis, idis, f., *Pyrrha,* daughter of Epimetheus, 1224.

epulae, ārum, f., *viands, feast, banquet,* 908, 1397.   *

equidem, adv. (quidem), *verily, truly, indeed, nay even,* 593, 959.   *

equus, ī, m., *horse, steed,* 396, 412, 466, etc.   *

Erebus, ī, m., *god of darkness; the under world,* 746.

ergō, conj., *therefore, accordingly, then,* 453, 877.   *

Ēridanus, ī, m., a river of western Europe, 635.

ērigō, 3, rēxī, rēctus (regō), *lift up, raise,* 213, 1464.

ēripiō, 3, ripuī, reptus (rapiō), *snatch away; take or tear away,* 626, 985, 1192, 1492, 1416;

rescue, 610, 803; pass., *escape,* 320.   *

errō, 1, *wander, rove, stray,* 154, 1269.   *

error, ōris, m., *wandering; uncertainty, doubt,* 387; *mistake in one's course,* 427.   *

ērudiō, 4, *teach, instruct,* 1591.

ēruō, 3, uī, ūtus, *draw out, tear out,* 1042.

et, conj., *and, also, too,* 9, 17, 19, etc.; *even,* 895, 1389.   *

etiam, adv., *now too, also, still, yet, even,* 405, 416, 495, etc.   *

etiamnum, adv., *even now, still,* 1376.

etsī, conj., *though, although,* 633.

Eumenides, um, f., *Eumenides, Furies,* 716.

Eumolpus, ī, m., a Thracian bard, founder of the Eleusinian mysteries, 763.

Eurus, ī, m., the southeast wind, 508.   *

Eurydicē, ēs, f., wife of Orpheus, 701.

ēvādō, 3, vāsī, vāsus, *go out; pass,* 1440.

ēvānēscō, 3, nuī, —, inch., *disappear, vanish,* 465.

ēvehō, 3, vēxī, vectus, *bear out; bear away,* 421.

ēventus, ūs, m., *occurrence; fate, lot, fortune,* 41.

ēvītābilis, e, adj. (ēvītō, *shun*), *avoidable,* 1023.

ēvocō, 1, *call out, summon,* 1263.

ēvolō, 1, *fly out, hasten forth,* 1105.

ex or (before consonants) **ē, prep.** w. abl., *from within; from, of, out from, out of,* 104, 176, **187,**

etc.; *on, in,* 558; *in accordance
with,* 40; ex ōrdine, *in order,*
457; ex aequō, *equally,* 129.   *

exāctus, see exigō.

exanimātus, a, um, adj (p. of ex-
animō, *put out of breath*), *lifeless, dead,* 579.

exanimis, e, adj. (anima), *lifeless,
dead,* 647, 1090.

exaudiō, 4, *hear from a distance;
listen to, overhear,* 211.   *

excēdō, 3, cessī, cessus, *go out, go
forth, depart,* 152; *go beyond,
preclude,* 986.   *

excidō, 3, cidī, — (cadō), *fall out;
fail (in),* 639.   *

excipiō, 3, cēpī, ceptus (capiō),
take out; leave out, except, 408;
receive, 416, 635, 1252, 1267,
1606.   *

exclāmō, 1, *cry out, exclaim,* 1538.

excūsō, 1, *excuse, apologize for,*
667.

exemplum, ī, n. *sample; representation,* 1200; *way, manner,*
1255, 1543.

exeō, īre, iī, itus, *go forth, go out,
depart,* 153, 463, 722; *come
forth, rise,* 1179, 1496; *issue,
flow,* 810.   *

exerceō, 2, uī, itus (arceō), *keep
busy; work, till,* 598.   *

exhālō, 1, *breathe out,* 748, 1036.

exhibeō, 2, uī, itus (habeō), *hold
forth; show, exhibit, display,*
1002.

exhorrēscō, 3, horruī, —, inch.
(exhorreō, *shudder*), *tremble,*
202.

exigō, 3, ēgī, āctus (agō); *drive,
plunge, thrust,* 1366; *finish,*

complete, perfect, 1240; *consider,
deliberate on, take counsel upon,*
28.   *

exiguus, a, um, adj., *exact; small,
little, too little, slight, short,* 203,
890, 1262, 1471.

exitiābilis, e, adj. (exitium), *destructive, fatal, deadly,* 1046.

exitium, ī, n., *destruction, ruin,*
601.

exitus, ūs, m. (exeō), *way out;
outcome, issue,* 678.

exōsus, a, um, p. (ōdī, *hate*), *hating, detesting,* 265.

(expallēscō), 3, palluī, —, inch.,
grow pale, turn pale, 173, 325.

expellō, 3, pulī, pulsus, *drive out;
thrust out, remove, deprive (of),*
624; *drive out, expel,* 1048,
1284.   *

experior, 4, pertus, *make trial of,
try, test,* 662.   *

expers, pertis, adj. (pars), *having
no part in; having nothing to do
with, renouncing,* 261; *without,*
651.

exsanguis, e, adj., *without blood,
bloodless, pale,* 711.

exserō, 3, uī, sertus, *stretch out,
thrust out, put forth,* 582.   *

exsilium, ī, n., *banishment, exile,*
1426, 1553, 1560.

exsistō, 3, stitī, —, *stand forth,
protrude,* 575, 1531.

exspatior, 1, *wander from the
track,* 543; *overflow,* 1126.

exspectō, 1, *look out for; await,*
1557; ante exspectātum, *sooner
than looked for,* 1421.

exspīrō, 1, *breathe forth,* 1542.   *

exstīnctus, a, um, adj. (p. of ex-

stinguō, *put out*), *deprived of
life; dead, lifeless*, 218.

exstō, 1,—,—, *stand forth, protrude,
extend above, tower*, 1025, 1173,
1364, 1499.

exstruō, 3, strūxī, strūctus, *heap
up; heap full, laden*, 790.

exsultō, 1, āvī, —, freq. (exsiliō,
leap up), *exult*, 1072.

extendō, 3, tendī, tentus and tēnsus, *stretch out, reach out*, 318,
819.

externus, a, um, adj. (exter, *on
the outside*), *outward;* as noun,
m., *outsider, foreigner*, 1281.

extrēmus, a, um, adj. (exter, *on
the outside*), *farthest, last;* lūna,
waning, in its last quarter, 465.*

exuviae, ārum, f., *that stripped off;
spoils, skins*, 258.

F

fabricō, 1 (fabrica, *joiner's shop*),
make, fashion, 906.

fābula, ae, f., *narration; rumor,
tale, story, fiction*, 2.

faciēs, —, em, ē, f., *appearance;
form, figure*, 979, 1246; *color,
appearance*, 193; *features*, 361;
beauty, 19.   *

facilis, e, adj., *easy to do; easy,
easily won*, 43.   *

faciō, 3, fēcī, factus, *make, con-
struct, fashion*, 136, 199, 347,
etc.; *make, render*, 163, 399,
471, etc.; *make, prove*, 45;
cause, bring about, 126, 251, 252,
etc.; *create, add to*, 31; *give*,
505, 770; *grant, allow*, 601; *do*,
78, 528; certum, *inform*, 1057. *

factum, ī, n. (p. of faciō), *deed,
act*, 805, 999, 1379, 1389, 1426.*

faex, faecis, f., *grounds; brine* (of
pickles), *sauce*, 902.

fagus, ī, f., *beech tree*, 906.

falcātus, a, um, adj. (falx, *sickle*),
sickle shaped; hooked, curved,
1359.

fallāx, ācis, adj., *deceitful; de-
ceptive, false*, 1225, 1422.

fallō, 3, fefellī, falsus, *trip; give the
slip to, escape the notice of*,
152, 161; *deceive, cheat*, 273, 958;
disappoint, 195; *beguile, pass
away*, 891.   *

falsus, a, um, adj. (p. of fallō),
feigned; false, pretended, lying,
385, 689; *groundless*, 1418.   *

fāma, ae, f., *report, rumor*, 698,
1056; fāma est, *they say, it is
said*, 579, 715.   *

famēs, is, f., *hunger*, 799.   *

famulus, ī, m., *attendant, servant*,
851, 875.   *

fāre, see for.

fās, indecl. noun, n., *divine law;* fās
esse, *be permitted*, 405.   *

fastīgium, ī, n., *top of a gable;* pl.,
roof, 351, 1207.   *

fateor, 2, fassus, *confess, own,
admit, acknowledge*, 84, 143,
659, etc.

fātidicus, a, um, adj. (fātum),
prophesying, prophetic, 1162.

fātifer, fera, ferum, adj. (fātum),
death dealing, fatal, 1040.

fatīgō, 1, *weary, tire out, worry*,
923.   *

fātum, ī, n. (p. of for), *utterance;
fate, ill fate, death*, 504, 616, 701,

935, 1192; pl., *the fates, fate,* 75, 708; fātum est, *it is fated,* 530. *

faucēs, ium, f., *throat, jaws,* 593.

fautrīx, īcis, f. (faveō), *patroness, protectress,* 1522.

faveō, 2, fāvī, fautūrus, *be favorable, be propitious,* 1334. *

favilla, ae, f., *cinders, hot ashes, embers,* 562, 595, 904.

favor, ōris, m., *good will; acclamation, cheering,* 97.

favus, ī, m., *honeycomb,* 914.

fax, facis, f., *torch,* 243, 676; *firebrand,* 275; *light wood,* 884.*

fēcundus, a, um, adj., *fertile; abounding, rich,* 1452, 1598.

fēlīx, īcis, adj., *fruitful; happy, fortunate, lucky,* 74, 675, 982, etc. *

fēmina, ae, f., *woman,* 20, 941, 1187; *womankind,* 1247. *

fēmineus, a, um, adj., (fēmina), *of a woman; the woman's,* 1247.

fera, ae, f. (ferus), *wild beast,* 173, 240, 363, etc. *

ferāx, ācis, adj., (ferō), *fruitful, fertile,* 1155.

feriō, 4, —, —, *strike, smite, beat,* 1540. *

ferō, ferre, tulī, lātus, *bear, bring, carry, take,* 90, 183, 1327; *take with one, have,* 393; *hold,* 972; *bear, endure,* 370, 563, 582, etc.; pass., *be borne, go, rush, fly,* 417, 512, 525, etc.; *turn, direct,* 201, 369, 1064; *experience,* 482; *direct, lead,* 1138; *say,* 642; *proffer, give,* 327, 616, 1214, 1329.

ferōx, ōcis, adj., *wild, fierce, savage,* 1354, 1489.

ferrum, ī, n., *iron, steel,* 1474, 1505; *sword, weapon, point,* 186, 230, 1025, etc.; *shears,* 850.   *

fertilitās, ātis, f. (fertilis, *fruitful*), *fruitfulness, abundance,* 596.

ferus, a, um, adj., *wild; fierce, cruel, savage,* 180, 409, 1071.

fervēns, entis, adj. (p. of ferveō, *be hot*), *warm, hot, burning,* 187, 890; *glowing,* 560.   *

fessus, a, um, adj., *wearied, tired, worn out, exhausted,* 1267.   *

festum, ī, n. (festus), *holiday; festival, feast,* 765.

festus, a, um, adj., *of holidays; festal, joyful, merry,* 39, 894, 1532.

fētus, ūs, m., *bearing; fruit,* 106, 192, 228.

fictilis, e, adj., *made of clay;* as noun, n. pl., *earthenware dishes,* 905.

fidēs, ē, f., *faith,* 1549; *genuineness, reality,* 777, 1527; *fulfillment,* 948; *testimony, witness,* 805.   *

fidēs, is, f., *chord, string,* 975; *lyre,* 835.

fīdūcia, ae, f. (fīdus), *trust, confidence, assurance,* 1190, 1320. *

fīdus, a, um, adj., *trusty, faithful, steadfast,* 343, 1479.   *

fīgō, 3, fīxī, fīxus, *fix, fasten, set,* 42, 254, 1016, etc.; *pierce, transfix,* 245, 1513; *press, imprint,* 208, 1446; pass., *catch,* 1138; p. *fixed* (star), 545.   *

figūra, ae, f., *form, shape,* 843; *beauty,* 328, 739.

fīlia, ae, f., *daughter,* 263.   *

fīlius, ī, m., *son,* 245.

findō, 3,—, fissus, *cleave, part, divide*, 132, 552, 1300.

fingō, 3, fīnxī, fīctus, *touch, fashion; form mentally, imagine, suppose*, 422, 788, 986.

fīniō, 4, (fīnis), *limit, bound*, 820; *end, finish*, 329, 347, 451, 1061.

fīnis, is, m., *limit, bound*, 479; *end, termination*, 657, 1029; pl., *borders, land, premises*, 1281.   *

fīō, fierī, factus, used as pass. of faciō, *be made, be caused, become*, 20, 133, 414, etc.

fissus, see findō.   *

fistula, ae, f., *pipe*, 1568; *water pipe*, 189.

flagellō, 1, —,—, (flagellum, *whip*), *beat, lash*, 1515.

flagrō, 1, *flame; burn, be fired*, 452.   *

flāmen, inis, n. (flō, *blow*), *blast, wind*, 310, 1104.

flamma, ae, f., *blazing fire; blaze, flame*, 277, 350, 471, etc.   *

flammifer, fera, ferum, adj. (flamma), *flame bearing; burning, fiery*, 503.

flāvēns, entis, adj. (flāveō, *be yellow*), *yellow, golden*, 907.

flāvēscō, 3, —,—, (flāveō, *be yellow*), *grow yellow*, 938.

flāvus, a, um, adj., *golden yellow; yellow haired, blond*, 833, 1574. *

flectō, 3, flēxī, flexus, *bend, bow, curve*, 237, 537, 1096, 1243, 1570; *turn, direct*, 721, 727, 933, 1014, 1206; *turn aside, avert*, 1212; *guide*, 517.   *

fleō, 2, flēvī, flētus, *weep, cry,* *shed tears*, 1098, 1201; *bewail, lament*, 711.

flētus, ūs, m., *weeping, wailing*, 207, 1326; *tears*, 1307.

flōrēns, entis, adj. (p. of flōreō, *bloom*), *blossoming; of flowers, flowery*, 375.

fluctus, ūs, m., *flood; wave, billow*, 1151, 1175, 1360.   *

fluitō, 1, āvī, —, freq. (fluō), *flow*, 796.

flūmen, inis, n., *flowing; stream, river*, 364, 809, 813, etc.   *

fluō, 3, flūxī, fluxus, *flow, run*, 787, 1107.

focus, ī, m., *fireplace, hearth*, 881, 908; *altar*, 1385.

foedō, 1 (foedus, *foul*), *defile; stain, bespatter*, 1027.

foedus, eris, n., *league; agreement, stipulation, compact*, 40.   *

folium, ī, n., *leaf*, 882, 887, 1374. *

fōns, fontis, m., *spring, fountain, source*, 157, 165, 569, etc.   *

(for), fārī, fātus, defective, *speak, say*, 1401.   *

forāmen, inis, n., *opening, orifice, hole*, 190.

fore, foret, from sum. See grammar.

foris, is, f., *door, gate;* pl., *two leaves of a door, double door, folding door, entrance*, 152, 344, 366, 461, 939.   *

fōrma, ae, f., *form, shape, appearance*, 198, 426, 1236, 1239; *image*, 1414; *beauty, charm*, 4, 14, 55, etc.   *

formīdō, inis, f., *fearfulness; fear, terror, fright*, 414, 541.

fŏrmō, 1 (fōrma), *make, fashion*, 1198.

fŏrmōsus, a, um, adj. (fōrma), *beautiful, handsome*, 964; n. pl., *the beautiful*, 52.

fornāx, ācis, f., *oven, kiln*, 560.

fors, fortis f., *chance, fate*, 60, 235, 1138.

forsitan, adv. (for fors sit an), *it may be that, perhaps*, 1, 424.

forte, adv., *by chance, perchance, as it happened*, 90, 170, 275, etc. *

fortis, e, adj., *strong; warlike, of strong men, manly*, 238; *strong, stout, brave*, 216, 1400; *spirited, impetuous*, 1010; *threatening*, 1285. *

fortiter, adv. (fortis), *strongly; stoutly, vigorously, manfully*, 475.

fortūna, ae, f. (fors), *chance, fate, hazard*, 26, 44; *personified*, 488, 984. *

foveō, 2, fōvī, fōtus, *warm*, 650. *

fragor, ōris, m., *crash*, 1110. *

fragōsus, a, um, adj. (fragor), *crashing; broken, rough, precipitous*, 1409.

frangō, 3, frēgī, frāctus, *dash to pieces, shatter, break*, 628.

frāter, tris, m., *brother*, 602, 604, 1078, etc. *

frāternus, a, um, adj. (frāter), *of a brother, brother's*, 549, 1549.

fremēns, entis, adj. (p. of fremō, rage), ferae, *raging*, 1351. *

frēnum, ī, n., pl. m. or n., *bridle, curb, bit, reins*, 469, 532, 627, etc.; *helm*, 527.

frequēns, entis, adj., *often; abounding (in), swarming (with)*, 1253.*

frequentō, 1 (frequēns), *visit frequently; attend, throng*, 759.

fretum, ī, n., *strait; sea, water*, 95, 609, 818, 1419. *

frondeō, 2, —, —, (frōns, *leaves*), *put forth leaves, become leafy*, 951, 952.

frōns, frondis, f., *leafy branch; leaves, foliage*, 331, 346, 553, etc.

frōns, frontis, f., *forehead, brow*, 587, 1108, 1442. *

frūctus, ūs, m., *fruit, crops*, 596.

fruor, 3, frūctus, *enjoy*, 269.

frūstrā, adv., *in error; in vain, to no purpose*, 742, 1083. *

frutex, icis, f., *shrub, bush*, 956.

(frūx), frūgis, f., *fruit; pulse, grain*, 790, (pl.) 599. *

fuga, ae, f., *fleeing; flight, running*, 293, 312, 326, 1468. *

fugāx, ācis, adj., *apt to flee; fleeing, fugitive*, 323, 1416.

fugiō, 3, fūgī, fugitūrus, *flee, take flight, run away*, 167, 168, 284, etc.; *flee from, avoid, shun*, 6, 256, 288, 297, 308. *

fugō, 1 (fuga), *put to flight, chase away, frighten off, repel*, 10, 251, 253, 492; *drive away*, 1104. *

fulgeō, 2, fulsī, —, *flash, gleam, shine*, 252, 365.

fulica, ae, f., *coot*, 865.

fulmen, inis, n., *lightning flash, thunderbolt*, 409, 590, 619, etc. *

fulvus, a, um, adj., *deep yellow, golden, tawny*, 89, 773, 794, 1145. *

fūmō, 1, —, —, (fūmus), *smoke, steam*, 550, 606, 635, 636.

fūmus, ī, m., *smoke, steam,* 563, 676.

funda, ae, f., *sling,* 1342.

fundō, 3, fūdī, fūsus, *pour, pour out,* 1110.

fūnestus, a, um, adj. (fūnus), *deadly, fatal,* 436, 1470.

fungor, 3, fūnctus, *perform, discharge,* 1397; *enjoy, receive,* 684.

fūnus, eris, n., *funeral procession; burial, funeral,* 1071, 1074, 1558.
                                                    *

furca, ae, f., *fork, forked pole,* 887; *fork-shaped prop, brace,* 937.

(furō,) 3, —, —, *be furious, rage,* 1504, 1543.
                                          *

furor, ōris, m. (furō), *rage, fury, madness, frenzy,* 967.
                                          *

fūrtim, adv., (fūrtum), *stealthily, secretly,* 1407.

fūrtum, ī, n., *theft; artifice, deceit,* 1428.

fūsilis, e, adj., *molten, fluid, liquid,* 796.

G

Gallicus, a, um, adj., *Gallic,* 315.

gaudeō, 2, gāvīsus sum, *rejoice, exult, be glad,* 101, 258, 500, etc.
                                          *

gelidus, a, um, adj. (gelū, *frost*), *icy, cold, chilly,* 157, 208, 541, etc.

geminus, a, um, adj., *twin, double,* 957; *double, twofold, of two, two,* 228, 536, 734, etc.

gemitus, ūs, m. (gemō), *groaning, lamentation,* 40.
                                          *

gemma, ae, f., *bud; precious stone, gem,* 457, 835.
                                          *

gemō, 3, uī, —, *sigh, groan, lament,* 1515.
                                          *

genae, ārum, f., *cheeks,* 716, 1093, 1586.

gener, erī, m., *daughter's husband; son-in-law,* 263, 980, 1333, 1368.

generōsus, a, um, adj. (genus), *of noble birth, high born,* 1397.

genetrīx, īcis, f. (genitor), *one who has borne; mother,* 971.
                                          *

geniāliter, adv. (geniālis, *pleasure-giving*), *jovially, merrily,* 765.

genitor, ōris, m., *parent, father, sire,* 46, 268, 299, etc.
                                          *

genitus, ī, m. (p. of gignō, *beget*), *son,* 1010. Cf. **nātus.** *

gēns, gentis, f., *race, tribe, people, nation,* 556, 974, 1301, 1456. *

genū, ūs, n., *knee,* 521.

genuālia, ium, n. (genū), *garters,* 34.

genus, eris, n., *race, stock, family, ancestry,* 48, 524, 600, etc.; *kind of people,* 1398.
                                          *

gerō, 3, gessī, gestus, *bear about, wear, have,* 202, 346, 376, etc.; *contain,* 363.

gestāmen, inis, n. (gestō, *bear*), *burden;* pl., *arms,* 239.

gestiō, 4, īvī, — (gestus, *bearing*), *gesticulate; be eager, long,* 197.

gignō, 3, genuī, genitus, *produce, give birth to, beget,* pass., *be descended,* 438; p. as noun, m., *descendant, son (of),* 1010. *

glaciālis, e, adj. (glaciēs, *ice*), *icy, frozen,* 378.

glāns, glandis, f., *acorn,* 827.

glēba, ae, f., *lump of earth, clod,* 781, 1009, 1527.

glōria, ae, f., *pride; glory, fame, renown*, 247, 1272, 1282.

glōrior, 1 (glōria), *take pride in; boast, vaunt, brag*, 973.

Gorgō, onis, f., *a Gorgon; Medusa*, 1331.

Gorgoneus, a, um, adj., *of the Gorgons*, 1251.

gracilis, e, adj., *slender; light, thin, lean*, 1140.

gradior, 3, gressus (gradus), *take steps; walk, move, go*, 428, 847.   *

gradus, ūs, m., *step, pace*, 126, 929, 1457; *of a temple*, 950, 1209.   *

grāmen, inis, n., *grass*, 1140.

grātēs, —, f. pl., *thanks*, 500, 1445.   *

grātia, ae, f. (grātus), *favor; good will, esteem, friendship*, 1287; mea, *regard for me*, 604.

grātus, a, um, adj., *beloved; pleasing, agreeable, acceptable*, 770.

gravis, e, adj., *heavy, weighty*, 1012, 1107, 1353, 1361; *heavy, deep*, 329, 1415; *cruel, painful, harsh*, 617; *portentous*, 678.   *

gravitās, ātis, f. (gravis), *heaviness, weight*, 119, 510.

gravō, 1 (gravis), *make heavy, weigh down*, 212, 1581.

gressus, ūs, m., *step*, 1064, 1438.

grex, gregis, m., *flock, herd, drove*, 295, 1268.

gurges, itis, m., *raging abyss; gulf, sea, waters*, 1131.   *

gutta, ae, f., *drop*, 1251.

guttur, uris, n., *gullet, throat*, 692, 799, 1025, etc.

H

habēna, ae, f., *holder;* pl., *reins*, 435, 499, 517, etc.   *

habeō, 2, uī, itus, *have, hold*, 48, 228, 253, etc.; *contain, hold*, 123, 356, 443, 1195, 1196; *bear, wear*, 339.   *

habitābilis, e, adj. (habitō), *fit for an abode; habitable*, 864.

habitō, 1, freq. (habeō), *dwell, dwell in, inhabit*, 181, 815, 1405, 1430.

hāc, adv. (hīc; sc. viā), *by this way; this way, here*, 481, 545.   *

Haemonius, a, um, adj., *Haemonian, Thessalian*, 429.

Haemus, ī, m., *a range of mountains in Thrace*, 747.

haereō, 2, haesī, haesūrus, *hang, stock, cling, be fixed*, 267, 332, 1025, 1079, 1492; *hesitate, be uncertain*, 199.   *

hālitus, ūs, m. (hālō, *breathe*), *breath, vapor*, 1496.

hāmātus, a, um, adj. (hāmus), *furnished with a hook; barbed*, 252.

hāmus, ī, m., *hook; barb*, 1041; *crooked blade*, 1352.

harēna, ae, f., *sand, strand*, 573, 758, 1250, 1373; *track*, 94.   *

harundō, inis, f., *reed, cane*, 858, 1593; *shaft*, 253; *Pan's pipe*, 822.

hasta, ae, f., *spear, shaft*, 1528. *

hastīle, is, n. (hasta), *spear-shaft, javelin*, 1490.   *

haud, adv., *not*, 36, 382, 864.

hauriō, 4, hausī, haustus, *draw up, draw*, 1372; *drink up, drain, empty*, 916; *dig up*, 855.   *

haustus, ūs, m., *drawing; outpouring, shedding, stream,* 185.

Helicē, ēs, f., the Great Bear, 1583.

herba, ae, f., *grass, herb;* pl., *grass, sward,* 149, 678, 1268, etc.; *herbs,* 304, 305. *

hērēs, ēdis, m. and f., *heir,* 1028.

herōs, ōis, m., *hero,* 100, 720, 776.*

Hesperidēs, um, f., *daughters of Hesperus,* 784.

Hesperius, a, um, adj., *of Hesperus, of the west, western,* 490; as noun, f., *Hesperia, the western land* (Italy), 636. *

hesternus, a, um, adj., *of yesterday, yesterday's,* 882.

heu, interj., of grief or pain, *Oh! alas! ah!* 220, 1062.

hīc, dem. pron., *this* (near the speaker); *this, he, she, it,* 5, 15, 25, etc.; *the one, the latter,* (pl.) *some,* 251, 254, 316, etc.; *another,* 1137. *

hīc, adv., *in this place, here, there,* 295, 638, 696, etc. *

hiems, emis, f., *winter;* personified, 378. *

hinc, adv., *from this place, hence,* 90, 864; hinc . . . illinc, *on this side . . . on that,* 138, 820. *

hinnītus, ūs, m. (hinniō, *neigh*), *neighing,* 502.

Hippomenēs, is, m., son of Megareus, 16.

Hippotadēs, ae, m., *son of Hippotas, Aeolus,* god of the winds, 1296.

hirsūtus, a, um, adj., *rough, shaggy,* 378.

hīscō, 3, —, —, inch. (hiō, *yawn*), *yawn, open,* 327.

holus, eris, n., *kitchen herbs, vegetables, greens,* 887.

homō, inis, m. and f., *human being, man,* 846, 1200, 1239, etc. *

honor, ōris, m., *honor, praise, reward,* 346, 447, 596, 657. *

hōra, ae, f., *hour,* 223, 946; *time,* 1329; hōrae mediae, *interval,* 891; personified, 374, 466.

horrendus, a, um, adj. (p. of horreō, *stand on end*), *to be shuddered at; dreadful, terrible,* 1413, 1459.

horrēns, entis, p. of horreō, *stand on end; rough, bristling,* 1409. *

horridus, a, um, adj., *bristling; rough, unkempt,* 296. *

hortāmen, inis, n. (hortor), *exhortation,* 1118.

hortor, 1, *encourage, urge,* 1591.

hortus, ī, m., *garden,* 886.

hospes, itis, m., *host, guest,* 765, 922; *stranger,* 38, 61, 1272, 1328, 1550. *

hospitium, ī, n. (hospes), *entertainment,* 1275. *

hostis, is, m. and f., *stranger; enemy, foe,* 240, 286, 289, etc. *

hūc, adv. (hīc), *to this place; hither,* 179, 690, 704, 866; *to this,* 979, 1554; hūc . . . illūc, *this way and that, hither and thither,* 1255. *

hūmānus, a, um, adj. (homō), *of man, human, mortal,* 600, 705, 813, 843. *

humī, adv. (locative of humus), *on the ground,* 1210, 1526. *

humilis, e, adj. (humus), *low, humble,* 878, 1451.

humus, ī, m., *earth, ground,* 188, 780, 834, etc.

Hymēn, —, m., god of marriage, 262.

Hymēnaeus, ī, m., *Hymen,* 672, 1390.   *

Hypaepa, ōrum, n., a small town near Mt. Tmolus, in Lydia, 820.

I

iaceō, 2, cuī, —, *lie, lie prostrate, lie dead,* 188, 520, 627, etc.; *be fallen, fall, drop,* 542, 1035; *droop,* 211.   *

iaciō, 3, iēcī, iactus, *throw, cast, hurl,* 116, 1228.   *

iactō, 1, freq. (iaciō), *throw, hurl, toss,* 619, 1217, 1221, 1381; *fling about, toss, blow,* 33; *move, ply, flap,* 1332, 1420; *show off, display, parade,* 821.   *

iactus, ūs, m., *throwing,* 112, 1247.

iaculum, ī, n., *dart, javelin,* 1475, 1486, 1540.

iaculor, 1 (iaculum), *hurl (as a javelin),* 409.

iam, adv., *at the moment, immediately, at once, soon,* 1176; *now, already, at last,* 64, 79, 212, etc.; *iust,* 102; neque, *no longer,* 562, 1607; iam iamque, *continually, every moment,* 317. *

Iapetīonidēs, ae, m., *son of Iapetus, Atlas,* 1265.

ibi, adv., *in that place, there,* 156, 821, 858, etc.

Īcarus, ī, m., son of Daedalus, 1571.

(icō), 3, īcī, ictus, *strike, hit, smite,* 1044.

ictus, ūs, m., *blow,* 1508; *force,* 1485; *beating, jet,* 191.

Īdē, ēs, f., *Mt. Ida,* near Troy, 741.

īdem, eadem, idem, dem. pron., *the same,* 159, 224, 508, etc.; *also, too,* 343.   *

ideō, adv., *for this reason, on that account, therefore,* 297.

iecur, oris, n., *liver,* 713.

iēiūnium, ī, n. (iēiūnus, *fasting*), *fasting, starvation,* (pl.) 1153.

igitur, adv., *then, therefore, accordingly,* 67.

ignārus, a, um, adj. (gnārus, *knowing*), *ignorant, not knowing, unaware, inexperienced,* 504, 532, 1052, 1424, 1572; *blind,* 235; *infatuated,* 448.   *

īgnifer, fera, ferum, adj. (īgnis) *fire-bearing, fiery,* 407.

īgnipēs, pedis, adj. (īgnis; pēs), *fiery-footed,* 662.

īgnis, is, m., *fire, flame, flames, heat,* 23, 82, 131, etc.; pl., *stars,* 148; *flame, love, passion,* 1308; *light,* 280, 1262.   *

ignōrō, 1, *not know, be unaware,* 78.

ignōscō, 3, nōvī, nōtus (nōscō) *overlook; pardon, forgive,* 21.

ignōtus, a, um, adj. (nōtus), *unknown, unfamiliar,* 544, 1446, 1564, 1585.

īlex, icis, f., *oak, holm oak,* 779. *

Īlioneus, eī, m., son of Niobe, 1050.

īlia, ōrum, n., *groin, flanks,* 186, 1366, 1488.

illāc, adv., *that way, there,* 1562.

ille, illa, illud, dem. pron., *that yonder, that, he, she, it,* 3, 14, 31,

etc.; *the one, the former, the
other,* 251, 254, 316, etc.   *

illīc, adv. (ille), *in that place,
yonder, there,* 353, 424, 875,
etc.; repeated, *in one place . . .
in another, yonder . . . yonder,*
627.   *

illinc, adv. (illim, *thence*), *from that
place, thence;* hinc . . . illinc,
*from this side . . . from that,
from* or *on both sides,* 138, 820.

illūc, adv. (illīc), *to that place;*
hūc . . . illūc, *hither . . .
thither, this way and that,* 1255.

imāgō, inis, f., *imitation; likeness,
representation,* 365, 1422; *appearance,* 1093; *sight, vision,*
1309; *representation* (of fact),
385.   *

imber, bris, m., *rain, shower,* 621,
1020, 1500.   *

imitor, 1, freq., *copy after; re-
semble, be like,* 350, 1571.

immānis, e, adj., *monstrous, im-
mense, large,* 358.   *

immēnsus, a, um, adj., *immeasur-
able; boundless, vast, endless,
enormous,* 383, 505, 671, etc.;
as noun, n., *the boundless air,
space,* 1254; in immēnsum, *to
enormous size,* 1294.

immeritus, a, um, adj., *undeserv-
ing, guiltless, innocent,* 1303.

immineō, 2, —, —, *overhang, lean
over,* 324; *overarch,* 355, 1323. *

immītis, e, adj., *not mellow; harsh,
hard, stern, cruel,* 14, 1304.

immittō, 3, mīsī, missus, *send in;
let go, loose, relax,* 1121; p.
immissus, *flowing,* 965; immissō
volātū, *with a plunge,* 1350.

immorior, 3, mortuus, *die in;
die on, fall dying upon,* 1084.

immōtus, a, um, adj., *unmoved;
immovable, motionless,* 1093. *

immūnis, e, adj., *not bound;
exempt from, free from,* 927, 1432.

immurmurō, 1, *whisper in,* 855.

impār, paris, adj., *unequal, ill-
matched,* 824; *too short,* 898.   *

impatiēns, entis, adj., *intolerant,
impatient,* 261.

impediō, 4, *hinder, retard,* 119, 1576.

impellō, 3, pulī, pulsus, *strike
against, beat, drive,* 311, 1442. *

imperfectus, a, um, adj., *unfinished,* 308.

imperō, 1 (parō), *command, order,
bid,* 466, 1425; *control, govern,*
518.

(impes, petis), m., *force, violence,*
1500.

impetus, ūs, m., *assault; rapid
motion, force,* 421; *rush, fury,
impulse,* 544.

impiger, gra, grum, adj., *nimble,
active, after a rapid flight,* 249. *

impius, a, um, adj., *undutiful;
wicked, impious,* 927.   *

impleō, 2, plēvī, plētus, *fill up,
fill full, complete,* 503, 844, 1317,
1368.   *

impōnō, 3, posuī, positus, *place,
put* or *lay upon,* 365, 472, 893,
1375; *put, make,* 1029, 1577;
press upon, 1080.   *

importūnus, a, um, adj., *unfit;
cruel, harsh, unkind,* 75.

impulsus, ūs, m., *blow, shock,
force,* 1340, 1482.

imputō, 1, *attribute, ascribe, charge,*
670.

īmus, a, um, adj. (īnfimus), *inmost, lowest*, 1535; *lowest part of*, 229, 1535, 1569; *below, at the base, at the roots*, 845; pars, *end*, 1514; n. pl. (sc. aequora), *depths, bottom*, 576; *lower world*, 717. *

in, prep. w. acc. and abl., *in;* w. acc., *into, to*, 66, 167, 170, etc.; *into, toward*, 115, 1259; *into, over*, 538; *upon, against*, 407, 623; *for*, 216, 217, 396, 593; *in respect to, in*, 846; in vicēs, *in turn*, 139; in adversum, *against*, 420; in oblīquum, in latus, *sidewise, slantwise*, 478, 1018; w. abl., *in, on, upon*, 42, 72, 92, etc.; *on, over*, 35, 360, 372, 490; *in, on the part of*, 828; *in, at*, 1155. *

Īnachidēs, ae, m., *son of Inachus, king of Argos; Perseus*, 1352.

inamoenus, a, um, adj. (amoenus, *lovely*), *unpleasant, gloomy*, 685.

inānis, e, adj., *empty, void*, 514; *unpeopled*, 1184; *vain*, 1504; as noun, n., *empty air, void, space*, 1019, 1350. *

incalēscō, 3, caluī, —, inch., *grow warm, become heated*, 435.

incēdō, 3, cessī, cessus, *come on, advance*, 719, 1371.

incendium, ī, n., *burning; fire, conflagration*, 556, 642. *

incertus, a, um, adj., *not fixed; undecided, doubtful, uncertain*, 199.

incipiō, 3, cēpī, ceptus (capiō), *take on; begin*, 1044. *

inclūdō, 3, clūsī, clūsus (claudō), *inclose, confine, imprison*, 1110.

incognitus, a, um, adj., *not examined; not looked upon, unseen*, 394. *

incola, ae, m. and f., *inhabitant, resident*, 294, 957.

incrēmentum, ī, n. (incrēscō, *grow on*), *growth, increase, addition*, 1524.

incumbō, 3, cubuī, cubitus, *lay oneself; fall upon, fall on*, 230, 649, 1066; *bend to one's task, put forth all one's strength*, 98. *

incursō, 1, freq. (incurrō, *run into*), *dash against, strike against*, 546, 1144.

incursus, ūs, m., *running to; assault, onset*, 1503.

incurvō, 1 (incurvus, *bent*), *bend up;* pass. *be doubled up, writhe*, 1034.

incustōdītus, a, um, adj., *not watched, unguarded*, 1436.

indāgō, 1 (indu = in), *trace, search out, track*, 244.

inde, adv., *from that place, thence*, 379, 500; *then, next*, 671, 881, 1205, etc. *

indēiectus, a, um, adj., *not cast down*, 1130.

indicium, ī, n., *notice; testimony, evidence*, 856.

indicō, 1 (index, *one who points out*), *point out; declare, disclose, make known*, 1321.

indigena, ae, adj. (indu = in), *sprung from the land;* m., *native*, 85.

indīgnandus, a, um, adj. (p. of indīgnor), *to be despised; unworthy (of), unsuited (to)*, 896.

indīgnor, 1 (indīgnus), *deem un-*

*worthy, resent, be offended, be
angry,* 45, 993. *

indīgnus, a, um, adj., *unworthy;
undeserved, cruel,* 68; *unde-
serving,* 205, 290.

indolēscō, 2, doluī, —, *feel pain;
mourn, grieve, be pained,* 775.

indōtātus, a, um, adj., *without
dowry, portionless,* 1390.

indūcō, 3, dūxī, ductus, *lead in;
bring on, draw over, collect,
gather,* 618, 620, 665, 1104.

induō, 3, uī, ūtus, (indu = in), *put
on, assume, clothe,* 847, 1111. *

indūrēscō, 3, dūruī, —, *harden,*
1377.

Indus, a, um, adj., *of India, In-
dian;* dentēs, *ivory,* 835.

ineō, īre, īvī and iī, itus, *go into,
enter,* 1396.

iners, ertis, adj. (ars), *unskillful,
incompetent,* 43; *inactive, sluggish,* 915.

īnfaustus, a, um, adj., *unpropi-
tious, hapless,* 1457.

īnfectus, a, um, adj. (factus,
faciō), *not done; unfinished, un-
done,* 991.

īnfēlīx, īcis, adj., *unfruitful, unhappy, unlucky, hapless, ill-
starred,* 216, 520, 729, etc. *

īnferior, ius, gen. ōris, adj. (īnferus, *below*), *lower; inferior,*
1286.

īnferius, adv. (n. of īnferior), *lower
down, below,* 549; *too low,* 485.

īnfernus, a, um, adj. (īnferus, *below*), *lower; of the lower regions,
infernal,* 572.

īnfēstus, a, um, adj., *made unsafe;
infested,* 1253.

īnficiō, 3, fēcī, fectus (faciō), *stain,
tinge; paint,* 37; *befoul,* 1497.

īnfitior, 1 (īnfitiae, *denial*), *not to
confess; deny,* 382.

īnfrā, adv. (for īnferā, sc. parte),
*on the under side; below, be-
neath,* 1301; quam, *lower than,*
588.

īnfundō, 3, fūdī, fūsus, *pour into;
breathe into, put into, infuse,*
1198.

ingemō, 3, gemuī, —, *groan over;
give a groan,* 1034. *

ingenium, ī, n., *that born in one;
mind, nature,* 816.

ingēns, gentis, adj., *not natural;
huge, vast,* 700, 1264. *

ingrātus, a, um, adj., *unpleasant;
ungrateful, unthankful,* 143.

inhaereō, 2, haesī, haesus, *stick
fast; fasten (on),* 317.

inhibeō, 2, uī, itus (habeō), *hold
in; restrain, check curb, stay,* 293,
476; *hinder, prevent,* 543.

inimīcus, a, um, adj. (amīcus), *un-
friendly, hostile;* as noun, f., *enemy, foe, rival,* 1072. *

inīquus, a, um, adj. (aequus), *unequal, one-sided, cruel,* 16; *un-
friendly, hostile,* 52; *discontented,
complaining,* 874. *

iniūstus, a, um, adj., *unreasonable;
unfair, unjust,* 841.

inlinō, 3, lēvī, litus, *smear over;
spread upon, lay on,* 907.

inlitus, see **inlinō**.

inlūstris, e, adj., *light; bright, shining, brilliant,* 398.

innātus, a, um, adj. (p. of innāscor,
grow on), *grown on, native,* 1173.

innītor, 3, nīxus, *lean on, support oneself by*, 1594.

innocuus, a, um, adj., *harmless, innocent, inoffensive*, 1168.

innubus, a, um, adj., *unmarried, unwedded, single*, 8.

innumerus, a, um, adj., *countless, numberless*, 242, 1301.

innūptus, a, um, adj., *unmarried, unwedded, single*, 258.

inops, opis, adj. (ops), *insufficient, meager*, 1153; *destitute (of);* mentis, *frantic, crazed*, 541.

inōrnātus, a, um, adj., *unadorned, without ornament*, 279.

inquam, defective verb, *say*, 10, 26, 52, etc. *

inquīrō, 3, quīsīvī, quīsītus (quaerō), *try to find out, inquire, ask*, 294.

inquit, see **inquam**.

inrequiētus, a, um, adj., *restless, without repose*, 656.

inritus, a, um, adj. (ratus, *deciding*), *undeciding; in vain, ineffectual, unavailing, useless*, 722, 1114.

inrōrō, 1 *bedew, sprinkle*, 1205.

īnscius, a, um, adj., *not knowing, ignorant*, 496, 1308. *

īnsequor, 3, secūtus, *follow after, pursue*, 286, 293, 322. *

īnserō, 3, seruī, sertus, *put in, thrust in*, 442, 1538.

īnsidiae, ārum, f., *snares, hidden dangers, pitfalls*, 426. *

īnsonō, 1, sonuī, —, *sound upon; play on*, 829; *roar, resound*, 1322.

īnspīrō, 1, *breathe into*, 1175. *

īnstabilis, e, adj., *unsteady*, 512; *movable*, **845.**

īnstar, indecl., n., *likeness;* w. gen., *like*, 202.

īnstō, 1, stitī, statūrus, *stand upon; pursue, beset*, 9, 1503; *urge, press, entreat, insist*, 1318.*

īnstrictus, a, um, p. of īnstringō, *bind; bound; inlaid*, 835.

īnstruō, 3, strūxī, strūctus, *build in; prepare, set*, 1395; *teach*, 1579. *

īnsum, esse, fuī, —, *be in one, one has*, 57.

intemptātus, a, um, adj., *untouched, untried*, 26.

intendō, 3, tendī, tentus, *stretch out, extend*, 728.

inter, prep. w. acc., *between, among*, 488, 584, 719, etc.; inter sē, *together*, 1223, 1312. *

interdum, adv., *sometimes, at times, occasionally*, 531, 632, 1499. *

intereā, adv. (inter ea), *in the meantime, meanwhile*, 501, 651, 891, etc. *

intereō, īre, iī, itūrus, *go among; perish*, 65, 617.

interius, adv. (n. of interior, *inner*), *within*, 1094. *

internōdium, ī, n. (nōdus, *knot*), *place between two joints*, 1045.

interritus, a, um, adj., *undismayed, undaunted, not afraid*, 57.

intexō, 3, texuī, textus, *weave in, interweave*, 963.

intibum, ī, n., *endive, succory*, 903.

intimus, a, um, adj., *inmost*, 1040.*

intonō, 1, uī, —, *thunder*, 622.

intōnsus, a, um, adj., *unshorn, with long hair*, 345, 1043.

intrā, adv., *on the inside; within*, 1097.

intremō, 3, tremuī, —, *tremble, shake to the center*, 521, 1125.

intrō, 1, *go into, enter*, 368, 878, 1118, 1476.

introitus, ūs, m. (intrō), *going in; entrance*, 1405.

intus, adv., *on the inside; within*, 442. *

inūtilis, e, adj., *useless; unserviceable, harmful, injurious*, 770.

inveniō, 4, vēnī, ventus, *come upon; discover, find*, 170, 677, 751, 1425.

inventum, ī, n. (p. of inveniō), *invention, discovery*, 303.

invideō, 2, vīdī, vīsus, *look askance at; grudge, refuse, deny*, 224.

invidia, ae, f., *envy; jealousy*, 25; *ill will, hate, unpopularity*, 69.

invidiōsus, a, um, adj. (invidia), *full of envy; to be envied, enviable*, 758, 1065.

invidus, a, um, adj., *envious, envying*, 83; *stingy, hateful*, 140.

invīsus, a, um, adj. (p. of invideō), *detested, hateful*, 800. *

invītus, a, um, adj., *against the will; unwilling, reluctant*, 103, 500.

invocō, 1, *call upon, appeal to*, 81.

involvō, 3, volvī, volūtus, *roll upon; enwrap, envelop*, 563.

ipse, a, um, dem. pron., *self, himself, herself, in person, very, even*, 7, 27, 91, etc. *

īra, ae, f., *anger, passion*, 654, 964, 1115; *spite*, 235. *

īrāscor, 3, īrātus (īra), *be angry, be in a rage*, 1058.

Īris, idis, f., *goddess of the rainbow, messenger of the gods*, 1112.

is, ea, id, dem. pron., *this, that*, 13, 134, 459, etc. *

Ismēnos, ī, m., *one of the sons of Niobe*, 1013.

iste, a, ud, dem. pron., *that, that of yours*, 239, 270, 327, 402; *such*, 1311.

ita, adv., *in this manner, thus, so*, 52, 525, 589, etc.

iter, itineris, n., *going; way, road, course*, 426, 481, 518, 1601; *passage way, channel*, 136. *

iterō, 1 (iterum), *repeat;* iactāta, *throw repeatedly*, 1381.

iterum, adv., *a second time, again*, 111, 730, 742, 1588.

iuba, ae, f., *mane*, 1026.

iubeō, 2, iussī, iussus, *command, bid, order*, 88, 389, 812, etc.; *bid, prompt*, 53, 178. *

iūdex, icis, m. and f., *judge, umpire*, 54, 824, 825, 828.

iūdicium, ī, n. (iūdex), *judgment, decision*, 840, 943.

iugālis, e, adj. (iugum), *of a yoke; marriage, nuptial*, 265.

iūgerum, ī, n., *juger, a measure of land, acre*, 241.

iugulum, ī, n., *throat, neck*, 1047.

iugum, ī, n., *yoke*, 457, 510, 626, 1432; *mountain peak, ridge*, 1291, 1365; *slope, side*, 808. *

iungō, 3, iūnxī, iūnctus, *yoke, harness*, 466; *join, unite*, 141, 223, 480, etc.; *in marriage*, 872; *join, clasp*, 1033; ōrdine iūnctus, *continuously, in succession,* 766; iūnctissimus, *closely joined,* 740. *

Iūnō, ōnis, f., *Juno, sister and wife of Jupiter,* 996. *

Iūnōnius, a, um, adj., *of Juno, sacred to Juno,* 1596. *

Iuppiter, Iovis, m., *Jupiter, king of the gods,* 299. *

iūrō, 1 (iūs), *swear, take an oath,* 394, 397; *swear by,* 449.

iūs, iūris, n., *bond, rites,* 127; *power, authority,* 707, 1059; *control,* 396. *

iussum, ī, n. (p. of iubeō), *order, command,* 467, 1219. *

iūstē, adv. (iūstus), *rightly, justly,* 1325.

iūstus, a, um, adj. (iūs), *just, righteous, upright,* 941, 1211; *proper, regular,* 511; *allotted,* 706. *

iuvenālis, e, adj. (iuvenis), *youthful,* 345, 498, 872.

iuvenāliter, adv. (iuvenālis), *like a youth, with youthful strength,* 116.

iuvenca, ae, f. *young cow, heifer,* 1436.

iuvenīlis, e, adj. (iuvenis), *of youth; youthful,* 1030.

iuvenis, is, adj., *young, youthful,* 313, 769; as noun, *young man, youth,* 18, 24, 30, etc. *

iuventūs, tūtis, f., *youth;* = iuvenēs, 1545. *

iuvō, 1, iūvī, iūtus, *help, aid, assist,* 27, 489, 1116. *

Ixīōn, onis, m., *king of the Lapithae,* 712.

L

labefaciō, 3, fēcī, factus (labō), *make totter; wrench loose, loosen,* 1491.

labō, 1, *totter; roll,* 511.

lābor, 3, lāpsus, *slip down* or *off, fall,* 168; p. lābēns, as adj., *flowing,* 808. *

labor, ōris, m., *labor, toil, exertion, effort,* 326, 657, 1114, 1371; *exercise,* 1029; *trouble, difficulty,* 476. *

labōrō, 1 (labor), *toil, be in distress, suffer,* 607. *

lāc, lactis, n., *milk,* 903.

lacer, era, erum, adj., *torn; broken, shattered,* 629.

lacertus, ī, m., *upper arm, arm,* 205, 267, 283, etc.

lacrima, ae, f., *tear,* 184, 207, 650, etc. *

lacrimōsus, a, um, adj. (lacrima), *tearful; filling the eyes with tears,* 676.

lacus, ūs, m., *lake, pool,* 569.

laedō, 3, laesī, laesus, *hurt, wound,* 255, 290, 1221, 1353, 1509; *injure, scar,* 1373; *insult, offend,* 328. *

laetus, a, um, adj., *joyful, cheerful, happy, rejoicing,* 341, 675, 1393; pred., *gladly, rejoicing,* 768, 776. *

laevus, a, um, adj., *left, on the left,* 1386, 1596; as noun, f., sc. manus, *left hand, left arm,* 1413; ā laevā, *on the left side,* 373, 836, 1288.

lambō, 3, —, —, *lick, lap,* 1478.

lāmina, ae, f., *thin plate* (of metal); *gold leaf,* 794.

lancea, ae, f., *light spear, lance,*
1474.

laniō, 1 (lanius, *butcher*), *tear in
pieces, rend, mangle,* 171, 206,
646, 1037.

lapis, idis, m., *stone,* 741, 1227,
1233, etc. *

lāpsus, ūs, m., *falling; course,
flight,* 1005.

largus, a, um, adj., *abundant,
bountiful,* 1391. *

lascīvus, a, um, adj., *wanton,
sportive, playful, frolicsome,* 238.

lassō, 1 (lassus), *make faint, weary,
exhaust,* 1149.

lassus, a, um, adj., *weary, faint,
exhausted,* 104.

lātē, adv. (lātus), *far and wide, on
all sides,* 629, 818, 1007, 1109. *

latebra, ae, f., *hiding place; con-
cealment, riddle,* 1222.

lateō, 2, uī, —, *lie hid, hide, be con-
cealed,* 155, 284, 580, 1084,
1131. *

Latius, a, um, adj., *of Latium,
Latin,* 341.

Lātōna, ae, f., the mother of
Apollo and Diana, 968.

Lātōus, a, um, adj., *of Latona,*
1063.

lātus, a, um, adj., *wide, broad,* 154,
478, 618, 1156, 1323. *

latus, eris, n., *side, flank,* 115,
1358, 1444; in latus, *sidewise,*
1018. *

laudō, 1 (laus), *praise, commend,
extol,* 23, 282.

laurea, ae, f. (laureus, *of laurel*),
laurel tree, 347.

laurus, ī, f., *laurel tree, laurel,* 340,
833, 990.

laus, laudis, f., *praise, commenda-
tion, glory, honor,* 244; *title to
praise, achievement* (i.e. *swiftness*), 4. *

lavō, 1 or 3, lāvī, lautus or lōtus,
wash, bathe, 786.

lea, ae, f., *lioness,* 169.

leaena, ae, f., *lioness,* 164.

Lebinthos, ī, f., an island of the
Aegean, 1598.

lectus, ī, m., *couch, bed,* 893, 896.

legō, 3, lēgī, lēctus, *gather; read,*
649; *trace,* 1438. *

Lenaeus, a, um, adj., *of the wine
press,* an epithet of Bacchus,
802.

lēnis, e, adj., *soft, gentle,* 860.

lentē, adv. (lentus), *slowly, de-
liberately,* 847, 1436.

lentus, a, um, adj., *pliant; tough,*
1487.

leō, ōnis, m., *lion,* 181, 287, 1145,
1473, 1502; the constellation
Leo, 429.

lepus, oris, m., *hare,* 315.

Lēthaea, ae, f., wife of Ōlenos, 740.

lētō, 1, (lētum), *kill, slay,* 1476.

lētum, ī, n., *death, destruction,* 57,
218, 709, 1085, 1541.

levis, e, adj., *light, slight,* 274,
285, 311, etc. *

levitās, ātis, f. (levis), *lightness,*
512.

leviter, adv. (levis), *lightly, slowly,*
904.

levō, 1 (levis), *lift up, raise,* 507;
support, 930, 1588; *take down,*
887; *lighten, mitigate, alleviate,*
592. *

lēx, lēgis, f., *law; condition, stipulation, terms,* 13, 15, 720, 1336;

sine lēge, *carelessly,* 259; *recklessly,* 545. *

līber, era, erum, adj., *free; permitted, allowed,* 491.

Līber, erī, m., an Italian god identified with Bacchus, 775.

liber, brī, m., *inner bark,* 330.

līberō, 1 (līber), *free; shake free, clear,* 826.

lībō, 1, *pour as a libation; dedicate, consecrate,* 1205; *draw,* 1448; *touch lightly, graze,* 94. *

lībrō, 1 (lībra, *balance*), *poise,* 622, 1577.

Libycus, a, um, adj., of Libya, *Libyan, African,* 1250.

Libyē, ēs, f., *Libya, Africa,* 568. *

licentia, ae, f. (licēns, p. of licet), *freedom, license, unrestrained liberty,* 1150.

licet, 2, licuit and licitum est, *it is lawful; it is permitted, it is allowed,* 61, 399, 401, etc. *

līgnum, ī, n., *gathered wood; wood,* 337.

ligō, 1, *unite; bind, fasten,* 740, 1298.

limbus, ī, m., *border, fringe,* 34.

līmes, itis, m., *path, track,* 367, 478, 1579.

līmus, ī, m., *slime, mud,* 1183.

lingua, ae, f., *tongue,* 1002, 1094, 1303, etc.

līnum, ī, n., *flax; thread, cord,* 1569.

liquidus, a, um, adj., *flowing, running,* 786; *watery liquid,* 1165; *transparent,* 902, 1300; *clear, clear, settled,* 1204.

liquor, 3, —, *be fluid; melt, dissolve,* 1100. *

liquor, ōris, m., *fluid; liquid, water,* 1205.

lītus, oris, n., *shore, seashore,* 490, 1133, 1180, 1367. *

līvēns, entis, adj. (p. of līveō, *be dark*), *dark, livid,* 1068, 1347.

locus, ī, m., pl. loca, ōrum, n., *place, spot, region,* 150, 198, 536, etc.; *place for rest, lodging,* 868; pl., *land, ground,* 1181; *region,* 1398; locum dare, *make room,* 910; medius locō, *in the center,* 379.

longē, adv. (longus), *long, far, far off,* 105, 603, 1049, etc. *

longus, a, um, adj., *long, continued, extended,* 84, 134, 176, etc.; *great,* 909; *deep,* 1458; *tall,* 1499. *

loquor, 3, locūtus, *speak, say,* 130, 145, 307, etc. *

lōrīca, ae, f., *corselet, cuirass,* 1484.

lōrum, ī, n., *thong;* pl., *reins,* 475, 493, 541, 626.

lūceō, 2, lūxī, —, *be light; shine, glitter, sparkle,* 372.

Lūcifer, ferī, m. (m. of lūcifer, *light-bringing*), the morning star, son of Aurora, 463; hence *day,* 768.

luctor, 1 (lucta. *wrestling*), *wrestle, struggle, contend,* 1031. *

lūctus, ūs, m., *sorrow, mourning, grief,* 227, 472, 640, 654, 1070.

lūcus, ī, m., *sacred grove; wood, grove,* 424, 1142, 1456; *clump,* 858. *

lūgubris, e, adj., *sorrowful, sorrowing, mourning,* 645, 1324.

lūmen, inis, n., *light,* 352, 371,

458, etc., *eye*, 721, 977, 1036.*

lūna, ae, f., *moon*, 166, 465; personified, 549. *

luō, 3, luī, —, *loose; pay, suffer*, 926. *

lupus, ī, m., *wolf*, 287, 1145.

lūstrō, 1 (lūstrum, *purification*), *purify; traverse, wander through*, 261. *

lūsus, ūs, m. (lūdō, *play*), *play, sport*, 1575.

lūx, lūcis, f., *light*, 158, 383, 653; *sunlight, daylight*, 276; *life*, 1061.*

Lȳdus, a, um, adj., *of Lydia* (in *Asia Minor*), *Lydian*, 768.

Lyncīdēs, ae, m., *descendant of Lynceus*, father of Atlas; *Perseus*, 1399.

lyra, ae, f., *lyre*, 1392.

M

mactō, 1 (mactus, *honored*), *honor; sacrifice, slay*, 922, 1387.

madefaciō, 3, fēcī, factus (madeō, *be wet*), *make wet, drench, steep*, 193.

madēscō, 3, maduī, — (madeō, *be wet*), *become wet, be soaked* or *moistened*, 716, 1361, 1586.

madidus, a, um, adj., *wet, moist, dripping*, 539, 1105.

maestus, a, um, adj., *full of sadness, sorrowful, gloomy*, 1092. *

magis, adv., *more, all the more*, 31, 101, 131. *

māgnanimus, a, um, adj. (māgnus; animus), *great souled, high spirited, presumptuous*, 459. *

māgnus, a, um, adj., *large, great, mighty*, 49, 402, 555, etc. *

māior, māius, gen. māiōris, comp.

of māgnus, *greater*, 410, 984, 1527. *

male, adv. (malus,) *ill, poorly, not aright*, 496, 772, 806.

mālō, mālle, māluī, — (magis; volō), *prefer, wish*, 51, 523.

mālum, ī, n., *apple*, 118, 912.

malus, a, um, adj., *bad, wicked, evil;* as noun, n., *evil, misfortune, calamity*, 643, 645, 776, etc.

mandō, 1 (manus), *put in hand; deliver, consign, commit*, 488.

māne, adv. (māne, *morn*), *in the morning*, 411.

maneō, 2, mānsī, mānsus, *stay, remain, tarry, wait*, 286, 287, 806, etc.; *wait for, await*, 1328; *be left*, 1200. *

mānēs, ium, m., *departed spirits, shades, world below*, 614.

manifēstus, a, um, adj. (manus), *plainly seen, clear, distinct*, 481, 1238.

mānō, 1, āvī, —, *flow, drip, trickle*, 1100, 1307, 1506.

manus, ūs, f., *hand*, 21, 91, 215, etc. *

mare, is, n., *sea*, 413, 444, 512, etc. *

margō, ginis, f., *edge, border, margin*, 725, 1535.

marītus, a, um, adj., *married;* m., *husband*, 975.

marmor, oris, n., *marble*, 939, 1239; *gravestone*, 649; pl., *stone*, 1100.

marmoreus, a, um, adj., *made of marble, marble*, 1308.

Mārs, Mārtis, m., *the god of war; strife*, 1544. *

Mārtius, a, um, adj. (Mārs), *of Mars, sacred to Mars,* 1453.

massa, ae, f., *lump, mass,* 903; *nugget,* 782.

māter, tris, f., *mother,* 585, 1013, 1057, etc.   *

māteria, ae, f. (māter), *stuff, matter, material,* 353; *means, source,* i. e. *fuel,* 554.

māternus, a, um, adj. (māter), *of a mother, maternal,* 1221, 1303, 1320.

mātūrēscō, 3, mātūruī, —(mā- tūrō, *ripen*), *become ripe, ripen,* 859.

mātūrus, a, um, adj. *ripe; of ripe age,* 706.

māximus, a, um, adj. (māgnus), *greatest, largest,* 1152; *great, mighty,* 634, 971.   *

medicāmen, inis, n. (medicō, *drug*), *drug, ointment,* 470.

medicīna, ae, f. (medicus, *physi- cian*), *the art of healing, medicine,* 303.

medius, a, um, adj., *middle, cen- tral, middle of,* 88, 379, 412, etc.; *in the midst,* 344; *enclosed,* 354; *intervening,* 1342; hōrae, *interval,* 891; parte, *half,* 283, 1464; n. as noun, *middle,* 42, 485, 735, etc.   *

medulla, ae, f., *marrow,* 255; *pith,* 1376.

Medūsa, ae, f., a Gorgon, 1288.

Medūsaeus, a, um, adj. *of Medusa, Medusan,* 692.

Megarēius, a, um, adj., *of Mega- reus, son of Megareus,* 100.

Megareus, eī, m., son of Onches-

tius and father of Hippomenes, 46.

mel, mellis, n., *honey,* 1598.   *

melior, ius, adj., comp. of bonus, *better, more upright,* 1163; *more gentle, better disposed,* 756; *more sensible,* 775; *fairer, more beau- tiful,* 284.   *

melius, adv., comp. of bene, *better; more wisely,* 489.   *

membrum, ī, n., *limb, member* (of the body), 201, 336, 538, etc.   *

memor, oris, adj., *mindful of, re- membering,* 1275.   *

memorābilis, e, adj. (memorō), *notable, famous, glorious,* 49, 1248.

memorō, 1 (memor), *bring to re- membrance; relate, tell,* 1321.

mēns, mentis, f., *mind, heart, soul,* 57, 129, 817, etc.; mentis inops, *frantic,* 541.   *

mēnsa, ae, f., *table,* 789 (pl.), 897, 898; pl., *feast, banquet,* 970; se- cunda, *dessert,* 910.   *

mēnsis, is, m., *month;* personified, 373.   *

menta, ae, f., *mint,* 900.

mentior, 4, *invent; state falsely,* 698; *falsely boast,* 1283.

Mercurius, ī, m. (merx, *wares*), *Mercury,* god of trade, messen- ger of the gods, 1386.

mereō, 2, uī, itus, *deserve, be worthy of,* 590, 601, 602, 663.

mergō, 3, mersī, mersus, *plunge, sink, submerge,* 933, 1136; *over- whelm,* 1214.

mergus, ī, m., *diver* (a water fowl), 865.

meritum, ī, n. (p. of mereō), *thing*

deserved; deserts, kindness, services, 1334. *

meritus, a, um, adj. (p. of mereō), *deserved, merited,* 926; *deserved (ly),* 800.

Merops, opis, m., a king of Ethiopia, 525.

merum, ī, n. (merus, *pure*), *pure or unmixed wine, wine,* 760. *

messis, is, f., *gathering* (of crops); *harvest, sheaf* (of grain), 783.

mēta, ae, f., *cone; goal,* a conical column at the end of the course, 105; *turning point, bounds,* 490; *course, race,* 38. *

mētior, 4, mēnsus, *measure, estimate,* 529.

metuēns, entis, adj. (p. of metuō), *fearing;* deōrum, *god-fearing,* 1164.

metuō, 3, uī, — (metus), *fear, be afraid,* 726, 974, 1279. *

metus, ūs, m., *fear, alarm, dread, apprehension,* 178, 195, 440, 986.*

meus, a, um, poss. pron. (mē), *my, mine,* 20, 62, 70, etc. *

micāns, antis, adj. (p. of micō), *shining, flashing, glittering, sparkling,* 280, 350, 388. *

micō, 1, uī, —, *vibrate; glitter, flash,* 1454. *

Midas, ae, m., a king of Phrygia, son of Cybele, 762.

mīlle, adj., indecl., *a thousand,* 868, 869, 1166, 1167, 1268. *

minae, ārum, f., *threats, menaces,* 667, 1284.

Minerva, ae, f., goddess of wisdom, 901.

minimus, a, um, adj. (parvus), *smallest, least,* 137, 1087, 1088,

1566; *very small, very slight, tiny,* 921, 1054.

minister, trī, m., *servant, attendant,* 789, 1447. *

ministrō, 1 (minister), *serve, supply, furnish,* 600. *

minitor, 1 (minor, *jut forth*), *threaten,* 540.

minor, minus, gen. ōris, comp of parvus; *smaller, less,* 247. *

Mīnōs, ōis, m., king of Crete, 1563.

minuō, 3, uī, ūtus, *make small; cut into small pieces, break up,* 885.

minus, adv. (minor), *less,* 392. *

mīrābilis, e, adj. (mīror), *marvelous, wonderful,* 1379, 1575. *

mīrāculum, ī, n. (mīror), *strange sight, monster,* 534.

mīrātor, ōris, m. (mīror), *admirer,* 1274.

mīror, 1 (mīrus), *marvel at, wonder at, wonder,* 31, 459, 935, etc. *

misceō, 2, miscuī, mixtus, *mix, mingle, blend, join,* 208, 795, 911, 1285, 1360. *

miser, era, erum, adj., *wretched, unfortunate, poor, miserable,* 73, 218, 222, etc.; *sad, grieving,* 1325. *

miserābilis, e, adj. (miseror, *lament*), *wretched, miserable,* 225, 640.

miserandus, a, um, adj. (p. of miseror, *lament*), *to be pitied,* 1065; *wretched,* 177, 1193. *

misereor, 2, miseritus (miser), *pity, have compassion,* 605, 803.

mītis, e, adj., *mild, gentle, merciful,* 804, 1214, 1237; *delicate,* 599.

mittō, 3, mīsī, missus, *let go, send, shoot*, 933; *let fall, throw, hurl*, 106, 623, 666, etc.; *send forth*, 1459; *furnish, give up*, 908.   *

moderāmen, inis, n. (moderor), *control, management, guidance*, 396, 415.

moderātē, adv. (moderātus, p. of moderor), *with moderation; slowly, gently*, 292, 293.

moderor, 1 (modus), *set a measure; manage, guide, control*, 1012.

modestus, a, um, adj. (modus), *keeping due measure; modest*, (pred.) *modestly*, 1315.

modicus, a, um, adj. (modus), *in proper measure; of a tolerable size, moderate*, 863.

modo, adv. (modus), *by a measure; only, merely*, 641, 928; *if only, provided*, 1334; *just now, but now, a little while ago*, 22, 241, 352, etc.; modo . . . modo (nunc), *now . . . now, at one time . . at another*, 547, 752, 1353, etc.

modulor, 1 (modus), *accompany*, 822.

modus, ī, m., *measure; manner, way*, 1484; quō modō, *how?* 1194.   *

moenia, ōrum, n., *defensive walls, city walls*, 555, 976, 1007, etc. *

molāris, is, m. (mola, *mill stone*), *large stone*, 1480.   *

mōlēs, is, f., *mass, weight, pile*, 1404; *bank, dike*, 360, 1120. *

mōlior, 4 (mōlēs), *make exertion; drive, guide*, 483.   *

molliō, 4 (mollis), *make soft, soften*, 1009, 1236, 1573, 1602; *carpet*, 1374.   *

mollis, e, adj., *yielding; soft, tender, softened*, 50, 330, 892, 1045.   *

moneō, 2, *advise, warn*, 1580.

monitum, ī, n. (p. of moneō), *advice, warning, counsel*, 474, 1231.

monitus, ūs, m. (moneō), *advice, warning, command*, 451, 1548, 1586.

mōns, montis, m., *mountain, mountain range*, 294, 557, 575, etc.   *

mōnstrum, ī, n., *divine omen; monster*, 692, 1248, 1377.

montānus, a, um, adj. (mōns), *of mountains, mountain-*, 815,1151.

monumentum, ī, n., *that which reminds; memorial, reminder*, 228.

mora, ae, f., *delay*, 84, 100, 110, etc.; *slowness*, 119; *lapse of time, time*, 1236.   *

mordeō, 2, momordī, morsus, *bite, bite into*, 1490.

moribundus, a, um, adj. (morior), *expiring, dying*, 1080.

morior, morī, mortuus, *expire, die*, 187, 730; moriēns, as adj., *dying*, 1017, 1061.

moror, 1 (mora), *delay*, 702; *go more slowly*, 102.   *

mors, mortis, f., *death*, 13, 212, 219, etc.   *

morsus, ūs, m., (mordeō), *bite; teeth, jaws*, 180. 320, 1356, 1469.   *

mortālis, e, adj. (mors), *subject to death; mortal, human*, 404, 688, 866, 1101, 1190; *man-producing*, 1526.   *

mōrum, ī, n. (mōrus), *fruit of the mulberry tree, mulberry,* 194.

mōrus, ī, f., *mulberry tree,* 157.

mōs, mōris, m., *way, manner,* 1354; pl., *character, nature,* 1399. *

mōtus, ūs, m., *moving; movement, motion,* 677, 1125; mōtūs reddere, *move,* 1096.

moveō, 2, mōvī, mōtus, *move, stir, set in motion,* 506, 619, 860, etc.; *toss, shake,* 964; *ply,* 710, 1300; *prompt,* 313; *affect, influence, touch,* 56, 84, 1053, 1215, 1229; *plow,* 1523; pass. *move,* 845, 1527.*

mox, adv., *soon, presently, afterward, later,* 226, 647, 980, etc.

mucrō, ōnis, m., *sharp point,* 229.

mūgītus, ūs, m. (mūgiō, *bellow*), *bellowing, lowing,* 1442.

mulceō, 2, mulsī, mulsus, *stroke, calm, soothe,* 1172, 1225. *

Mulciber, erī, m., an epithet of Vulcan, 353.

multifidus, a, um, adj. (multus), *divided into many pieces, many-cleft,* 884.

multō, adv. (abl. n. of multus), *by much, by far, much,* 985.

multus, a, um, adj., *much, abundant, copious,* 169; *great,* 1491; pl., *many,* 1088; as noun, m., *many (men),* 260; n. sing., *much,* 528; pl., *many things, a great deal,* 151, 985; multum as adv., *very,* 222. *

mundus, ī, m., *world, universe,* 383, 443, 464, etc.

mūnīmen, inis, n. (mūniō, *defend*), *means of defense; defense, protection,* 1404.

mūnus, eris, n., *duty, function,* 1397; *reward, gift, boon,* 114, 392, 403, etc. *

mūrex, icis m., *purple-fish,* a prickly shellfish, 1173; *purple* made from the murex, 834.

murmur, uris, n., *murmuring, whisper,* 137, 150; *prayer,* 992. *

mūrus, ī, m., *wall,* 125, 863. *

mūscus, ī, m., *moss,* 1208.

mūtābilis, e, adj. (mūtō), *changeable, open to persuasion,* 493.

mūtō, 1, freq. (moveō), *change, transform, alter,* 328, 1243. *

mūtus, a, um, adj., *speechless, dumb, still, deep* (silence), 723.

mūtuus, a, um, adj. (mūtō), *borrowed; with one another, mutual,* 954, 1544.

N

nāis, —, pl. nāides, um, f., *water nymph, Naiad,* 636, 679.

nam, conj., *for, you know,* 232, 353, 640, etc.

namque, conj. (nam que), *for, and in fact,* 46, 1195. *

nāris, is, f., *nostril,* 433.

nārrō, 1 (gnārus, *knowing*), *make known; tell, relate,* 197, 951, 959, 1403.

nāscor, 3, nātus, *be born, be produced, spring,* 1374, 1417. *

nāta, ae, f. (nātus), *daughter,* 264, 359, 580, etc. *

nātālis, e, adj. (nātus), *of birth, native,* 1560.

natō, 1, freq. (nō), *swim, float,* 579.

nātūra, ae, f., *birth; nature, character,* 737, 1237, 1382, 1565.

nātus, a, um, adj. (p. of nāscor),

sprung from; as noun, m., *son,* 400, 437, 470, etc.; pl., *children,* 1000. *

nāvigō, 1 (nāvis), *sail, cruise,* 1137. *

nāvis, is, f., *boat,* 511, 1338. *

-ne, enclitic particle; as adv., in an interrogative sentence, 422, 596; as conj., in indirect question, *whether, or,* 4, 875. *

nē, conj., *not; that not, lest,* 24, 195, 290, etc.; as adv., *not,* 449, 1537.*

nebula, ae, f., *mist, vapor, cloud,* 507, 1108.

nec or **neque,** conj., *not, and not, but not,* repeated, *neither . . . nor,* 10, 48, 55, etc.; *not even,* 220; neque iam, *no longer,* 562. *

necō, 1, *kill, put to death, destroy,* 925, 1470.

nefās, indecl., n. (fās), *impiety; wrong, outrage,* 1226.

negō, 1, *say no; deny, refuse,* 60, 75, 323, etc.; *deny* (a fact), 390, 695, 982.

nēmō, —, nēminī, m. and f. (nē; homō), *no one, nobody,* 659, 1558.

nemus, oris, n., *woodland, grove,* 261, 1465, 1476. *

nepōs, ōtis, m., *grandson, descendant,* 264, 504, 1555.

Neptūnius, a, um, adj., *of Neptune, Neptunian,* 80, 106.

Neptūnus, ī, m., *god of the sea,* 47. *

neque, see **nec.**

nequeō, 4, īvī, —, *be unable, cannot,* 1243. *

nēquīquam, adv. (quisquam), *in vain, to no purpose,* 145, 673.

Nērēis, idis, f., *daughter of Nereus, Nereid, sea-nymph,* 1143.

Nēreus, eī, m., a sea god, 579.

nervōsus, a, um, adj. (nervus), *sinewy, muscular,* 1045.

nervus, ī, m., *sinew; cord, bowstring,* 237, 1032, 1075; *string,* pl., *lyre,* 300, 686, 710.

nēsciō, 4, īvī, —, *not know, be ignorant,* 296, 565; w. quis, quid, *some one, something,* 243. *

nēscius, a, um, adj., *unknowing, in one's ignorance,* 406. *

neu or **nēve,** adv., *and not, nor, and that not, and lest,* 120, 154, 665, etc.; repeated, *and not . . nor,* 486, 487. *

nex, necis, f., *death,* 68, 182, 663, 734.

(nexus, ūs) m. (only abl. sing. and pl., and nom. pl.), *binding together; grapple, clasp, embrace,* 1031, 1462.

nīdus, ī, m., *nest,* 1590.

niger, gra, grum, adj., *dark, black,* 539, 567, 888, 1497.

nihil, indecl., n., *nothing,* 1093.

nil, for nihil, *nothing,* 729; as adv., *in no respect, not at all,* 6.

nimbus, ī, m., *rain storm; rain cloud,* 1102, 1107, 1110, 1169. *

nimis, adv., *beyond measure; overmuch, too* (*much*), 276.

nimius, a, um, adj. (nimis), *beyond measure; too much, too great,* 142, 512; *too eager, too ardent,* 18.

Ninus, ī, m., a king of Assyria, husband of Semiramis, 155.

Niobē, ēs, f., daughter of Tantalus, wife of Amphion, 962.

nisi, conj. (nē; sī), *if not,* 616,

1234; *unless, except,* 10, 91,729, etc.

niteō, 2, nituī, —, *shine, glitter, gleam,* 88.   *

nitidus, a, um, adj. (niteō), *gleaming, sparkling, shining,* 107, 116, 351, 1030.

nītor, 3, nīxus and nīsus, *exert oneself, struggle, strive,* 420, 931, 1365.

nitor, ōris, m. (niteō), *brightness; beauty, charm,* 333.

niveus, a, um, adj. (nix, *snow*), *snowy; snow-white,* 156.

nō, 1, āvī, —, *swim, float,* 359, 1145.   *

nocēns, entis, adj. (p. of noceō), *hurting; guilty, culpable,* 177, 739.

noceō, 2, cuī, citūrus, *do harm, hurt, injure,* 774, 816, 984, 1231.

nocturnus, a, um, adj. (nox), *of night,* 148.

nōlō, nōlle, nōluī, —(volō), *wish . . . not, be unwilling,* 63, 73, 709, 1319.

nōmen, inis, n., *means of knowing; name,* 85, 256, 384, etc.; *fame, reputation,* 49.   *

nōminō, 1 (nōmen), *call by name, call,* 211.

nōn, adv., *not, by no means,* 2, 3, 41, etc.   *

nōndum, adv., *not yet,* 22, 195, 496, 1204, 1321.

nōscō, 3, nōvī, nōtus, *get knowledge of;* pf., *know,* 533.

noster, tra, trum, poss. adj., *of us; our, my,* 59, 69, 82, etc.   *

nōtitia, ae, f. (nōtus), *being known; acquaintance,* 126.

notō, 1 (nota), *mark; scratch,* 291; *mark, notice, observe,* 38, 134.

nōtus, a, um, adj. (p. of nōscō), *known,* 22; *well known, familiar,* 184, 696; *customary, usual,* 1204.   *

Notus, ī, m., the south wind, 1105.*

novitās, ātis, f. (novus), *newness, novelty,* 379; *strangeness, unusualness,* 797, 918.   *

novō, 1 (novus), *make new, change,* 1565.

novus, a, um, adj., *new, fresh,* 679, 1378, 1536; *new-formed,* 335; *new, strange,* 1151; *early,* 375; superl., *last,* 38, 223, 463.   *

nox, noctis, f., *night,* 146, 151, **159,** etc.   *

nūbēs, is, f., *cloud, vapor, mist,* 618, 620, 1006, etc.   *

nūbila, ōrum, n. (nūbilus, *cloudy*), *clouds, rain-clouds,* 550, **1109,** 1169, 1191.

nūbō, 3, nūpsī, nūptus, *be married, wed,* 62.

nūdō, 1 (nūdus), *lay bare, expose, uncover,* 309; *strip, despoil,* 1182.   *

nūdus, a, um, adj., *bare, exposed, uncovered,* 283, 376, 1025, 1603. *

nūllus, a, um, adj. (ūllus), *not any, none, no,* 62, 305, 427, etc.; as noun, m., *no one,* 91, 134, 543, 996.   *

nūmen, inis, n., *nod; divine will, command, power,* 1202, 1245; *divinity, god,* 364, 665, 687, etc.; *shrine, oracle,* 969, 1168.   *

numerō, 1 (numerus), *count, reckon, number,* 58.

numerus, ī, m., *number,* 988.   *

numquam, adv. (nē; umquam), *at
no time, never,* 523.

nunc, adv. (num), *now, at present,*
98, 99, 114, etc.   *

nūntia, ae, f. (nūntius, *messenger*),
messenger, 1111.

nūper, adv., *newly, recently,* 236,
1135.

nūpta, ae, f. (p. of nūbō), *wife;*
nova, *bride,* 678.

nurus, ūs, f., *daughter-in-law,* 980.

nūtō, 1, *nod, wave to and fro,* 1529.

nūtriō, 4, *nourish, foster, keep alive,*
278, 883.

nūtus, —, ū, m., *nodding; nod,* 130.

nux, nucis, f., *nut,* 911.

nympha, ae, f., *bride; young woman, nymph,* 254, 286, 287, etc.*

O

O, interj , *O, oh,* 102, 181, 222, etc.*

obdūcō, 3, dūxī, ductus, *draw
before; cover, conceal, veil,* 640.

obeō, īre, īvī, itus, *go to meet; come
upon, cover,* 333.

obiectō, 1, freq. (obiciō, *throw
before*), *throw against; cast up,
charge, reproach with, accuse of,*
670.

obitus, -ūs, m., *going to; death,*
1558.

oblinō, 3, lēvī, litus, *smear over, be-
daub,* 164.

oblīquus, a, um, adj., *sidelong;* ab
oblīquō, *sideways,* 116; in oblīquum, *obliquely,* 478.

oblitus, see oblinō.

oblītus, see oblīvīscor.

oblīvīscor, 3, lītus, *forget,* 1310.

oborior, 4, ortus, *rise, spring up,
appear,* 522, 737, 1186, 1317.

obruō, 3, ruī, rutus, *overwhelm'*
1150; *cover over, bury,* 857, 861. *

obscūrus, a, um, adj. *dark, dusky,*
167, 724; *hidden, obscure,* 1222. *

obsequor, 3, secūtus, *follow com-
ply, yield,* 270.

observō, 1, *watch, guard, keep,* 296.

obsitus, a, um, p. of obserō, *sow;
covered, strewn,* 1357.

obstipēscō, 3, stipuī, —, *stand
amazed, be astounded, be thunderstruck,* 21, 107, 1218, 1595.   *

obstō, 1, stitī, —, *stand in the way
of, thwart, resist, oppose,* 140,
507, 1501, 1513.   *

obstruō, 3, ūxī, ūctus, *build
against; block, bar,* 1562.

obtūsus, a, um, adj. (p. of ob-
tundō, *beat against*), *blunt, dull,*
253.

obvius, a, um, adj. (via), *in the
way, to meet,* 310, 423, 808.   **

occāsus, ūs, m., *setting* (sc. sōlis),
sunset, west, 531, 1188, 1259.   *

occidō, 3, cidī, cāsus (cadō), *fall
dead, perish; die,* 67, 680, 1054,
1089.

occupō, 1, *take possession of; take,
seize,* 329, 498, 1134, etc.

occurrō, 3, currī, cursus, *run
against; meet* 1431.   *

ōcior, ius, adj., *swifter, fleeter,*
284, 323.

oculus, ī, m., *eye,* 196, 212, 281,
etc.   *

ōdī, ōdisse, ōsūrus, *hate,* 653, 798.

odor, ōris, m., *scent, incense,* 1391.*

odōrātus, a, um, adj. (p. of
odōrō, *make fragrant*), *fragrant,*
1602.

Oetaeus, a, um, adj., *of Mt. Oeta in Thessaly; Thessalian,* 1154.

officium, ī, n. (opus), *service, kindness, offices,* 597, 655; *duty, function, office,* 1039. *

Ōlenos, ī, m., husband of Lēthaea, 739.

ōlim, adv., *once upon a time, formerly,* 132, 864. *

Olympus, ī, m., a high mountain on the border of Thessaly, the home of the gods, 408. *

ōmen, inis, n., *foreboding; sign, portent,* 675. *

omnipotēns, entis, adj. (omnis, potēns), *all-powerful, almighty,* 615.

omnis, e, adj., *all, the whole, every,* 130, 388, 571, etc.; as noun, m. pl., *everybody, all,* 306, 841, 1052, etc.; n., *everything,* 245, 380, 588, etc. *

Onchestius, a, um, adj., *of Onchestus, son of Onchestus,* 46.

onerō, 1 (onus), *load, laden,* 1530 *

onus, eris, n., *load, burden,* 119, 513. *

opācus, a, um, adj., *shaded, dark, thick,* 8, 585, 690, 724.

operiō, 4, peruī, pertus, *cover, cover over,* 857, 1364.

opifer, era, erum (ops), *aid-bringing, helper,* 303.

opifex, icis, m. and f. (opus), *workman, artisan,* 1577.

oppōnō, 3, posuī, positus, *place against; put to, hold out,* 587.

oppressus, a, um, p. of opprimō, *press against; buried, fallen, sinking,* 586. *

(ops), opis, f., *aid, help, support,*

84, 327, 616, 1214, 1329; pl., *riches, wealth, resources,* 798, 814, 978. *

optimus, a, um, adj. (bonus), *best, fairest, most fertile,* 86. *

optō, 1, *choose, select, wish for, desire,* 24, 63, 182, etc.; *hope, pray,* 489; p. optāta, n. pl., *choice,* 774. *

opus, eris, n., *work, labor, toil,* 1297 (pl.), 1550, 1576, 1586; *exercise,* 1030; *work, statue,* 1308; *workmanship,* 353, 459; *aim, purpose,* 251; *need, use,* 6, 1120. *

ōra, ae, f., *shore,* 672; *region, world,* 696. *

ōrāculum (ōrāclum), ī, n. (ōrō), *divine announcement, oracle,* 273, 1162, 1226, 1429.

orbis, is, m., *ring; circle, disk,* 652, 1014, 1462, 1498; *earth* (with or without terrārum), 303, 355, 558, etc.; *course,* 421; *region* (of the earth), 634; *shore,* 1261; *wheel,* 712. *

orbō, 1 (orbus), *bereave,* 661.

orbus, a, um, adj., *deprived, robbed, bereaved,* 989, 1001, 1089.

ōrdō, inis, m., *row, line, circle,* 456; *row, order,* 457, 516, 1455, 1565; iūnctus ōrdine, *in succession, without intermission,* 766; nūllō ōrdine, *wildly, passionately,* 1066. *

orgia, ōrum, n., *orgies, rites* (of Bacchus), 763.

Oriēns, entis, m. (p. of orior), *the rising sun, the East,* 123. *

orīgō, inis, f. (orior) *beginning, source, origin,* 58. *

Orīōn, onis, m., the constellation *Orion,* 1583. *

orior, 4, ortus, *arise, begin; rise, start,* 508, 1298. *

ōrō, 1 (ōs), *speak; pray, entreat,* 292, 701, 717, etc. *

Orpheus, eī, m., a Thracian bard, son of Apollo and Calliope, 734.

Orphēus, a, um, adj., *of Orpheus,* 673.

ortus, ūs, m. (orior), *rising* (sc. sōlis), hence *east,* 460, 531, 1188, 1259; *source,* 809; *birth,* 391.

ōs, ōris, n., *mouth, lips,* 104, 139, 433, etc.; *jaws,* 171, 320, 1015, 1503; *face, features, head,* 72, 173, 333, etc. *

os, ossis, n., *bone,* 255, 647, 648, etc. *

ōsculum, ī, n. (ōs), *little mouth;* pl., *lips,* 281; *kisses,* 142, 147, 184, etc. *

ostendō, 3, tendī, tentus (tendō), *stretch out; point out, show, disclose,* 956, 1170, 1183, 1533. *

ovis, is, f., *sheep,* 1145.

ōvum, ī, n., *egg,* 904.

P

pābulum, ī, n., *food;* pl., *grass, fodder,* 553. *

pacīscor, 3, pactus, *agree together; bargain, stipulate, agree,* 1335.

Pactōlos, ī, m., a river of Lydia, with sands of gold, 757.

pactum, ī, n. (pactus), *thing agreed; agreement, stipulation,* 158.

pactus, a, um, adj. (p. of pacīscor), *agreed on, appointed,* 183.

Paeān, ānis, m., *Apollo,* god of healing, 347.

paene, adv., *nearly, almost,* 1310.

paenitet, 2, uit, —, impers., *it repents one, one is sorry,* 397. *

palaestra, ae, f., *wrestling school; wrestling place, palaestra,* 1030.

palātum, ī, n., *roof of the mouth, palate,* 1094, 1506.

palla, ae, f., *pallium* (a long robe), *cloak, mantle,* 834. *

Pallas, adis, f., a surname of Athene (the Roman Minerva), 1523. *

palleō, 2, uī, —, *be pale; be discolored,* 1208.

pallēscō, 2, palluī, —, (palleō), *grow pale* or *yellow, be yellow,* 521, 780.

pallidus, a, um, adj., *pale, pallid,* 202. *

palma, ae, f., *palm* (of the hand), *hand,* 786, 787; *palm tree, fruit of the date palm,* (dried) *dates,* 911. *

palūs, ūdis, f., *swamp, bog, marsh,* 394, 933, 1165.

palūster, tris, tre, adj. (palūs), *marshy, swampy,* 865, 870.

Pān, Pānos, m., god of the woods and shepherds, 815.

pandō, 3, pandī, passus, *spread out; declare, tell,* 1313; p. passus, *disheveled, loose,* 569. *

Panopē, ēs, f., a city of Phocis, 1440.

pār, paris, adj., *equal, alike,* 899, 1286, 1543. *

parātus, ūs, m. (parō), *provision; splendor,* 1395; nūllīs parātibus, *lack of preparation,* 920.

parcō, 3, pepercī, parsus, *spare,
refrain from*, 475, 1053, 1152.

parēns, entis, m. and f. (p. of
pariō), *father, mother, parent,*
222, 231, 368, etc.   *

pāreō, 2, uī, —, *appear; be
obedient, obey*, 474, 876, 930,
etc.   *

pariēs, ietis, m., *wall, house wall,*
133, 140.

parilis, e, adj. (pār), *equal*, 871.

pariter, adv. (pār), *equally, at the
same time, together*, 119, 623,
1061, etc.   *

Parnāsis, idis, adj., f., *of Parnasus,*
833.

Parnāsius, a, um, adj., *of Parnasus*, 1276.

Parnāsus, ī, m., *Mt. Parnasus*, in
Thessaly, 249, 1158.

parō, 1, *make ready, prepare,*
1467; *intend, be minded*, 922;
attempt, 793, 1536.   *

Paros, ī, f., one of the Cyclades,
1597.

pars, partis, f., *part, piece, portion,
share*, 86, 113, 846, etc.; *slice,
rasher*, 889; *side*, 146, 1288,
1597; *place, direction, quarter,*
508, 558, 628; *some*, 359, 360,
1010; ab utrāque parte, *both,*
1299.   *

partior, 4, partītus (pars), *share,
divide*, 1406.   *

parvus, a, um, adj., *small, little,
slight*, 150, 820, 870, etc.;
short, 908; *low*, 855; gen. of
value, *of little account*, 1287; as
noun, n. pl., *small matters*, 555.

pāscō, 3, pāvī, pāstus, *feed;* pass.,
satiate oneself, gloat, 1069, 1070.*

passim, adv. (passus, pandō),
here and there, all around, 534,
1410.

passus, a, um, see pandō, patior.

passus, ūs, m., *step, pace*, 28, 95,
314, 752.

pāstor, ōris, m, *herdsman, shep-
herd*, 295, 1594.

Pataraeus, a, um, adj., *of Patara,*
a city in Lycia, containing a
temple of Apollo, 298.

patefaciō, 3, fēcī, factus (pateō;
faciō), *lay open, open*, 460; *expose, lay bare*, 1125, 1525.

pateō, 2, uī, —, *stand open, lie
open, open*, 142, 1395, 1562;
be exposed, be revealed, 300,
1357, 1535; p. patēns as adj.,
broad, spreading, 1007.   *

pater, tris, m., *father, sire*, 79, 263,
264, etc.; pl., *parents*, 128.   *

paternus, a, um, adj. (pater), *of a
father, fatherly, paternal*, 395,
474, 523, etc.

patior, 3, passus, *bear, support, endure*, 434; *suffer, experience*, 68,
445, 695, 1085, 1432; *suffer,
allow*, 843; p. patiēns, as adj.,
able to endure, 471.   *

patria, ae, f. (patrius, sc. terra),
fatherland; native land, country,
634, 1099, 1428.   *

patrius, a, um, adj. (pater), *of a
father; a father's, paternal*, 369,
440, 442, 1587, 1605.   *

patulus, a, um, adj., *spreading;
broad, wide*, 912.

paucus, a, um, adj., *few;* n. pl.,
a few things (words), 942.   *

paulātim, adv. (paulum), *little by*

little, gradually, 1018, 1534, 1568.   *

paulum, adv. (paulus, *little*), *a little, somewhat*, 588, 702, 910, 1502.

pauper, peris, adj., *poor, humble, stingy*, 915.

paupertās, ātis, f. (pauper), *small means, poverty*, 873.

paveō, 2, pāvī, —, *be struck with terror, quake with fear, be afraid*, 379, 517, 668, etc.

pavidus, a, um, adj. (paveō), *trembling, quaking, timid*, 1220, 1520; *making timorous*, 414.

pavor, ōris, m., *trembling; fear, fright*, 736.

pāx, pācis, f., *agreement; peace*, 1549.   *

peccō, 1, *miss; do wrong, sin*, 802, 804.

pectus, oris, n., *breast, heart*, 229, 277, 302, etc.   *

pecus, oris, n., *cattle, flocks*, 599, 828.

pecus, udis, f., *sheep;* pl., *flocks*, 1127.   *

Pēgasos, ī, m., *the winged horse of the Muses*, 1417.

pelagus, ī, n., *sea*, 584, 1172, 1372, 1561.   *

pellis, is, f., *skin, hide*, 1474, 1485.

pellō, 3, pepulī, pulsus, *beat, strike*, 686, 747; *drive away, put aside, avoid*, 100.   *

penātēs, ium, m., *household gods; house, home*, 877.   *

pendeō, 2, pependī, —, *hang, be suspended*, 194, 279, 888, etc. *

pendō, 3, pependī, pēnsus, *weigh; pay, suffer*, 40, 1303.

Pēnēis, idos, f. adj., *of the Peneus*, a river in Thessaly, 326; *daughter of Peneus*, the river god, 254.

Pēnēius, a, um adj., *of the Peneus*, a river in Thessaly; as noun, f., *daughter of Peneus*, the river god; *Daphne*, 234.

penetrālis, e, adj. (penetrō), *piercing;* as noun, n. pl., *inner rooms, shrines*, 1128.

penetrō, 1, *enter, penetrate*, 571. *

penitus, adv., *inwardly;* penitus penitusque, *far, far below*, 520. *

penna, ae, f., *feather;* 1047, 1565, 1581, etc.; *wing*, 248, 288, 322, etc.

pepercī, see **parcō.**

per, prep. w. acc., *through, across, over, along, traversing*, 33, 255, 477, etc.; *through, throughout, among*, 8, 134, 303, 426, 997, 1067; *through, about*, 1268; *for*, 766; *by means of, by*, 17, 136, 299, etc.; *between*, 428; per sē, *of itself*, 917.   *

peragō, 3, ēgī, āctus, *carry out, accomplish, obey*, 467, 706.

percēnseō, 2, uī, —, *count over; go over, travel through*, 646.

percipiō, 3, cēpī, ceptus (capio), *take wholly; take on, receive*, 1378, 1604.

percurrō, 3, cucurrī and currī, cursus, *run through; run over*, 96.

percutiō, 3, cussī, cussus (quatiō), *strike through; strike, pierce*, 1055; *strike, beat*, 205, 248, 1124.

perdō, 3, didī, ditus, *make away with, destroy*, 53, 175, 216, 328, 1102; *lose*, 1521; *waste*, 313.

peregrīnus, a, um, adj. (peregre, abroad), *from foreign parts, foreign, strange, alien,* 648, 1445.

pereō, īre, iī, itūrus, *pass through; fall, die, perish, be destroyed,* 60, 555, 591, etc.

pererrō, 1, *wander through, roam over,* 1427.

perfundō, 3, **fūdī, fūsus,** *pour over; bathe, moisten, wet, bedew,* 650.

perīculum, ī, n., *trial; risk, danger, peril,* 17, 197, 1418, 1572. *

perimō, 3, **ēmī, ēmptus** (emō, take), *take away; destroy, kill, slay,* 64, 177, 1518.

permātūrēscō, 3, **mātūruī, —,** inch.; *ripen fully,* 232.

perōsus, a, um, adj. (p. of perōdī, hate fully), *hating greatly, detesting,* 814, 1559.

perpetuus, a, um, adj., *eternal, perpetual, lifelong,* 268, 346.

perquīrō, 3, **—, sītus** (quaerō), *seek thoroughly, make eager search for,* 1424.

Persephonē, ēs, f., *Proserpina,* 685.

persequor, 3, secūtus, *follow after, follow,* 218.

Perseus, eī, m., son of Jupiter and Danaë, the Gorgon slayer, 1272.

perspiciō, 3, **spēxī, spectus,** *look through, examine, inspect,* 460.

perveniō, 4, **vēnī, ventus,** *come up; go through, reach,* 147; *come to, arrive at,* 162.

pēs, pedis, m., *foot,* 94, 167, 316, etc.; *leg,* 506, 893, 898; *hoof,* 503; *swiftness, running,* 4, 11;
pedem retrō ferre, *start back,* 201. *

pestifer, fera, ferum, adj. (pestis, plague), *pestilent, noxious, destructive,* 241, 1495.

petō, 3, **petīvī and iī, petītus,** *seek, make for, go to,* 117, 547, 576, etc.; *seek, try to win, try for,* 17, 23, 54, 316, 1330; *woo,* 260; *look for,* 381, 868; *ask,* 392, 402, 439, 775, 1275; *rise toward,* 1157: w. terrās, *set,* 464. *

Phaedimus, ī, n., a son of Niobe, 1028.

Phaëthōn, ontis, m., son of Phoebus and Clymene, 382.

pharetra, ae, f., *quiver,* 250, 340, 1019. *

Philēmōn, onis, m., an aged Phrygian, 871.

Phlegōn, ontis, m., one of the sun's horses, 502.

phōca, ae, f., *seal,* 578, 1141.

Phōcis, idis, f., a country between Boeotia and Thessaly, 1154.

Phoebē, ēs, f., *Diana,* 258.

Phoebēus, a, um, adj., *of Phoebus, of Apollo,* 1551.

Phoebus, ī, m., *Apollo,* the sun god, 234. *

Phoenīces, um, m., *the Phoenicians,* 1467.

Phorcis, idis, f., *daughter of Phorcus, Gorgon,* 1406.

Phorcȳnis, idis, f., *daughter of Phorcys, Medusa,* 1375.

Phrygius, a, um, adj. (Phryx), *Phrygian,* 863, 963. *

Phryx, ygis, adj., *of Phrygia,* in Asia Minor, *Phrygian,* 761. *

piceus, a, um, adj. (pix, *pitch*),
pitchy, pitchy black, 564, 1106.

pictus, a, um, adj. (p. of pingō,
paint), *colored,* 1529; *orna-
mented, embroidered,* 34.   *

piger, gra, grum, adj., *unwilling;
clinging, tenacious,* 332.

piget, 2, guit and gitum est, impers., *it pains, afflicts, grieves
one,* 524, 656.

pignus, oris and eris, n., *pledge,
assurance,* 386, 439, 1555.

pinguis, e, adj., *fat; slow, stupid,*
816.   *

pīnus, ī, f., *pine; ship,* 526.

piscis, is, m., *fish,* 361, 576, 1137,
1359, 1593.

pius, a, um, adj., *dutiful, con-
scientious, devout,* 750, 871, 961,
etc.   *

placeō, 2, cuī or citus sum, *please,
be acceptable, suit,* 158, 294, 406,
etc.   *

placidus, a, um, adj., *gentle, quiet,
still, calm,* 940, 1224, 1285;
steady, 1534.   *

plāga, ae, f., *blow, stroke,* 1509.

plangō, 3, plānxī, planctus, *strike,
beat,* 1037, 1546.

plangor, ōris, m. (plangō), *beating
of the breast in sorrow, hence,
wailing, shrieks,* 205, 1327.

planta, ae, f., *sprout; sole* (of the
foot), *foot, heel,* 32.

plānus, a, um, adj., *even, flat, level,*
1007.

plausus, ūs, m. (plaudō, *strike*),
clapping (of hands), *applause,*
109, 1367.   *

plēctrum, ī, n., *quill* (for playing
on the lyre), *plectrum,* 836.

Plēias, adis, f., *Pleiad,* one of the
seven daughters of Atlas, 971.

plēnus, a, um, adj., *full, filled,* 178,
461, 699, 1180, 1494; *fulfilled,
completed,* 859.

plūma, ae, f., *feather,* 1574.

plumbum, ī, n., *lead,* 189, 253;
leaden ball, bullet, 1342.

plūrimus, a, um, adj. (multus),
*very much, copious(ly), in fullest
flood,* 810.   *

plūs, plūris, adj. (multus), *more;*
pl., *many,* 1380; as noun, n.,
307, 405, 529, etc.; as adv.,
more, 283, 1464.   *

pōculum, ī, n., *drinking cup,* 907. *

poena, ae, f., *compensation; pen-
alty, punishment,* 40, 446, 447,
etc.   *

pollex, icis, m., *thumb,* 838, 1574.

polliceor, 2, itus, (liceor, *bid*), *hold
forth; offer, promise,* 777.   *

polus, ī, m., *end of an axis; pole,
heavens,* 423, 479, 606.   *

pōmārium, ī, n. (pōmārius, *of
fruit*), *fruit garden, orchard,*
1279.

pompa, ae, f., *solemn procession,*
342.

pōmum, ī, n., *fruit, apple,* 91, 107,
112, etc.

pondus, eris, n., *weight,* 118, 509,
1514; *ballast,* 511.   *

pōnō, 3, posuī, positus, *put, place,
set up, set in position,* 334, 490,
687, etc.; w. corpora, *lie,* 1141;
arrange, order, 259, 374, 457;
plant, set, 931; *put down* or
away, lay aside, take off, 19, 195,
661, etc.; *found,* 1551.

pontus, ī, m., *sea, ocean,* 574, 583, 1133, etc. *

poples, itis, m., *knee,* 34, 1045.

populor, 1, *lay waste; consume,* 630.

populus, ī, m., *people, nation,* 79, 556, 567, etc. *

porrigō, 3, rēxī, rēctus (regō), *stretch out, extend,* 538.

porta, ae, f., *gate, entrance,* 683. *

portitor, ōris, m., *carrier; ferryman, boatman,* 743.

portō, 1, *bear, carry,* 658, 735. *

poscō, 3, poposcī, —, *ask urgently; beg, request,* 79, 445, 447, etc.; *demand, require,* 492. *

possideō, 2, sēdī, sessus (sedeō), *have and hold; hold, occupy,* 1323, 1563; *contain, possess, cover,* 1189.

possum, posse, potuī, (potis, *able;* sum), *be able, can, may,* 3, 55, 63, etc.; dare posse, *give the power,* 845. *

post, prep. w. acc., *of place, behind,* 111, 528, 905, etc.; *of time, after,* 831, 1074, 1182. *

(posterus), a, um, adj. (post), *coming after; next, following,* 148.

postis, is, m., *door, door post,* 343, 784, 785; pl., *door,* 878.

postpōnō, 3, posuī, positus, *put after, esteem less,* 1000.

postquam, conj., *after, as soon as, when,* 204, 214, 504, etc.

potēns, entis, adj. (p. of possum), *able; strong, mighty,* 44, 781. *

potentia, ae, f. (potēns), *power, influence,* 14, 304.

potior, 4 (potis, *able*), *become master of; gain, win,* 10. *

prae, prep. w. abl. (prae, adv., *in front of*), *before; in comparison with,* 823.

praebeō, 2, uī, itus (habeō), *hold forth; furnish, afford,* 554, 643; *offer, show, turn,* 1347.

praecēdō, 3, cessī, cessus, *go before, lead the way,* 753.

praeceps, cipitis, adj. (caput), *headforemost, headlong,* 417, 548, 631, 1350; *swift, rushing,* 526.

praecepta, ōrum, n. (p. of praecipiō, *advise*), *directions, instructions,* 1584.

praecipitō, 1 (praeceps), *throw headlong;* pass., *sink rapidly, hasten down,* 159.

praecordia, ōrum, n. (cor), *breast, waist,* 330, 1040; *mind, so thoughts,* 817.

praecutiō, 3, —, — (quatiō), *shake before, brandish in front,* 1391.

praeda, ae, f., *booty, spoil, prey,* 316, 1278. *

praeferō, ferre, tulī, lātus, *bear before; place before, prefer,* 1333; p. praelātus, *surpassing,* 123.

praefīgō, 3, fīxī, fīxus, *fasten before, fix in front, tip with,* 1338.

praelātus, see praeferō.

praemium, ī, n., *advantage; reward, prize,* 12, 22, 121, 1389. *

praepes, petis, adj., *outstripping;* as noun, m., *swift bird,* 1346.

praepōnō, 3, posuī, positus, *set before; prefer,* 967.

praesaepe, is, n. (saepēs), *inclosure; stable, stall,* 468. *

praesāgus, a, um, adj., *foreboding, prophetic (of)*, 472.

praescius, a, um, adj., *foreknow-ing, foreseeing*, 1020.

praesīgnis, e, adj. (signum), *dis-tinguished, wonderful*, 1453.

praestāns, stantis, adj. (p. of prae-stō), *standing before; conspicu-ous, famous*, 4, 1475.   *

praestō, 1, stitī, stitus, *stand be-fore; surpass, excel*, 1264.   *

praetentus, a, um, p. of praetendō, *hold before; stretched forth, thrust forward*, 1504.

praeter, prep. w. acc. (praeter, adv., *besides*), *past; except, be-sides*, 1076.

praetereō, īre, iī, itus, *go by, pass, outstrip*, 109, 121, 508.

praevius, a, um, adj. (via), *going before, in advance, ahead*, 753.

prātum, ī, n., *meadow*, 1138.

precēs, see (prex).

precor, 1 (prex), *ask, beg, pray, supplicate*, 286, 803, 1050, 1201, 1401.

premō, 3, pressī, pressus, *press; de-press, bear down*, 483; *stand upon, load*, 496; *ride*, 1012; *cover*, 241, 794; *alight on*, 1351; *sink*, 1131; *overpower*, 594; *grasp, squeeze*, 357, 1109; *press, urge*, 452, 1512; *shut in*, 1269; p. pressus, *deep-set*, 1525; *low-lying*, 487; *slow*, 1438.   *

prēndō, 3, ēndī, ēnsus, *take hold of, grasp, seize*, 728.

pretium, ī, n., *price; reward, prize*, 13, 68, 1371.

(prex, precis), f., *prayer, entreaty*, 83, 329, 667, etc.

prīmō, adv. (prīmus), *in the begin-ning, at first, first*, 647, 1314.   *

prīmum, adv. (prīmus), *first*, 715, 1533; ut prīmum, *as soon as*, 859.   *

prīmus, a, um, adj., *first, the first, foremost*, 77, 126, 135, etc.; *first part of*, 411.

prīncipium, ī, n. (prīnceps, *chief*), *beginning*, 656.

prior, prius, ōris, adj., *former; first (of two), earlier*, 179, 737, 1219.   *

prīscus, a, um, adj. (prius), *of former times;* as noun, m. pl., *ancients, men of old*, 86.

prius, adv. (n. of prior), *before, sooner, first*, 11, 151; *at first*, 516.

prō, prep. w. abl., *before; instead of, for*, 447, 707, 1089, etc.; *for, as*, 1234.   *

probō, 1 (probus, *good*), *make good; prove, show*, 440.

(procer, eris), m., *nobleman, prince*, 1396.   *

procul, adv., *in the distance; at a distance, afar*, 166, 370, 634, etc.   *

prōcumbō, 3, cubuī, cubitum, *fall prostrate*, 1209, 1444.

procus, ī, m., *wooer, suitor*, 9, 15, 65.

prōdō, 3, didī, ditus, *put forth; ex-hibit, display, show forth*, 1289; *betray*, 851, 860.   *

prōdūcō, 3, dūxī, ductus, *lead forth*, 1590; *raise, bring*, 883.

prōficiō, 3, fēcī, fectus (faciō), *accomplish, effect, avail*, 1050.

proficīscor, 3, profectus, *set out; come*, 1456.   *

profugus, a, um, adj., *in flight;* as noun, m., *exile,* 1428. *

profundus, a, um, adj., *vast, deep,* 560; as noun, n., *the deep,* 578, 1172. *

prōgeniēs, —, em, ē, f., *descent; offspring, child,* 382. *

prohibeō, 2 (habeō), *hold before; hold back, check, hold spellbound,* 1468. *

prōlēs, is, f., *offspring, descendant,* 80, 106, 367, 994, 1590. *

Promēthiadēs, ae, m., *son of Prometheus, Deucalion,* 1224.

prōmissum, ī, n. (p. of prōmittō), *that promised; promise,* 393, 399.

prōmittō, 3, mīsī, missus, *let go; promise,* 1337.

prōmō, 3, prōmpsī, prōmptus (emō, *take*), *take out, draw out,* 250; p. prōmptus, *practicable, easy,* 1517.

(**prōmptus**, ūs), m., only abl. (prōmō), *readiness;* in prōmptū, *in one's power, easy,* 434.

pronepōs, ōtis, m., *great-grandson,* 47.

prōnus, a, um, adj., *leaning forward,* 1026; *swiftly, headlong,* 93, 290, 1210; *steep,* 415. *

propāgō, inis, f., *shoot; descendant, offspring,* 386.

prope, prep. w. acc., *near,* 1007.

properō, 1 (properus, *quick*), *hasten, make haste, run,* 99, 292, 476, 703; p. properātus, *too quickly run,* 701. *

propior, propius, ōris, adj. (prope), *nearer,* 370, 389, 548, 614.

prōpositum, ī, n. (p. of prōpōnō, *set forth*), *plan, purpose,* 452.

prōsiliō, 4, uī, — (saliō, *leap*); *burst forth, start out,* 1049.

prōspiciō, 3, spēxī, spectus, *look forward, look ahead and see,* 531, 934; *look out over,* 818. *

prōsum, prōdesse, prōfuī, *be useful; benefit, profit, help,* 306, 1147.

Prōteus, eī, m., *a sea god of changeable shape,* 357.

prōtinus, adv., *right onward; at once, directly, then,* 256, 369, 727, 1103, 1389.

proturbō, 1, *drive on; repulse, sweep down,* 1501.

proximus, a, um, adj., superl. of prope, *next, nearest,* 1019. *

pruīnōsus, a, um, adj. (pruīna, *hoar frost*), *frosty, icy,* 149.

prūnum, ī, n., *plum,* 912.

pūblicus, a, um, adj. (populus), *public, universal, common,* 383.

pudor, ōris, m., *shrinking from blame; shame, disgrace,* 848.

puella, ae, f., dim. (puer), *girl, maiden, lass,* 63, 123.

puellāris, e, adj. (puella), *girlish, youthful,* 35.

puer, erī, m., *boy, lad,* 56, 238, 475, etc. *

puerīlis, e, adj. (puer), *boyish, youthful,* 72, 403.

pulcher, chra, chrum, adj., *beautiful, fair, handsome,* 122, 266, 1395. *

pullus, a, um, adj., *dark colored, dark,* 227.

pulmō, ōnis, m., *lung,* 1041.

pulsō, 1, freq. (pellō), *beat upon,*

strike, 200, 503, 1144; *dash against*, 1151; *tread, stamp* (upon), 1008.

pulvis, eris, m., *dust*, 173. *

pūniceus, a, um, adj. (Pūnicus, *Phoenician*), *purple, red*, 194, 1360.

purpureus, a, um, adj., *purple colored, dark red, crimson*, 37, 371, 461, 849, 913. *

pūrus, a, um, adj., *pure, clear*, 795.

putō, 1 (putus, *clean*), *clear up; think, consider*, 59, 95, 284, etc.

Pyramus, ī, m., *a Babylonian youth*, 122.

Pyroïs, entis, m., *one of the sun's horses*, 501.

pyrōpus, ī, m., *gold bronze, firestone*, 350.

Pyrrha, ae, f., *wife of Deucalion*, 1186.

Pȳthōn, ōnis, m., *a huge serpent slain by Apollo*, 242.

Q

quā, adv. (abl. of quī), *on which side; by what way, where, wherever*, 292, 544, 907, etc.; *as far as, as long as*, 453; *how*, 517, 518; indef., *in any way*, 1022. *

quadriiugus, a, um, adj. (quattuor, *four;* iugum), *of a team of four;* m. pl., *four-horse team*, 516.

quadrupēs, pedis, adj. (quattuor, *four;* pēs), *with four feet; horse, steed*, 432, 469, 1015.

quaerō, 3, quaesīvī, quaesītus, *seek, hunt for*, 750, 1148; *try to gain*, 43; *ask*, 981, 1202, 1399. *

quālis, e, pronom. adj., *of what

sort, 854; *such as, like*, 20, 362, 652. *

quam, adv. (quī), *in what manner; how*, 72; *than*, 36, 189, 405, etc. *

quamquam, conj., *though although*, 29, 1229

quamvīs, conj., *as you will; although, though*, 757,

quantus, a, um, adj., *of what size, how great, how much*, 141, 197, 1320, 1401, 1465; quantus erat, *of just his size*, 1290; tantum . . . quantum, *so far as*, 932, 1341; as adv., quantum, *as far as*, 964; quantum dīstat, *how far removed*, 989, 1062; quantō . . . tantō, *by as much as, by so much*, 246. *

quartus, a, um. num. adj. (quattuor, *four*), *fourth*, 58, 502.

quater, num. adv. (quattuor, *four*), *four times*, 397, 1366. *

quatiō, 3, —, quassus, *shake, move*, 1310, 1603.

-que, conj., *and, also*, repeated, *both . . . and* 7, 12, 21, etc. *

quercus, ūs, f., *oak, oak tree*, 344, 826, 862, 1512.

querella, ae, f., *complaint*, 1004.

queror, 3, questus, *express grief, lament, utter complaints*, 151, 555, 731, 746. *

quī, quae, quod, gen. cūius, rel. pron., *who, which, what*, 22, 23, 29, etc. *

quia, conj., *because*, 67, 1508.

quīcumque, quae-, quod-, rel. pron., *whoever, whatever, whatsoever, all that*, 181, 450, 644, etc. *

quid, interrog. adv., *in what re-

spect? why? 43, 140, 448, 590, 1518.　＊

quīdam, quae-, quid- and quod-, indef. pron., *a certain, some,* 361; as adj., 1238.

quidem, adv., *assuredly, to be sure, certainly, of course, indeed,* 14, 270, 301, etc.

quīlibet, quae-, quod- (quid-), indef. pron., *any one, whom you will,* 658.

quīnque, num. adj., indecl., *five,* 477, 766, 1547.

quis (**quī**), quae, quid (quod), interrog. pron., *who? which? what?* 52, 57, 58, etc.; indef., *some one, any one,* 24; nēscio quis, *some,* 243.　＊

quisquam, quicquam, indef. pron., *any, any one, anything,* 17, 407, 730, 1163.　＊

quisque, quaeque, quidque and quodque, indef. pron., *whoever it be, each, every, everybody,* 147, 289, 406, etc.

quisquis, quicquid or quodquid, indef. rel. pron., *whoever, whatever,* 443, 688, 772.　＊

quīvīs, quae-, quid-, indef. pron., *whom you please, any one, any,* 392.

quō, adv. (abl. and dat. of quī), *that* (= ut, eō), 392; of time, *when,* 1277; of degree, *by as much as, the* (more), 131; of place, *to which, whither, where,* 115, 367, 564.　＊

quod, conj. (quī), *that, in that, the fact that,* 57, 58, 59, 144, etc.; *that, because, since,* 56, 597, 599, 775; *but,* 74, 604.

quondam, adv., *at some time; once, formerly,* 740, 1013, 1567.　＊

quoniam, adv. (iam), *since now, since, whereas,* 65, 71, 338, etc.

quoque, conj., *also, too,* 55, 127, 153, etc.; *even,* 1074, 1133.　＊

quotiēns, adv. (quot, *how many*), *how many times, how often,* 102.

R

radiō, 1, —, — (radius), *gleam, shine,* 352, 785, 1270.

radius, ī, m., *staff; spoke,* 456, 628; *beam, ray,* 149, 166, 389, 472.

rādīx, īcis, f., *root,* 193, 332; *radish,* 903.

rādō, 3, rāsī, rāsus, *scrape,* 1496; *pass over, skim,* 95.

rāmālia, ium, n. (rāmus), *twigs, sticks,* 884.

rāmus, ī, m., *branch, bough,* 89, 225, 331, etc.

rapidus, a, um, adj., *tearing away; devouring, raging,* 471; *swift, rapid,* 421; *scorching,* 1601.　＊

rapīna, ae, f., *seizure, ravishing,* 698.

rapiō, 3, rapuī, raptus, *seize and carry off, snatch away, catch up, seize,* 1099, 1424; *wash away,* 1128, 1152; *bear along,* 418, 546; *take away,* 568, 1390; *catch,* 1377.　＊

raptō, 1, freq. (rapiō), *seize and carry off; hurry away, drag on,* 565.　＊

rāstrum, ī, n., pl. rāstrī, m., *toothed hoe, mattock,* 598.

ratis, is, f., *raft, boat,* 1160.　＊

ratus, see **reor.**

recēdō, 3, cessī, cessus, *go back; depart, take flight,* 748.

recēns, centis, adj., *fresh, recent,* 163, 718, 960, 1376, 1494; *fresh, untired,* 411. *

recidō, 3, cidī, cāsūrus (cadō), *fall back; recoil, rebound, be visited,* 688, 1001.

recingō, 3, —, cīnctus, *ungird, loosen,* 1232.

recipiō, 3, cēpī, ceptus (capiō), *take back; receive,* 680; *recover,* 771; *receive, take in, welcome,* 869; sē, *return,* 747. *

recognōscō, 3, gnōvī, gnitus, *know again, see again,* 750.

recondō, 3, didī, ditus, *put up again; close again,* 213.

rēctor, ōris, m., *guide; ruler, master,* 408, 1172; *pilot, skipper,* 527, 1021.

rēctus, a, um, adj. (p. of regō), *straight, erect,* 1499. *

recūsō, 1 (causa), *make an objection against; refuse,* 1219.

reddō, 3, didī, ditus, *give back, restore,* 769; *reflect,* 458; *bring back, return,* 1184; w. mōtūs, *move,* 1096; *repeat, utter, exchange,* 954. *

redeō, īre, iī, itus, *go back, come back, return,* 115, 170, 196, 709, 1122.

redigō, 3, ēgī, āctus, (agō), *drive back; bring down, reduce,* 988.

redolēns, entis, adj., *fragrant,* 912. *

referō, ferre, rettulī, relātus, *bear back, bring back,* 32, 1248; *repeat,* 855, 861; *reply,* 383; *relate, narrate,* 1003; *repay, show,*

give, 597; *turn back,* 614; *carry off,* 909. *

rēfert, ferre, tulit, —, impers., *it concerns, it matters,* 875.

refugiō, 3, fūgī, —, *flee back; shrink from,* 337.

refugus, a, um, adj. (refugiō), *fleeing back, receding,* 712.

rēgāliter, adv. (rēgālis, *of a king*), *regally, splendidly,* 667.

regerō, 3, gessī, gestus, *carry back; heap* or *throw back,* 856.

rēgia, ae, f. (rēgius, *royal*), sc. domus, *palace,* 349, 609; sc. urbs, *royal city, residence, capital, kingdom,* 298, 974.

regiō, ōnis, f., *direction; district, region,* 544, 1608. *

rēgius, a, um, adj. (rēx), *of the king, royal,* 716. *

rēgnum, ī, n., *kingdom, rule, realm, sway,* 685, 700, 705, 1261, 1337. *

regō, 3, rēxī, rēctus, *keep straight; control, manage,* 434, 663; *rule, govern,* 717, 976. *

relābor, 3, lāpsus, *slip back,* 727.

relanguēscō, 3, languī, —, inch., *sink down, collapse,* 1080.

relaxō, 1, *stretch out; unloose, open, open wider,* 1122.

relevō, 1, *lift up; mitigate, relieve, lessen,* 799; *rest,* 879.

religō, 1, *bind back; bind fast, fasten,* 1305, 1316.

relinquō, 3, līquī, līctus, *leave behind, leave,* 26, 103, 111, etc.; *give up, abandon,* 61, 276.

remaneō, 2, mānsī, —, *stay behind, remain,* 333, 1382.

rēmigium, ī, n., *rowing apparatus,*
i. e., *wings,* 1604.   *

remittō, 3, mīsī, missus, *loosen,*
relax, let go, relinquish, 526, 532,
541, 1017.

remollēscō, 3, —, —, *become soft,*
soften, 1212.

remoror, 1, *hold back; stay back,*
wait, be delayed, linger, 112, 204.

removeō, 2, mōvī, mōtus, *move*
back; drive away, disperse, 148,
1120, 1169.   *

rēmus, ī, m., *oar,* 1135.   *

renīdeō, 2, —, —, *shine back,*
beam, smile, 1573.

reor, 2, ratus, *reckon, think,* 1228,
1308.

repāgula, ōrum, n., *barriers,* 503.

reparābilis, e, adj., (reparō), *that*
may be repaired; reparable, 1213.

reparō, 1, *get again; renew, re-*
store, 1197, 1247.

repellō, 3, reppulī and repulī, re-
pulsus, *drive, throw* or *shove*
back, put aside, 505, 1485;
spurn, 1343.

repercussus, a, um, adj. (p. of
repercutiō, *strike back*), *shining*
back, reflected, 458, 1414.

reperiō, 4, repperī, repertus, *find*
again; find, discover, 175, 648.

repetō, 3, petīvī, petītus, *fall upon*
again, attack repeatedly, 1366;
heave again and again, 473; *go*
over, review, 1222; *repeat,* 1588. *

repleō, 2, ēvī, ētus, *fill again, refill,*
916.

repūgnō, 1, *fight back; resist, object*
(to), rebel (at), 271, 435, 451.

repulsa, ae, f. (repellō), *rejection;*
refusal, denial, 445.

requiēs, ētis, f., *rest, repose,* 323,
868, 1262, 1275.

requiēscō, 3, quiēvī, quiētus, *rest,*
repose, 233, 1295, 1433.

requīrō, 3, quīsīvī, quīsītus
(quaerō), *seek again; look for,*
ask for, 196, 647, 875, 1430,
1608; *ask,* 1313.

rēs, reī, f., *thing, object, matter,*
affair, circumstance, 379, 437;
pl., (heroic) *deeds,* 1274, 1282;
things, universe, world, 665,
1214; rērum summa, *the uni-*
verse itself, 611.   *

resecō, 1, secuī, sectus, *cut loose;*
cut off, 850, 889.

reserō, 1, *unbar, throw back,* 1394.

resideō, 2, sēdī, — (sedeō), *sit*
back, sit down, 1089.

resistō, 3, stitī, —, *withstand, op-*
pose, 1129; *stop, stay,* 285.   *

resolvō, 3, solvī, solūtus, *untie;*
unloose, loosen, 1216; *open,* 593;
free, release, 1370.

resonō, 1, āvī, —, *ring, resound,*
109.

respiciō, 3, spēxī, spectus, *look*
back at, 531, 754, 1443, 1592.

respondeō, 2, spondī, spōnsus,
answer, reply, 210.   *

restituō, 3, uī, ūtus (statuō),
restore to one's former state, 805.

restō, 1, stitī, —, *withstand; re-*
main, be left, 114, 1086, 1199.   *

resūmō, 3, sūmpsī, sūmptus, *take*
up again, resume, 1298.

resupīnus, a, um, adj., *bent back;*
with head thrown back or *raised,*
1064; *fallen backward, on one's*
back, 188, 578.   *

retardō, 1, *keep back; restrain, hold in check,* 1503.

retexō, 3, xuī, xtus, *weave back; unravel,* 701.

reticeō, 2, cuī, — (taceō), *keep silence, be silent,* 853.

retineō, 2, tinuī, tentus (teneō), *hold back; keep, hold,* 533, 843.

retorqueō, 2, torsī, tortus, *twist back; turn round,* 831, 1348, 1489.

retrahō, 3, trāxī, trāctus, *draw back, withdraw,* 1508.

retrō, adv., *backward, back,* 201, 311, 721, 1509, 1512.

retrōversus, a, um, adj., *turned back, averting oneself,* 1289.

rettulī, see **referō.**

revellō, 3, vellī, volsus, *pull away; tear off,* 627; *tear away, separate,* 219, 220.

revocābilis, e, adj. (revocō), *that may be recalled, revocable,* 1053.

revocō, 1, *call back,* 285; *recall,* 1176.   *

revolvō, 3, volvī, volūtus, *roll back;* pass., *fall back, return,* 733.

rēx, rēgis, m., *king, ruler, monarch,* 47, 572, 762, etc.   *

Rhodopē, ēs, f., a Thracian mountain range, 747.

Rhodopēius, a, um, adj., *Rhodopean, Thracian,* 681.

rictus, ūs, m., *open mouth, gaping jaws,* 164, 796, 1495.

rigeō, 2, —, —, *be stiff; stiffen, become solid,* 792; *stand out, project, rise,* 818, 1521.   *

rigidus, a, um, adj., *stiff; rough, hard,* 1539.

rigor, ōris, m., *stiffness, rigidity,* 1235, 1378.

riguus, a, um, adj., *well watered,* 886.

rīma, ae, f., *cleft, crack, chink, fissure,* 132, 552, 571.   *

rīpa, ae, f., *bank, shore,* 648, 744.   *

rōbur, oris, n., *hard wood, oak,* 1513; pl., *trees,* 1144; *trunk,* 1515.

rogō, 1, *ask, ask for,* 221, 395; *implore, entreat,* 524, 666, 1089, 1220; *pray to,* 1052.

rogus, ī, m., *funeral pile, pyre,* 233.

rōrō, 1 (rōs, *dew*), *drip, stream,* 1108.

rosa, ae, f., *rose,* 461.

rōstrum, ī, n. (rōdō, *gnaw*), *beak of a ship, prow,* 1338; *muzzle,* 318.

rota, ae, f., *wheel,* 456, 481, 487, 628, 1008; pl., *chariot,* 623.   *

rotō, (tota), *turn round, whirl,* 422.

rubēns, entis, adj. (p. of rubeō, *be red*), *red, crimsoned,* 1011.

rubēscō, 3, rubuī, —, inch. (rubeō, *be red*), *grow red, redden,* 464.

rubor, ōris, m., *flush, blush,* 35, 266.

rudis, e, adj., *unformed; rough, in the rough, unwrought,* 1240; *inexperienced,* 77; *coarse,* 880.

rūgōsus, a, um, adj. (rūga, *wrinkle*), *wrinkled,* 911.

ruīna, ae, f., *rushing down; disaster, destruction, ruin,* 1057.   *

rūmor, ōris, m., *rustle; mere report, idle tale, hearsay,* 2.

rumpō, 3, rūpī, ruptus, *burst; break,* 1218; *cleave,* 191; *pierce,* 1040.

ruō, 3, ruī, rūtus, *fall with violence, fall,* 607; *rush away, rush,* 515, 545, 1126. *

rūpēs, is, f., *rock, cliff,* 181, 1365. *

rūricola, ae, m. and f., *husbandman; countryman, peasant,* 761.

rūrsus, adv. (for revorsus, p. of revertō, *turn back*), *back, again,* 112, 733, 817, 909.

rūs, rūris, n., *country, fields,* 364, 814, 1423. *

rūsticus, a, um, adj. (rūs), *of the country; rural, rustic,* 1567.

rutilus, a, um, adj., *red, golden red, ruddy,* 460, 630.

S

sacer, cra, crum, adj., *consecrated, sacred, reverend,* 470, 589, 831, etc.; n. pl., as noun, *sacred rites,* 764, 991, 1447; *sacred utensils,* 1128.

sacerdōs, ōtis, m. and f. (sacer), *priest, priestess,* 944. *

sacrō, 1 (sacer), *consecrate, dedicate,* 87.

saeculum, ī, n., *generation, age,* 134, 997; personified, 374. *

saepe, adv., *often, frequently,* 138, 263, 264, etc.; comp., *again and again,* 1318. *

saepēs, is, f., *hedge,* 275.

saeviō, 4 (saevus), *be fierce; be angry, be furious,* 670; *rush furiously* (upon), 1345.

saevus, a, um, adj., *raging, fierce, savage, furious, cruel,* 169, 235, 430, 624, 1348. *

sagitta, ae, f., *arrow, shaft,* 29, 242, 301, etc. *

sagittifer, fera, ferum, adj. (sa-gitta), *arrow-bearing, arrow-laden,* 250.

salignus, a, um, adj. (salix, *willow tree*), *of willow, willow,* 893, 896.

saltem, adv., *saved; at any rate, at least,* 474, 660. *

(saltus, ūs), m., *leaping, leap, bound,* 513, 625, 1463.

salūs, ūtis, f., *safety, deliverance, life,* 316. *

salūtō, 1 (salūs), *wish health; greet, salute,* 1368, 1446.

Samos, ī, f., an island in the Aegean, 1597. *

sānābilis, e, adj. (sānō, *make sound*), *able to be healed, curable,* 305.

sānctus, a, um, adj. (sanciō, *make sacred*), *sacred, venerable, revered,* 840, 1206. *

sanguinens, a, um, adj. (sanguis), *bloody, stained with blood,* 1478, 1546.

sanguis, inis, m., *blood,* 174, 185, 193, etc. *

sapiēns, entis, adj. (p. of sapiō, *have taste*), *sensible, clever, discreet,* 63.

sapienter, adv. (sapiēns), *wisely, prudently,* 450.

sarcina, ae, f., *package; burden, care,* 1013.

Sardēs, ium, f., *Sardis,* capital of Lydia, in Asia Minor, 807.

satiō, 1 (satis), *fill; sate, satiate,* 1070, 1071; *feed,* 1391.

satis, adj., n., indecl., as noun, *enough, sufficient,* 282, 755; as adv., *sufficiently, fully, enough,* 655, 681, 990, 1191, 1240.

satum, ī, n. (p. of serō, *sow*), *that sown;* pl., *crops,* 1127.

satur, ura, urum, adj., *full, sated, having eaten one's fill,* 468.

Sāturnius, a, um, adj., *of Saturn; son of Saturn, Jupiter,* 940.   *

saturō, 1 (satur), *fill full; dye, color richly,* 834.

satyrus, ī, m., *Satyr,* a forest god with goat's legs, 759.

saxum, ī, n., *large stone, rock,* 637, 714, 737, etc.   *

scelerātus, a, um, adj. (p. of scelerō, *pollute*), *polluted; impious, accursed,* 180, 1002; *cruel,* 1426.

Schoenēïus, a, um, adj., *of Schoeneus;* as noun, f., *daughter of Schoeneus, Atalanta,* 50, 101.

scīlicet, adv. (for scīre licet), *you may know; certainly, forsooth, of course,* 438, 1556.

scindō, 3, scidī (late), scissus, *cut; cut through, part,* 507; *burst open,* 190.   *

sciō, 4, *know, understand,* 518, 662.   *

scītor, 1, freq. (sciō), *seek to know, ask, inquire,* 5.

scopulus, ī, m., *projecting point of rock; rock, cliff,* 1341, 1363. *

Scorpios, ī, m., the constellation *Scorpion,* 431, 537.

scrobis, is, m. and f., *trench, ditch,* 857.

Scythicus, a, um, adj., *of Scythia,* in Asia, *Scythian,* 29.

sēcēdō, 3, cessī, cessus, *go apart, go off by oneself, withdraw,* 853.

secō, 1, secuī, sectus, *cut, cut through, cleave,* 478, 890, 1204. *

secundus, a, um, adj. (sequor), *following; second,* 112; mēnsae, *dessert,* 910.   *

secūris, is, f., *axe,* 1449.

sed, conj., *but, on the contrary, still,* 14, 25, 56, etc.   *

sedeō, 2, sēdī, sessum, *sit, sit down, sink down, rest,* 16, 162, 360, etc.   *

sēdēs, is, f., *seat; place, position,* 145, 703; *footing,* 495.   *

sedīle, is, n., *seat, chair,* 879.   *

sēdulus, a, um, adj., *buy, bustlings,* 880.

sēdūcō, 3, dūxī, ductus, *lead aside: set aside, remove, withdraw,* 910; *remove,* 1256.

seges, etis, f., *cornfield, standing grain, field,* 96, 554, 1113, 1136, 1531.

semel, num. adv., *a single time, once,* 932.

sēmen, inis, n., *seed,* 1381, 1526.

Semīramis, idis, f., a queen of Assyria, 125.

semper, adv., *ever, always, at all times,* 228, 339, 346, 815, 1556. *

senecta, ae, f. (senex), *old age; age,* 909.

senex, senis, adj., *old, aged;* as noun, m., *old man,* 87, 879, 941, 959.

senīlis, e, adj. (senex), *of an old man, aged,* 1586.

senior, ius, ōris, adj. (senex), *aged, old,* 825, 952.

sententia, ae, f., *opinion, judgment, decision, verdict,* 840.   *

sentēs, ium, m., *thorns, briers,* 291.

sentiō, 4, sēnsī, sēnsus, *discern by sense; feel, perceive, be aware,* 78,

335, 515, 561; *find out, become aware,* 135.
*

sēparō, 1, *disjoin; part, separate, divide,* 1154, 1466.

septem, num. adj., indecl., *seven,* 743, 979, 1010, 1071.
*

sepulcrum, ī, n. (sepeliō, *bury*) *burial place, tomb,* 1610; *burial,* 684.

sepultus, a, um, p. of sepeliō, *bury;* m., *the buried youth,* 1611.

sequor, 3, secūtus, *come after, follow, pursue,* 289, 314, 753, etc.*

sera, ae, f., *bolt, bar,* 869.

serēnus, a, um, adj., *clear, fair, bright,* 632.

sērius, adv., comp. of sērō, *late; later,* 703; *at a later hour,* 172.

sermō, ōnis, m., *continued speech; talk, words, story,* 120, 842, 891.*

serpēns, entis, f. or m. (p. of serpō, *creep*), *creeping thing; snake, serpent,* 236, 680, 1483, etc.

sertum, ī, n. (p. of serō, *twine*), *wreath of flowers, garland,* 376, 960, 1392.
*

servātor, ōris, m. (servō), *deliverer, preserver,* 1369.

serviō, 4 (servus, *slave*), *be a slave; obey, be subject (to),* 298.

servitium, ī, n. (servus), *slavery; service, yoke,* 1437.
*

servō, 1, *save, deliver, preserve,* 1335; *watch, keep watch over,* 1280; *keep, save, treasure up,* 889.
*

sētius, adv., comp., *in a less degree:* nōn, *not otherwise, i.e., like,* 29.

seu, see sīve.

sex, num. adj., indecl., *six,* 366, 1085.

sī, conj., *if,* 20, 60, 74, etc.
*

sībila, ōrum, n., *hissing,* 1459.

sīc, adv., *thus, in this way, so,* 277, 287, 288, etc.; *still, yet,* 199, 1204, 1238.
*

siccō, 1 (siccus), *dry, dry up,* 149, 360.

siccus, a, um, adj., *dry,* 95, 573, 882.

sīcut, adv., *so as; just as,* 1033.

Sīdōnius, a, um, adj., *of Sidon* in Phoenicia, *Phoenician,* 1550.
*

sīdus, eris, n., *group of stars; constellation, star,* 281, 419, 1295, 1420.
*

sīgnō, 1 (sīgnum), *set a mark upon; mark, inscribe,* 637.

sīgnum, ī, n., *mark, token, sign,* 130, 227, 1175, 1437; *sign* (of the Zodiac), 366, 538; pl., *signal, sign,* 93; *figure,* 1533; *statue,* 1240.

silēns, entis, adj. (p. of sileō), *still, quiet, silent,* 151.
*

silentium, ī, n. (silēns), pl., *stillness, quiet. silence,* 700, 723, 1185, 1218.

Sīlēnus, ī, m., an old satyr, tutor of Bacchus, 760.

sileō, 2, uī, —, *be still, be silent,* 1314.

silex, icis, m. and f., *flint, stone,* 1412.
*

silva, ae, f., *wood, forest, woodland,* 8, 170, 257, etc.
*

similis, e, adj., *resembling; like, similar,* 281, 317, 514, 1240.
*

simplex, icis, adj., *simple, not complicated,* 1043.

simul, adv., *at the same time, to-gether, at the same time with* or *and,* 720, 811, 930, 955, etc.; *as soon as,* 367, 515 (w. ac), 764, 1041, 1305, 1400.   *

simulācrum, ī, n. (simulō, *make like*), *likeness; form, figure,* 535, 684, 1411.

simulātus, a, um, adj. (p. of simulō, *make like*), *imitated; artificial,* 37.

sincērus, a, um, adj., *pure,* 901.

sine, prep. w. abl., *without,* 170, 511, 642, etc.; sine lēge, *care-lessly,* 259; *recklessly,* 545.   *

singulī, ae, a, adj., *one at a time;* n., *various things, everything,* 777.   *

sinister, tra, trum, adj., *left, on the left,* 366; comp., *the left,* 487; as noun, f. (sc. manus), *left hand,* 1365.

sinō, 3, sīvī, situs, *let down; let, permit, allow,* 141, 437, 497, etc.

sinuō, 1 (sinus), *curve, wind,* 1463.

sinus, ūs, m., *curve; fold,* 1108; *robe, garment,* 646.   *

Sipylus, ī, m., a son of Niobe, 1020.

sīquis, qua, quid, etc. = sī quis, *if any, whatever,* 284, 611, 1129.

sistō, 3, stitī, status, *set up, place, set,* 906; *stand, alight,* 1148.

Sīsyphus, ī, m., a King of Corinth, 714.

sitis, is, f., *thirst,* 165, 169, 799.

situs, a, um, adj. (p. of sinō), *placed, laid at rest, buried,* 638.

sīve or **seu,** conj. *or if, if;* re-peated, *if . . . or if, whether*

. . . *or,* 44, 48; 791, 793; 1272, 1274, etc.   *

smaragdus, ī, m. and f., *emerald,* 372.

socer, erī, m., *father-in-law,* 973, 1553.

sociō, 1 (sōcius), *share,* 76.   *

socius, ī, m., *fellow, sharer, com-panion,* 764, 1472.   *

sōl, sōlis, m., *sun,* 149, 380, 502, etc.; *Sun god,* 349, 664, 1266. *

soleō, 2, solitus sum, *be wont, be accustomed,* 137, 417, 589, etc.; p. solitus, as adj., *wonted, ac-customed, usual,* 79, 150, 510, 1029, 1493.   *

solidus, a, um, adj., *firm, solid, steady,* 495, 1243, 1279, 1404.

solium, ī, n., *seat; throne,* 372. *

sollemnis, e, adj. (annus), *annual; sacred, hallowed,* 674.

sollers, sollertis, adj., *skillful; cun-ning, clever, artful,* 1407.

sollertia, ae, f. (sollers), *skill; cunning, cleverness, penetration,* 1225.

sollicitō, 1 (sollicitus), *disturb; stir, strike,* 838.

sollicitus, a, um, adj., *disturbed, troubled, anxious,* 80, 473.

sōlor, 1, *comfort, console, solace,* 1081.   *

solum, ī, n., *lowest part; ground, earth,* 201, 571, 1035.   *

sōlus, a, um, gen. īus, adj., *alone, single, only,* 220, 400, 970, etc.; *deserted,* 1431.   *

solvō, 3, solvī, solūtus, *loosen; impair, enfeeble, weaken,* 949; *annul, revoke,* 805; *give, pay,* 774.   *

somnus, ī, m., *sleep, slumber*, 1415. *

sonitus, ūs, m., *sound, noise*, 1019, 1458.

sonō, 1, sonuī, itus (sonus, *sound*), *make a noise; resound, sound*, 1075, 1394, 1496; p. sonāns, as adj., *resounding*, 1174; *clanking*, 469. *

sordidus, a, um, adj. (sordēs, *dirt*), *dirty, stained, soiled*, 377; *dark, dingy*, 888.

soror, ōris, f., *sister*, 362, 971, 1078, etc. *

sors, sortis, f., *lot; lot, fate, life*, 404, 602, 656; *response, prediction, oracle*, 8, 1202, 1215, 1223, 1276. *

sortior, 4 (sors), *cast lots; obtain, enjoy*, 1545.

spargō, 3, sparsī, sparsus, *strew, spread, scatter*, 324, 534, 575, 629, 1526. *

spatior, 1 (spatium), *walk abroad, wander*, 154, 752.

spatiōsus, a, um, adj. (spatium), *of great extent, huge, large*, 1477.

spatium, ī, n., *space, room*, 538; *distance, interval*, 374; *way*, 516; *region, place*, 548; *time*, 1245, 1545; *bulk*, 1516; in spatium, *lengthwise*, 844.

speciēs, —, em, ē, f., *form, likeness*, 866.

speciōsus, a, um, adj. (speciēs), *good-looking; splendid, glittering*, 803, 1441.

spectābilis, e, adj. (spectō), *that may be seen, beautiful, lovely*, 963.

spectāculum, ī, n. (spectō), *spectator's seat, grand stand*, 109.

spectātor, ōris, m., *looker on, spectator*, 16.

spectō, 1, freq., *look at, espy, behold, see*, 103, 279, 326, etc.

specus, ūs, m., *cave, grotto*, 1450.

spērō, 1 (spēs), *hope, hope for*, 273, 278, 318. *

spēs, speī, f., *hope*, 321, 788, 1230.*

spīna, ae, f., *thorn; spine, back*, 1487.

spīceus, a, um, adj. (spīca, *point*), *of ears* (of wheat), 376.

spīra, ae, f., *coil, fold*, 1498.

splendēns, entis, adj. (p. of splendeō, *shine*), *glittering, shining*, 1474.

splendidus, a, um, adj., *bright; shining, glittering*, 801. *

spoliō, 1 (spolium), *strip, despoil*, 988, 1277.

spolium, ī, n., *skin; hide, spoil*, 1248, 1502. *

sponda, ae, f., *bedstead*, 893. *

sponte, abl. of (spōns, spontis), f., *of one's own accord*, 476, 917.

spūma, ae, f. (spuō, *spit*), *foam, froth*, 1495. *

spūmāns, antis, adj. (p. of spūmō, *foam*), *foaming, covered with foam*, 164, 1015. *

spūmiger, era, erum, adj., *foam bearing; foaming*, 810.

squālēns, entis, adj. (p. of squāleō, *be rough*), *rough, unkempt, foul*, 1289.

squālidus, a, um, adj., *rough, unkempt, neglected*, 651, 744.

squāma, ae, f., *scale*, 1484, 1496.

squāmiger, era, erum, adj.

(squāma), *scale-bearing, scaly,*
1419.

squāmōsus, a, um, adj. (squāma),
scaly, 1462.

stāgnō, 1 (stāgnum), *be covered, be
overflowed,* 1165.

stāgnum, ī, n., *standing water;
marsh, pool, lake,* 864.   *

stāmen, inis, n., *foundation, thread,
warp; string* (of a lyre), 837.

statiō, ōnis, f., *standing; post, position, station,* 463.

statuō, 3, uī, ūtus (status), *determine, resolve,* 151, 1294.   *

status, ūs, m., *attitude, pose,* 837.

stella, ae, f., *star,* 462, 546, 632,
767.

sterilis, e, adj., *unfruitful, unre-
quited, hopeless,* 278.

sternō, 3, strāvī, strātus, *spread
out; arrange, prepare,* 895; *strew,
scatter,* 1375; *throw down, lay
low,* 242, 1113.   *

stimulus, ī, m., *prick, goad, spur,*
475, 669.

stīpes, itis, m., *log; trunk,* 334.

stipula, ae, f., *stalk, stem;* pl.,
straw, stubble, 274, 870.

stīva, ae, f., *plow-handle,* 1594.

stō, 1, stetī, status, *stand, stand
still,* 344, 375, 376, etc.; *be still
or quiet,* 1364; *stop, pause,
alight,* 1311, 1441; p. stāns, as
adj., *standing,* 96.   *

stolidus, a, um, adj., *slow, dull,
foolish,* 817, 843.

strāmen, inis, n., *straw,* 938.

strīdēns, entis, adj. (p. of strīdeō,
hiss), *hissing,* 190; *creaking,
beating, flapping,* 1249.   *

strīdulus, a, um, adj. (strīdō,
creak), *sputtering, hissing,* 676.

stringō, 3, inxī, ictus, *draw tight;
draw,* 1583; *touch lightly, graze,*
318; *stir, ruffle,* 203.   *

stupeō, 2, uī, —, *be amazed, be
astounded, stand aghast,* 532,
712, 734, 1309.   *

Stygius, a, um, adj., *of the Styx,
Stygian,* 449, 1497.

Styx, Stygis, f., *a river of the
lower world; the infernal regions,* 683.

suādeō, 2, suāsī, suāsus, *advise,
recommend,* 1226.   *

sub, prep. w. acc. and abl., *under;*
w. acc., *to a place under, under,*
229, 852; *toward, on the approach
of,* 146; w. abl., *under, beneath,*
155, 162, 335, etc.; *under, subject to,* 824, 975, 1244, 1266;
toward, about, 181, 276, 1259;
in, on, 253, 580.   *

subdō, 3, didī, ditus, *put under*
899; *spread beneath,* 1267;
plunge, 811, (sc. sē) 1354.

subeō, īre, iī and īvī, itus, *come
under* (to take the place of),
succeed, 937; *go under, enter,*
749.   *

sūbiciō, 3, iēcī, iectus (iaciō),
place beneath, put under, 304;
spread beneath, 416, 1009, 1139.

sūbitō, adv. (subitus), *suddenly,
immediately,* 1082, 1343, 1517. *

subitus, a, um, adj., *sudden,* 521,
1057, 1461; *sudden coming,
newly risen,* 1156, 1544.

sublātus, see tollō.

sublīmis, e, adj., *uplifted; high, on
high, lofty,* 349, 767, 1353.   *

submittō, 3, mīsī, missus, *let
down; lower (before), yield, sur-
render*, 839, 1444; pass., *bow,
stoop*, 878.

submoveō, 2, mōvī, mōtus, *move
from under; remove, disperse*,
1063.

subsequor, 3, secūtus, *follow after*,
1438.

subsīdō, 3, sēdī, sessus, *sit down;
sink down, fall, subside*, 588,
1179.

subsum, esse, —, *be beneath*, 34.

succēdō, 3, cessī, cessus, *go below;
go to, visit*, 812.   *

succīnctus, a, um, adj. (p. of suc-
cingō, *gird below*), *high girt;
with tucked up skirt*, 897.   *

succrēscō, 3, —, —, inch., *come
again, be supplied again*, 917.

succurrō, 3, currī, cursus, *run to
help, come to one's aid*, 998.   *

succutiō, 3, —, — (quatiō), *fling
up from below; toss up*, 514.

sūcus, ī, m., *juice, liquid, moisture*,
468, 552, 1241; *dye*, 1011.

sūdō, 1, sweat, 1339.

sūdor, ōris, m., *sweat;* venēnī,
liquid poison, 539.

suffundō, 3, fūdī, fūsus, *pour
below; overspread, suffuse*, 266.

suī, sibi, sē, reflex. pron., *himself,
herself*, etc., 27, 183, 576, etc.   *

sulcō, 1, āvī, — (sulcus), *furrow;
plow, cut through*, 1339.

sulcus, ī, m., *furrow*, 1525, 1528. *

sum, esse, fuī, futūrus, *be, exist,
live*, 3, 4, 6, etc.   *

summa, ae, f. (summus), *chief
place;* rērum, *universe*, 611.

summus, a, um, adj. (superus),

*uppermost; highest, top of, sur-
face of*, 94, 351, 542, etc.; *rim of*,
455; *greatest, chief*, 591, 1388;
as noun, n., *surface* (sc. aequor),
203; (pl.) 547; *summit*, 932.   *

super, adv., *above; on top, over, on*,
499, 1357; *in addition, besides*
(= īnsuper), 1337; *more* (than
enough), 990.

super, prep. w. acc., *over, upon,
above*, 36, 365, 576, etc.; *over and
above, besides*, 914.   *

superātor, ōris, m. (superō), *conqueror*, 1331.

superbia, ae, f., *pride*, 981.

superbus, a, um, adj., *haughty,
arrogant, proud*, 236, 966.   *

superīniciō, 3, iēcī, iectus (iaciō),
throw upon, throw over, 880.

superō, 1 (superus), *go over; tower
above, overtop*, 1158; *outshine,
surpass*, 353; *outstrip, vanquish,
defeat*, 2, 3, 43, 51.   *

superstes, itis, adj. (super), *surviv-
ing, remaining alive*, 1187, 1547.

supersum, esse, fuī, *be over and
above, be left, remain*, 233, 611,
1073, 1166, 1167.

superus, a, um, adj. (super),
above, on high, 681, 1367; *upper*,
696, 1522; m. pl., *the gods
above, gods*, 405, 615, 925, etc. *

supervolō, 1, —, —, *fly over*, 1257.

supīnus, a, um, adj., *backwards;
upturned, with upturned palms*,
918.

suppleō, 2, ēvī, ētus, *fill up; fill,
bathe*, 207.

supplex, icis, adj., *kneeling in
entreaty, suppliant*, 666, 1429. *

suppōnō, 3, posuī, positus, *put below, place beneath*, 1408, 1523.

suprā, prep. w. acc. (suprā, adv., *on the upper side*), *above*, 1172, 1477.

suprēmus, a, um, adj., superl. of superus, *highest, last; for the last time, dying*, 1035; *farewell, final*, 732, 1067, 1558.

surgō, 3, surrēxī and subrēxī, — (for subrigō, regō), *rise, arise*, 159, 858, 1181, 1533, 1568. *

sūs, suis, m. and f., *hog, swine*, 888. *

suscitō, 1, *revive, rekindle*, 882. *

suspīrium, ī, n., *sigh*, 473.

sustineō, 2, tinuī, tentus (teneō), *hold up, hold, bear*, 608, 717, 741, 836, 1503; *endure*, 312, 559.

sustulī, see tollō.

suus, a, um, adj. (suī), *of oneself; his, hers, its, theirs*, 121, 147, 204, etc.; as noun, m. pl., *one's family, friends*, 161, 935, 1056, 1065. *

T

tābēs, is, f., *wasting; poison, venom*, 1470.

tābēscō, 3, buī, — (tābeō, *melt*), *melt away*, 1603.

taceō, 2, cuī, citus, *be silent*, 1421.

tactiturnus, a, um, adj. (tacitus), *silent, quiet, still*, 1439.

tacitus, a, um, adj. (p. of taceō), *silent, in silence*, 857; *quiet, low*, 992. *

tāctus, (ūs), m. (tangō), *touch*, 1377.

taeda, ae, f., *pine torch; marriage torch*, 1390; *marriage*, 127, 265.

taedium, ī, n. (taedet, *it disgusts*), *disgust, loathing, weariness*, 66.

Taenarius, a, um, adj., *of Taenarus*, a town in Laconia, *Taenarian*, 683.

tālāris, e, adj. (tālus), *reaching to the ankles;* n. pl., *long robe*, 32; *sandals*, 1300, 1362.

tālis, e, adj., *such, of such a kind*, 994; n. pl., *such things, thus*, 27, 50, 145, etc. *

tālus, ī, m., *ankle*, 680.

tam, adv., *in such a degree; so, so much*, 332, 403, 1057. *

Tamasēnus, ī, m., a plain in Cyprus, 85.

tamen, adv., *notwithstanding, nevertheless, yet, but*, 7, 30, 41, etc.*

tandem, adv. (tam), *at length, at last*, 748, 924. *

tangō, 3, tetigī, tāctus, *touch, reach*, 320, 491, 877, etc.; *touch, move, affect*, 55, 77, 231, etc.; *partake of, eat at*, 970. *

Tantalis, idis, f., *descendant of Tantalus*, 1000.

Tantalus, ī, m., son of Jupiter and father of Niobe, 969; son of Niobe, 1029.

tantum, adv. (tantus), *so much, so greatly, so far*, 932, 1341; *only*, 826, 934; *now*, 595. *

tantus, a, um, adj., *of such size, so great*, 14, 17, 444, etc.; *such, such an one*, 45; as noun, n., *so much*, 1059; tantī, *of such importance, worth so much*, 54, 59; tantō . . . quantō, *(by) as much as*, 247. *

tardē, adv. (tardus), *slowly, re-luctantly, late,* 115, 158.

tardus, a, um, adj., *slow,* 13, 120, 923. *

Tartara, ōrum, n., *Tartarus,* the infernal regions, 571, 691.

taurus, ī, m., *bull,* 1388, 1422; the constellation *Taurus,* 428. *

tēctum, ī, n. (p. of tegō), *covering; roof,* 938, 1392; *garret,* 884; *covered building, house, dwelling,* 153, 484, 928, etc.; *palace,* 368. *

tegō, 3, tēxī, tēctus, *cover, cover over,* 131, 226, 351, etc.; *cover, thatch, roof,* 870; *cover, veil, shroud,* 564, 1006, 1106; *crown,* 39; *engulf,* 1159; *shade,* 1271.

tegumen (tegmen), inis, n. (tegō), *covering, protection,* 1473; capitum, *helmets,* 1529. *

tellūs, ūris, f., *land, earth, ground,* 86, 297, 551, etc.; *floor,* 939; *Earth,* 327, 583. *

tēlum, ī, n., *missile, dart, shaft, weapon,* 250, 1017, 1023, etc. *

temerārius, a, um, adj. (temerē, *rashly), rash, reckless, unthinking,* 15, 296, 398.

tēmō, ōnis, m., *pole, tongue* (of a chariot), 455, 627.

templum, ī, n., *temple, shrine,* 87, 937, 948, etc. *

temptō, 1, intens. (tendō), *handle; try, attempt,* 152, 660, 682, etc.; *test,* 1379. *

tempus, oris, n., *portion* (of time); *time, season,* 98, 110, 127, etc.; *occasion,* 894, 1326; pl., *temples* (of the head), 827, 849. *

tendō, 3, tetendī, tentus or tēnsus, *stretch,* sc. iter, *make one's way,*

673, 704; p. tentus, as adj., *stretched, tight, taut,* 1032. *

tenebrae, ārum, f., *darkness, sha-dows,* 160, 492, 665; *shady places,* 257; *darkness, blindness, blur,* 522.

Tenedos, ī, f., *an island in the Aegaean,* 298

teneō, 2, tenuī, —, *hold, keep, have,* 227, 639, 676, etc.; *clasp, grasp,* 448, 836, 1365; *keep to,* 427; *seize,* 317, 783; *make, take* (one's way), 488; *maintain,* 1162; *hold, occupy, live in,* 124, 1143, 1423; *take possession of,* 1415. *

tener, era, erum, adj., *soft,* 1444; *thin,* 1249; *tender, youthful,* 821, 1590.

tenor, ōris, m. *holding; motion,* 1534.

tenuis, e, adj., *drawn out; thin, delicate, fine,* 171, 330; *slight, small,* 132, 190, *slender,* 1358.

tenus, prep. with abl., *as far as, up to,* 586, 1047, 1352. *

tepeō, 2, —, —, *be warm,* 230.

tepidus, a, um, adj., *warm,* 580, 881, 1307, 1546.

ter, num, adv., *three times, thrice,* 397, 581, 582, 1258, 1366. *

terebrō, 1, —, ātus (terebra, *bore), pierce, cleave,* 1049.

tergeō, 2, tersī, tersus, *rub off, wipe clean,* 900.

tergum, ī, n., *back,* 33, 111, 358, etc.; *shoulders,* 168, 323; *side, flitch,* 888. *

tergus, oris, n., *back; side, strip, flitch,* 889. *

ternī, ae, a, adj., *three each, three*, 692. *

terō, 3, trīvī, trītus, *rub; graze, grate upon*, 1139.

terra, ae, f., *earth, land, ground*, 354, 363, 413, etc.; *earth, clay*, 1198; *Earth*, 1227. *

terrēnus, a, um, adj. (terra), *of the earth, earthy*, 1242.

terreō, 2, *frighten, alarm*, 8, 572, 1191, 1355, 1536. *

terribilis, e, adj., *frightful, dreadful*, 409, 1106.

terrigena, ae, adj., *earthborn*, 1539.

terror, ōris, m., *great fear, fright*, 668, 1521.

tertius, a, um, num. adj. (ter), *third*, 898. *

testa, ae, f., *baked clay; brick*, 899.

testis, is, m. and f., *witness*, 393, 1234.

testor, 1 (testis), *call to witness*, 615.

Tēthys, yos, f., *wife of Oceanus*, 417.

textum, ī, n. (p. of texō, *weave*), *web; piece of cloth, coverlet*, 880.

thalamus, ī, m., *inner room, bridal chamber, marriage*, 12, 61.

theatrum, ī, n., *theater*, 1532.

Thebae, ārum, f., *Thebes*, capital of Boeotia, 1552.

Themis, idos, f., goddess of law and of prophecy, 1162.

Thīnēius, a, um, adj., *of Thinaeum*, in Phrygia, 956.

Thisbē, ēs, f., *a Babylonian girl*, 122.

Thrācius, a, um, adj., *Thracian*, 762.

tiāra, ae, f., *tiara, cap, turban*, 849.

tibia, ae, f., *shin bone; pipe*, 1393.

tīgnum, ī, n., *timber, beam*, 888.

tigris, idis, pl., tigrēs, m. and f., *tiger, tigress*, 1146.

tilia, ae, f., *linden tree*, 862.

timeō, 2, uī, —, *fear, be afraid*, 25, 439, 1589. *

timidus, a, um, adj., *fearful, afraid, faint-hearted*, 182, 307, 735, 919.

Timōlus, ī, m., *Mt. Tmolus*, 756.

timor, ōris, m., *fear, dread, alarm, apprehension*, 321, 414, 521, etc. *

tinguō, 3, tīnxī, tīnctus, *wet, bathe, stain, dye*, 174, 194, 812, 1507. *

Tītan, ānis, m., one of the giants, son of Heaven and Earth, 466.

Tītānia, ae, f., *daughter of the Titans, Pyrrha*, daughter of the Titan Epimetheus, 1229.

titubō, 1, *stagger, reel*, 760.

titulus, ī, m., *inscription; mark, distinction, glory*, 1278; *honor*, 43.

Tmōlus, ī, m., a mountain in Lydia, 819.

tolerō, 1, *bear, endure*, 612.

tollō, 3, sustulī, sublātus, *lift, raise, take up*, 21, 108, 118, etc. *

tonitrus, ūs, m. (tonō, *thunder*), *thunder*, 619.

torpor, ōris, m., *numbness*, 329.

torqueō, 2, torsī, tortus, *turn, whirl, revolve*, 419, 1463; *torment*, 800. *

torreō, 2, torruī, tostus, *dry up; parch*, 790; *scorch, burn*, 594. *

tortus, a, um, adj. (p. of torqueō), *twisted; twisting, winding*, 486; plumbum, *sling shot*, 1341.

torus, ī, m., *bed, couch,* 892; *bier,* 1078; cōnsors torī, *spouse,* 1160.   *

torvus, a, um, adj., *staring; scowling, stern, savage,* 581.

tot, num. adj., indecl., *so many, such a number of,* 64, 65, 241, etc.

totidem, num. adj., indecl. (tot), *so many, the same number of,* 366, 980, 1268, 1385.   *

totiēns, num. adv. (tot), *so many times, so often,* 916.   *

tōtus, a, um, gen. īus, adj., *all, the whole, entire,* 99, 141, 173, etc.; *full, free,* 1121; *wholly,* 1395.

trabs, bis, f., *beam, shaft; tree-trunk,* 1499.   *

trāctō, 1 (trahō), *handle, touch,* 1572.

trāctus, ūs, m., *drawing; course, track, train,* 631.

trādō, 3, didī, ditus, *give up, hand over, pass to one,* 1407; *assign, give* by lot, 602; *commit, entrust,* 763, 1585.

trahō, 3, trāxī, trāctus, *draw, drag,* 187, 419, 561; *draw out,* 844, 1046, 1079; *cause,* 36; īgnēs, *breathe in, become inflamed,* 1308; *take on, assume, acquire,* 567, 738, 1246, 1606; *lead astray,* 427, 1600.   *

trāiciō, 3, iēcī, iectus (iaciō), *pierce, transfix,* 255, 1033.   *

trāmes, itis, m. (trāns), *crossway; way, path, road,* 723.

trānseō, īre, iī, itus, *go or pass through,* 137; *go over,* 1030; *go by, pass,* 102, 113, 742.

trānsitus (ūs), m., *going over; passage, way,* 144.

trānsmittō, 3, mīsī, missus, *send across; send, hurl,* 1342.

tremebundus, a, um, adj. (tremō), *quivering,* 200.

tremō, 3, uī, —, *tremble, shake,* 203, 897, 1587; *quiver,* 1024.   *

tremor, ōris, m., *shaking, trembling,* 1461; *earthquake,* 587.

tremulus, a, um, adj., *shaking; quivering, trembling,* 858, 1593.

trepidō, 1 (trepidus), *hurry with alarm; rush about,* 1084; *tremble, quiver, palpitate,* 288, 335, 414.

trepidus, a, um, adj., *restless; trembling, frightened,* 167, 535.

trēs, tria, num. adj., *three,* 90, 105, 479, etc.

tribuō, 3, uī, ūtus (tribus, *a third part*), *assign; give,* 393.

(tricuspis, idis), adj.(trēs; cuspis), *with three prongs, three-tined,* 1171.

tridēns, entis, adj. (trēs; dēns), *with three teeth;* as noun, m., *three-tined spear, trident,* 1124. *

trifidus, a, um, adj. (ter), *three-cleft, three-forked,* 636.

triplex, icis, adj. (ter), *threefold, triple,* 1455.

trīstis, e, adj., *sad, sorrowful, mournful,* 1478.   *

Trītōn, ōnis, m., *a sea god, son of* Neptune, 356.   *

Trītōnis, idis, f., *Minerva, from* Lake Triton in Africa, her birthplace, 1548.

trītus, a, um, adj. (p. of terō), *rubbed; oft-trodden, beaten,* 515.

triumphō, 1 (triumphus), *exult, triumph,* 1072.

triumphus, ī, m., *triumphal procession, triumph,* 341.

truncō, 1 (truncus), *strip, cut off,* 887.

truncus, ī, m., *trunk* (of a tree), 957.

tū, tuī, pron., *thou, you,* 6, 7, 62, etc.   *

tuba, ae, f., *trumpet,* 93.

tueor, 2, tūtus, *watch over, support,* 344; *care for, maintain,* 944. *

tum, adv., *then, at that time,* 105, 150, 309, etc.   *

tumeō, 2, —, —, *swell, puff up,* 1454.

tumēscō, 3, muī, — (tumeō), *begins to swell, swell,* 1494.

tumidus, a, um, adj., *swollen, swelling,* 242.   *

tumulō, 1 (tumulus), *cover with a mound, bury,* 947.

tumulus, ī, m., *mound, hill,* 1150; *tomb, grave,* 162, 224, 637.

tunc, adv. (tum), *then, at that time,* 416, 566, 621, etc.

tunica, ae, f., *under garment; shirt, tunic,* 1232.

turba, ae, f., *turmoil; crowd, throng, number,* 9, 15, 679, etc.; *pack* (of hounds), 1355.   *

turbō, inis, m. (turbō, *be in a whirl*), *tempest, hurricane,* 1098.*

turpis, e, adj., *ugly, foul, unsightly,* 848, 1207.

turris, is, f., *tower,* 1131, 1482.

tūs, tūris, n., *incense,* 600, 969. *

tūtēla, ae, f., *watching; guardian, keeper,* 948.

tūtō, adv. (tūtus), *with safety, in security,* 754.

tūtus, a, um, adj. (p. of tueor), *guarded; safe, secure, in safety,* pred., *safely,* 136, 401, 485, etc.*

tuus, a, um, adj. (tū), *thine, yours, your,* 20, 210, 215, etc.   *

tyrannus, m., *king, sovereign, monarch,* 1117.   *

Tyrius, a, um, adj., *of Tyre, Tyrian, purple,* 834, 1011, 1456.   *

U

ūber, eris, adj., *full, thickly laden,* 156; *plenteous,* 1452.

ubi, adv. (quī), *in which place, where,* 536, 1008, 1135, etc.; *when, whenever,* 124, 138, 232, etc.*

ubīque, adv., *in any place whatever; everywhere,* 1392.   *

ūllus, a, um, gen. īus, (ūnus), *any one, any,* 1164, 1604.   *

ulmus, ī, f., *elm, elm tree,* 1137.

ulna, ae, f., *elbow; arm,* 751.

ulterior, ius, ōris, *farther;* n. as adv., *farther, longer, more,* 613.

ultimus, a, um, adj. superl. of ulterior, *farthest; last,* 113, 704, 1050, etc.; *last part of,* 415.

ultor, ōris, m., *avenger,* 1479.

ultrā, adv., *on the other side; more, longer,* 312, 1362.

ulva, ae, f., *swamp grass, sedge,* 892.

umbra, ae, f., *shade, shadow,* 37, 155, 183, etc.; *shade, ghost, spirit,* 682, 686, 718, etc. *

umbrōsus, a, um, adj. (umbra), *full of shade; shady,* 249.

umerus, ī, m., *upper arm, shoulder,* 239, 608, 1173, etc. *

ūmidus, a, um, adj., *moist, wet,* 491, 741, 1241.

ūmor, ōris, m., *moisture,* 568.

umquam, adv., *at any time, ever,* 946.

ūnā, adv. (ūnus), *in the same place; near, by,* 1571; *at the same time, together,* 1324. *

uncus, a, um, adj. (uncus, *hook*), *curved, hooked,* 1299. *

unda, ae, f., *wave, billow, water, waters,* 165, 169, 326, etc. *

unde, adv., *from which place, whence,* 413, 618, 619, 1518; *from which (fact),* 1253. *

ūndecimus, a, um, adj. (ūnus; decimus, *tenth*), *eleventh,* 768.

undique, adv. (unde; que), *from every side, on all sides,* 563, 584, 1021.

unguis, is, m., *claw, talon,* 1349.

ungula, ae, f. (unguis), *hoof,* 1009.

ūnicus, a, um, adj. (ūnus), *single, the only, solitary,* 921.

ūnus, a, um, gen. īus, num. adj., *one, a single, only one, alone,* 76, 105, 216, etc.; *one and the same,* 361, 703. *

urbs, urbis, f., *walled town, city,* 125, 153, 363, etc. *

urna, ae, f., *jar,* 1458, 1460; *burial urn,* 233, 713.

ūrō, 3, ūssī, ūstus, *burn, consume,* 278, 553, 800. *

usque, adv., *all the way; continuously, ever,* 677; sequor, *follow up,* 1512.

ūsus, ūs, m., *use; practice, custom,* 6; *use, enjoyment,* 384, 1406; *ad-* *vantage, good,* 643; *use, purpose,* 92, 1242; *loan,* 707.

ut or **utī,** adv., *when, as soon as, just as,* 19, 169, 174, etc.; *as,* 184, 188, 274, etc.; *in proportion as,* 551; ut prīmum, *as soon as,* 859; *as, since,* 313, 583; *like,* 77, 336, 348; *though,* 198, 427, 985, 1204, 1238; *that, so that, in order that, to,* 141, 151, 223, etc. *

uterque, utraque, utrumque, gen. utrīusque, pron., *each, either, both,* 93, 133, 488, etc.; *on both sides,* 819; ab utrāque parte, *both,* 1299.

utinam, adv. (utī; nam), *oh that! I wish that! if only!* 70, 71, 399, 441, 1197. *

ūtor, 3, ūsus, *use, make use of,* 99, 772, 1119; *wield, ply,* 475; *take, adopt,* 494. *

utrimque, adv. (uterque), *on both sides, on either hand,* 537.

ūva, ae, f., *bunch of grapes, grapes,* 377, 913.

V

vacca, ae, f., *cow,* 1387.

vacō, 1, *be empty; be free* or *idle, rest,* 713. *

vacuus, a, um, adj., *empty, void,* 215, 315, 513; *lonely,* 302; *abandoned, deserted,* 1346.

vādō, 3, —, —, *walk, go, proceed,* 807; *depart,* 1282.

vādum, ī, n., *shallow; river bed, channel,* 1204, 1440. *

vagor, 1 (vagus), *wander, rove about,* 679.

vagus, a, um, adj., *wandering, roaming, unsettled,* 1149, 1573.

valē, imper. of valeō, *be strong; farewell, adieu,* 146, 732, 954.

valeō, 2, uī, itūrus, *be strong, be able, have power,* 408, 533; *succeed, prevail,* 524.

validus, a, um, adj., *strong, violent,* 1098, 1485. *

vallis, is, f., *valley, vale,* 722. *

valvae, ārum, f., *pair of door leaves, folding doors,* 352, 1394.

vānus, a, um, adj., *empty; nōn, veracious, trustworthy,* 958. *

vapor, ōris, m., *steam, vapor,* 594, 612.

varius, a, um, adj., *party-colored, mottled,* 1252; *various, changing,* 1111; *diversified, perplexing,* 534.*

vastus, a, um, adj., *huge, enormous, vast,* 408, 535, 700, etc. *

vātēs, is, m. and f., *prophet; bard, singer,* 682.

-ve, conj. enclitic, *or,* 290, 1594. *

vehō, 3, vēxī, vectus, *bear, carry,* 1145, 1146; pass., *be borne, ride,* 362, 1160. *

vel, conj. (volō), *choose; or if you will, or,* 20, 327, 493; repeated, *either . . . or,* 276. *

vel, adv. (vel), *or even; even,* 1065; *certainly, at least,* 142.

vēlāmen, inis, n. (vēlō), *covering; garment, robe,* 19, 168, 182. *

vēlō, 1 (vēlum), *cover, enfold, enwrap,* 371, 671, 894, 1216, 1232; *encircle,* 849.

vēlōciter, adv. (vēlōx), *swiftly, quickly,* 24.

vēlōx, ōcis, adj., *swift, quick, rapid, fleet,* 2, 12, 71, etc.

vēlum, ī, n., *sail; curtain, awning,* 36. *

velut or **velutī,** adv., *even as, as if, like,* 265, 465, 560, etc. *

vēna, ae, f., *vein,* 1095; *of earth,* 1244, 1494.

venēnifer, fera, ferum, adj. (venēnum), *poisonous, venemous,* 1506.

venēnum, ī, n., *poison,* 539, 693, 1454, 1470. *

veneror, 1, *reverence, worship,* 992.

venia, ae, f., *indulgence, grace,* 708, 920; *pardon,* 802, 1220. *

veniō, 4, vēnī, ventus, *come,* 15, 90, 104, etc. *

venter, tris, m., *belly,* 241.

ventus, ī, m., *wind,* 309, 748, 1098, 1254, 1296. *

Venus, eris, f., *goddess of love,* 245. *

vēr, vēris, n., *spring;* personified, 375.

(verber), eris, n., *lash, whip,* 669.

verberō, 1 (verber), *beat, strike,* 1359.

verbum, ī, n., *word, words,* 98, 144, 221, etc. *

verēcundus, a, um, adj. (vereor), *ashamed; shy, modest,* 266.

vereor, 2, veritus, *fear, be afraid, dread,* 1260; *be anxious,* 417. *

vērō, adv. (vērus), *in truth, in fact, to be sure,* 558, 791, 1493; *but, however,* 174, 519. *

verrō, 3, —, —, *sweep, brush,* 834.*

versō, 1, freq. (vertō), *turn (often), keep turning,* 160, 904, 1036; sc. sē, *turn (oneself),* 1355. *

vertex, icis, m., *summit, peak,*
993, 1157, 1363; *head,* 878. *

vertigō, inis, f., *turning round,*
whirling, 418.

vertō, 3, vertī, versus, *turn,* 193;
convert, change, 557, 773, 937,
1242. *

vērus, a, um., adj., *true, genuine,*
real, 386, 391, 446, 690, 1571. *

vester, tra, trum, adj. (vōs), *your,*
yours, 607, 707, 1119, etc. *

vestīgium, ī, n., *tracks, footprints,*
traces, 172, 481; *heels,* 318;
fragments, 629; *steps,* 314, 369,
etc.

vestīgō, 1, —, —, *follow in the*
track of, trace, 1473.

vestis, is, f., *covering; clothes, gar-*
ments, robe, 174, 184, 214, etc.;
bed clothes, 894, 896.

vetō, 1, uī, itus, *forbid, prohibit,*
128, 271, 925. *

vetus, eris, adj., *old, aged, advanced*
in years, 895, 936, 1449; *former,*
698. *

vetustās, ātis, f. (vetus), *old age;*
antiquity, tradition, 1234.

vetustus, a, um, adj. (vetus), *old,*
ancient, 1275.

via, ae, f., *way, road, path, course,*
411, 415, 427, etc.; *coming,*
voyage, 381, 693; pl., *channels,*
1125. *

viātor, ōris, m. (via), *wayfarer,*
traveler, 275.

vibrō, 1, *set in tremulous motion;*
flutter, 310; *hurl, wield,* 619;
dart, 1455.

vīcīnia, ae, f. (vīcīnus), *nearness,*
neighborhood, 126, 926, 1601;
neighbors, 1269.

vīcīnus, a, um, adj., (vīcus,
neighborhood), *neighboring, near-*
by, 165, 807, 957.

(vicis), is, f., *change;* in vicēs, *in*
turn, 139.

vīctor, ōris, m., *conqueror,* 121,
1250, 1516; as adj., *victorious,*
1477. *

vīctōria, ae, f. (vīctor), *victory,* 69.

vīctrīx, īcis, f. (vīctor), *victor,* 39,
1072, 1073; as adj., *conquering,*
victorious, 1372.

vīctus, ūs, m., *sustenance, food,*
1153. *

videō, 2, vīdī, vīsus, *see, discern,*
perceive, look upon, 19, 73, 135,
etc.; *see to it,* 65; pass., *be*
represented, 359; *seem, appear,*
30, 117, 158, etc.; *seem best,* 1200;
p. videndus, *to be seen, visible,*
seen, 91. *

vigil, ilis, adj., *on the watch; watch-*
ful, 460.

vīlis, e, adj., *of small price; poor,*
mean, 895.

villa, ae, f., dim., *country house,*
farm house, 921, 1136.

villōsus, a, um, adj. (villus),
hairy, shaggy, 691.

villus, ī, m. *tuft of hair;* pl., *hairs,*
844. *

vīmen, inis, n., *twig, withe,* 1384,
1450.

vinciō, 4, vinxī, vinctus, *bind,*
wind, entwine, 692, 761, 833;
bind, chain, 1327. *

vincō, 3, vīcī, vīctus, *overcome,*
vanquish, overpower, conquer, 11,
45, 48, etc.; *be victorious,* 1074;
win over, move, 1212; *exhaust,*
326; p. vīctī, *the vanquished,* 40.*

vinculum, or **vinclum,** ī, n. (vinciō), *means of fastening,* 1602; pl., *bonds, chains,* 1314. *

vīnētum, ī, n. (vīnum), *plantation of wine; vineyard,* 756, 1139.

vīnum, ī, n., *wine,* 909, 917. *

violentus, a, um, adj., *forcible; harsh, savage,* 429; *impetuous,* 9.

violō, 1 (vīs), *treat with violence; dishonor, profane,* 1449.

vīpera, ae, f., *serpent, snake,* 694.

vīpereus, a, um, adj. (vīpera), *of vipers, snaky,* 1248, 1524.

vir, virī, m., *male, man,* 2, 363, 1127, etc.; *youth,* 113; *husband,* 261, 976, 1090; *hero,* 1522. *

virēns, entis, adj. (p. of vireō, *be green*), *green,* 778, 900, 1270.

virga, ae, f., *slender green branch, sprout, twig,* 779, 1374, 1376, etc.

virgineus, a, um, adj. (virgō), *of a maiden; girlish,* 72.

virginitās, ātis, f. (virgō), *maidenhood,* 269.

virgō, inis, f., *maid, maiden, girl,* 28, 42, 101, etc.; bellica virgō, *Minerva,* 1386. *

viridis, e, adj., *green,* 360, 1138, 1507.

virtūs, ūtis, f. (vir), *manliness, bravery, courage, prowess,* 48, 57, 1335, 1401. *

vīs, —, vim, vī, f., *strength, force, power,* 1491, (pl.), 99, 217, 325, etc.; *violence,* 1284; aurea, *golden virtue, magic gold,* 812. *

vīscus, eris, n., *bowels, inwards, entrails,* 180, 1079, 1097; *center, heart,* 585. *

vīsō, 3, sī, sus, freq. (videō), *look*

at attentively; look upon, view, 342.

vīta, ae, f., *life,* 53, 66, 176, etc.

vitiō, 1 (vitium), *injure, ruin,* 606; p. vitiātus, *defective, containing flaws,* 189; *polluted,* 1497.

vītis, is, f., *vine, grapevine,* 913.

vitium, ī, n., *fault, defect, flaw, crack,* 134.

vītō, 1, *shun, avoid, flee from,* 197, 1429.

vitta, ae, f., *band, fillet,* 259.

vitulus, ī, m., *calf, bull calf,* 1388.

vīvō, 3, vīxī, —, *live,* 9, 67, 74, 1542. *

vīvus, a, um, adj., *alive, living,* 7, 1093, 1376, 1448. *

vix, adv., *with difficulty, hardly, scarcely,* 329, 395, 411, etc. *

vocō, 1, *call, summon,* 673, 718, 1174; *name,* 1434; *draw out,* 566; *declare,* 841. *

(volātus, ūs), m. (volō, *fly*), *flight,* 1599; volātū immissū, *swooping,* 1350.

volō, velle, voluī, —, *wish, will,* 53, 67, 476, etc.; *be willing,* 70, 76. *

volō, 1, āvī, ātūrus, *fly,* 28, 1582, 1584, 1589. *

volūbilis, e, adj., *turned round; spinning, whirling, rolling,* 108, 1462.

volucer, cris, cre, adj., *flying, winged,* 501, 565; as noun, f., *flying creature, bird,* 713, 1149. *

volūmen, inis, n., *that rolled; whirling, spinning,* 419.

voluntās, ātis, f., *will; wish,* 401; *good will,* 915.

volūtō, 1, freq. (volvō), *roll; turn over, consider, weigh*, 1223. *

volvō, 3, volvī, volūtus, *make revolve;* pass., *roll, be hurled*, 631, 1027; *roll, rush*, 1123. *

vomō, 3, uī, itus, *throw out, vomit forth*, 467, 1361.

vōtum, ī, n. (p. of voveō), *promise* (to a god); *prayer*, 231, 271, 437, 527, 948; *desire, hope*, 1114. *

voveō, 2, vōvī, vōtus, *vow; pray for*, 798

vōx, vōcis, f., *voice*, 80, 342, 589, etc.; *words*, 136, 399. *

Vulcānius, a, um, adj., *of Vulcan*, 454.

vulnus, eris, n., *wound*, 187, 207, 240, etc. *

vultus, ūs, m., *expression of countenance, looks*, 50, 72, 675; *features, face*, 103, 161, 208, etc ; *gaze*, 42, 832; *face, presence*, 369. *

Z

zōna, ae, f., *girdle; zone*, 479.